£8.50  8188

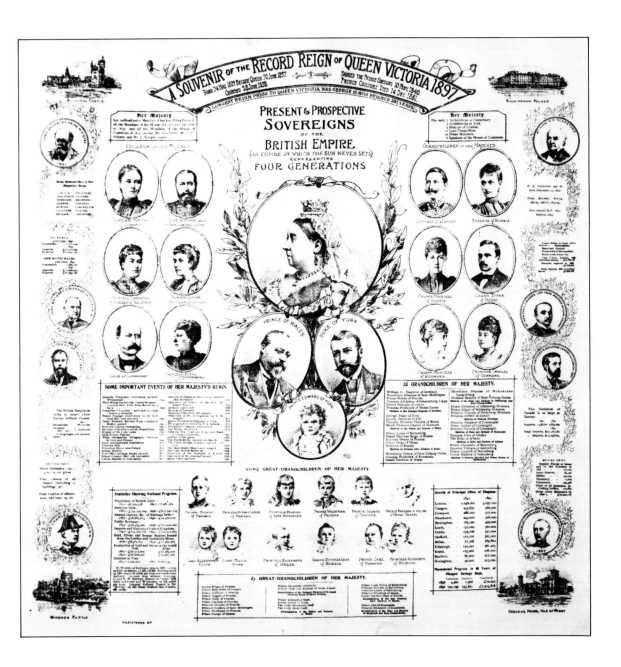

# ·THE·ILLUSTRATED·
# QUEEN VICTORIA

## LYTTON STRACHEY

With an Introduction by
Michael Holroyd

## BLOOMSBURY

# To Virginia Woolf

*Queen Victoria* first published 1921

This illustrated edition first published 1987 by
Bloomsbury Publishing Ltd, 4 Bloomsbury Place,
London WC1A 2QA

An Albion Book

Conceived, designed and produced by The Albion Press Ltd,
P.O. Box 52, Princes Risborough, Aylesbury, Bucks., HP17 9PR

*Designer: Emma Bradford*
*Editor: Jane Havell*
*Historical Adviser: Julia Courtney*
*Picture Researchers: Elizabeth Loving, Thea Philcox*

Introduction copyright © 1987 by Michael Holroyd
Design and editorial matter copyright © 1987 The Albion Press Ltd

*British Library Cataloguing in Publication Data*
Strachey, Lytton
    Lytton Strachey's Queen Victoria: the
    illustrated edition.
    1. Victoria, *Queen of Great Britain*
    2. Great Britain — Kings and rulers —
    Biography
    I. Title
    941.081'092'4    DA554

    ISBN 0–7475–0089–4

The illustrations in this book are reproduced courtesy of: Bodleian
Library (John Johnson Collection) Half-title, 72, 187; Bridgeman
Art Library 160; Forbes Magazine Collection, New York 153;
Hulton Picture Library 20, 35, 74, 79, 104, 122, 167, 180; Mansell
Collection 12, 15; Mary Evans Picture Library 10, 38, 58, 69, 70,
115, 118, 120, 131, 161, 162, 174, 184, 186; Museum of British
Transport, London 155; Punch 65, 106, 124; reproduced by
gracious permission of Her Majesty The Queen 50, 154, 158/159;
Royal Academy, London 156/157; Windsor Castle, Royal
Archives, copyright reserved, reproduced by gracious permission of
Her Majesty The Queen 40, 41, 133, 136, 151, 191, 192, 203,
204, 206; Windsor Castle, Royal Library, © Her Majesty The
Queen 27, 34, 49, 51, 52/53, 54, 55, 56, 62, 81, 87, 95, 97, 121,
125. All other pictures are from private collections.

A small asterisk in the text indicates a note on page 207.

HALF-TITLE ILLUSTRATION: *A commemorative handkerchief from
Queen Victoria's Diamond Jubilee in 1897.*

TITLE PAGE ILLUSTRATION: *Queen Victoria aged seventy-eight by
von Angeli.*

Typeset by Dataset, Oxford
Printed and bound in Great Britain by Oxford University Press

# CONTENTS

# INTRODUCTION

'We want your method for some stately Victorians who have waited long for it,' Professor Walter Raleigh wrote to Lytton Strachey in May 1918, a few days after *Eminent Victorians* was published. 'First the great Panjandrum—Victoria herself.' It was not until the end of that year, after reading through a good number of stout Victorian volumes, that Strachey at last decided to 'penetrate the various veils of discretion' and make his next book 'The Life of Her Late Majesty'.

*Queen Victoria* proceeds by means of a series of interconnected chapter–scenes that stand halfway between the essay form of *Eminent Victorians* and the psychological melodrama of *Elizabeth and Essex* (1928), which was to be based on a Shakespearian theatrical model. An attempt to broaden the scope of biographical narrative, it reads like a romantic novel beneath the surface of which moves a subversive current of irony. 'You've discovered a new style which gives the essential and all-pervading absurdity of most human and all official life without losing anything of its pathos,' Roger Fry wrote to Strachey. 'You're so kind and so unsparing. It seems to me more nearly a true perspective than anything yet found.'

The characters in *Queen Victoria* arrange themselves neatly into three categories. There are a number of unseen powers and immaterial beings who lurk in the shadowy recesses and mysteriously control the event-plot; there are some highly-coloured and acute portraits-in-miniature of 19th-century Prime Ministers; and finally there are the heroine and hero, Victoria and Albert.

The Duchess of Kent, Baroness Lehzen, King Leopold I and Baron Stockmar are all used by Strachey as mechanical tricks of his trade to orchestrate, with maximum aesthetic effect, the battle for political power behind the scenes. As latent supremacy passes from one to the other, so the kaleidoscope of the biography shifts between one pattern and the next. While Victoria is growing up a fierce struggle develops between the child's mother and her governess—and it is the governess, Lehzen, who emerges triumphant. 'Discreet and victorious, she remained in possession of the field,' Strachey writes. 'More closely than ever did she cleave to the side of her mistress, her pupil, and her friend; and in the recesses of the palace her mysterious figure was at once invisible and omnipresent.' In international affairs Victoria's uncle, King Leopold of the Belgians, tries to gain ascendency over the young queen. It is, however, Leopold's 'confidential agent', Baron Stockmar, who at length carries all before him. If Victoria is the Baroness's pupil, Albert is the genie whom the Baron summons out of his bottle to enact his every wish. After Albert and Victoria's marriage a kind of Punch-and-Judy show starts up, Stockmar and Lehzen violently activating the royal marionettes upon the stage until Punch–Albert–Stockmar is acclaimed by Strachey the winner. Lehzen 'lost ground perceptibly', he records. Then Stockmar gives the Prince the annihilating powers of his magic: 'He spoke, and Lehzen vanished for ever.'

Strachey's creation of Stockmar as an Invisible Man who holds prodigious sway over Albert was based on the mythical version which Stockmar himself conceived in the self-hypnotic throes of retrospective optimism. With his trap-door exits and entrances, he becomes the good fairy of Strachey's pantomime, while the royal couple are reduced to two mandarin figures nodding or shaking their heads as their master pleases. The satisfaction of Stockmar's 'essential being lay in obscurity, in invisibility', we are told, '—in passing, unobserved, through a hidden entrance, into the very central chamber of power, and in sitting there, quietly, pulling the subtle strings that set the wheels of the whole world in motion.' The end of Stockmar is heralded by the death of Albert.

Deprived of his medium, the Baron is suddenly redundant: a magician without a wand; a ventriloquist without a dummy. 'The Baron, by his fireside at Coburg, suddenly saw the tremendous fabric of his creation crash down into sheer and irremediable ruin. Albert was gone, and he had lived in vain.' Then, for the last time, the kaleidoscopic pattern alters. No longer animated to new life by the master puppet-maker, Victoria can only go through her old tricks once again. Her friendship with Disraeli is a distorted mummery of her earlier love for Melbourne; her dislike of Gladstone recalls her coldness to Peel. With sedate majesty she enters her second childhood.

Strachey likened Victoria's early years, under her mother the Duchess of Kent's domination, to those of a novice in a convent. 'The child grew into the girl, the girl into the young woman; but still she slept in her mother's bedroom; still she had no place allowed her where she might sit or work by herself. An extraordinary watchfulness surrounded her every step'. Above all, the young Victoria was protected from the contaminating presence of men. Yet the female atmosphere that enclosed her, Strachey suggests, may have given rise to an unforeseen reaction: 'perhaps, after all, to the discerning eye, the purity would not be absolute. The careful searcher might detect, in the virgin soil, the first faint traces of an unexpected vein.' For all the care taken over her upbringing, 'there was something deep within her which responded immediately and vehemently to natures that offered a romantic contrast with her own.'

It is this hidden sexuality that Strachey explores in describing Victoria's relationships with her Prime Ministers. He makes the romantic contrast between the young queen and the flippant, sceptical, absent-minded Lord Melbourne particularly striking. We see Lord M. not only through the fascinated eyes of Victoria, but also with the admiring gaze of her biographer. The result is the most satisfying impressionistic study in the book. Charles Greville described Melbourne as 'a man with a capacity for loving without having anything in the world to love'. This undirected capacity for loving suddenly focusses upon the Queen. Strachey picks out images that suggest the romantic sexuality of their attachment: 'the autumn rose, in those autumn months of 1839, came to a wondrous blooming. The petals expanded, beautifully, for the last time. For the last time in this unlooked-for, this incongruous, this almost incredible intercourse, the old epicure tasted the exquisiteness of romance.' Robert Peel possessed none of Melbourne's sophisticated sex-appeal. Reserved by nature, he seemed embarrassed by women and his manner became unattractively pompous in their company. Since he made little impression on Victoria, he occupies little space in her biography.

After her marriage, Victoria (whose simple pleasures, Strachey tells us, were mostly physical) lost her 'bold and discontented' look, and her platonic infatuation for Lord Melbourne gently faded away. Completely obsessed by her husband, her response to any man was decided by his opinion alone. The jaunty and volatile Palmerston, to whom she might otherwise have been attracted, repelled her because he was the very antithesis of the Prince Consort, representing all that was most hostile to him in the spirit of England. But Strachey features the gaudy and gipsyish figure of Tsar Nicolas I of Russia to remind us that Victoria was naturally appreciative of any strikingly handsome man.

After Albert's death this power of appreciation blossomed again: whenever Victoria's strong sexual instinct came into play Albert's posthumous endorsement was taken for granted. He had preferred Gladstone to Disraeli, yet because Gladstone behaved towards her more like a public meeting than a woman, she could never warm to him. Disraeli's oriental personality, with its flattery and charm, gave the Queen back her self-confidence. Strachey passes swiftly over Gladstone as he had done over Peel, but his portrait of Disraeli is almost as detailed and sympathetic as his Melbourne. 'After the long gloom of her bereavement, after the chill of Gladstonian discipline, she expanded to the rays of Disraeli's devotion like a flower in the sun.'

Strachey's Victoria is a woman who becomes dependent on men in order to experience a sense of physical security. Though shrewd, she had none of the political genius of Queen Elizabeth. Her politics belonged to the 18th century and her interest in them was simply personal. She suspected political zeal and was more at ease in her later years with her Highland gillie John Brown and her Indian attendant Munshi Abdul Karim than with prominent politicians. To overcome Albert's mute protest from the grave, she constructed an obscure spiritual bridge—'the gruff, kind, hairy Scotsman was, she felt, in some mysterious way, a legacy from the dead. She came to believe at last—or so it appeared—that the spirit of Albert was nearer when Brown was near.'

Victoria's deepest happiness came from her marriage to Albert, which forms the central panel in Strachey's biography. Albert is introduced early in the story when he visits England with his brother Ernest. 'The Princess shared her ecstasies and her italics between them,' Strachey wrote; 'but it is clear enough where her secret preference lay. "Particularly Albert"!' Albert out of sight was Albert out of mind: but when he came to England again, danced with her, talked with her, she was swept off her feet by a violent sexual upheaval which Strachey gives us in highly charged romantic language: 'Albert arrived; and the whole structure of her existence crumbled into nothingness like a house of cards. He was beautiful—she gasped—she knew no more. Then, in a flash, a thousand mysteries were revealed to her'.

Although the Prince was a mirror of manly beauty in the eyes of the Queen, his constitution was not strong and 'owing either to his peculiar upbringing or to a more fundamental idiosyncrasy he had a marked distaste for the opposite sex.' The prospect of marriage to the adoring Victoria filled him with depression. Strachey confirmed to Hesketh Pearson that he had intended to suggest that Albert was homosexual. This must be taken as the key to several passages which bring out Albert's melancholy and isolation: 'A shy young foreigner, awkward in ladies' company, unexpansive and self-opinionated, it was improbable that, in any circumstances, he would have been a society success. . . . Really, they thought, this youth was more like some kind of foreign tenor. . . . From the support and the solace of true companionship he was utterly cut off.'

Strachey portrayed in Albert a man partially akin to himself and revealed something of his own loneliness. Albert is seen as having the power of arousing an idolatry that in no sense meets his emotional needs. But he could not turn elsewhere, as his biographer could, for companionship. This was his 'curious position' to which Strachey returns in a later paragraph: 'The husband was not so happy as the wife. In spite of the great improvement in his situation, in spite of a growing family and the adoration of Victoria, Albert was still a stranger in a strange land, and the serenity of spiritual satisfaction was denied him. . . . Victoria idolized him; but it was understanding that he craved for, not idolatry. . . . He was lonely.' The peculiar fascination which this marriage exerted over Strachey is clearly disclosed when he asks: 'was he the wife and she the husband?' and answers his question—'It almost seemed so.' From resembling a foreign tenor Albert changes during the course of his marriage into an idealised butler. By adapting himself body and soul to the rôle of the Prince Consort, he sacrifices what is original in his character to become the caricature of a worthy man. What pricked Strachey's curiosity was the underlying ascendency of Victoria. Only when we come to see Victoria through the eyes of her declining husband are we made to feel a repugnance for her. 'Beside Victoria, he presented a painful contrast. . . . If only, by some sympathetic magic, she could have conveyed into that portly, flabby figure, that desiccated and discouraged brain, a measure of the stamina and the self-assurance which were so pre-eminently hers!'

After the death of Albert, and during Victoria's old age, Strachey's attitude softens to the Queen. His last two chapters contain a full inventory of her shortcomings—her imperialism and religious obscuranticism, her disapproval of the memoirs of Greville, her insistence on etiquette, her complacency, pride, egotism, insensitivity. It is a formidable list—but Strachey seems more amused than censorious. Many of Victoria's failings are presented sympathetically. Her middle-class morals were really, we are led to believe, a development of a genuine family affection. Her passion for John Brown contributes to her humanity and that most loved of English qualities, eccentricity. Her collecting instinct, which is described in terms of an obsessional neurosis, is seen to have its roots in her fear of death, so that our hearts are touched. Even her indefensible insistence upon changing the form of the verdict in criminal cases involving insanity is partly excused as being due to her memory of Albert's feelings on the subject.

Strachey frames his picture of the Queen's old age with the abiding love of her people. In many ways she did not merit such devotion. She was out of step with her times and often insufferable to her family. Yet the extraordinary loyalty persisted, so that each limitation of character Strachey points to only serves to increase our wonder at the spell of her personality. 'The Queen was hailed at once as the mother of her people and as the embodied symbol of their imperial greatness,' he writes in his penultimate chapter; 'and she responded to the double sentiment with all the ardour of her spirit. England and the people of England, she knew it, she felt it, were, in some wonderful and yet quite simple manner, *hers*. . . . At last, after so long, happiness—fragmentary, perhaps, and charged with gravity, but true and unmistakable none the less—had returned to her.'

This tenderness, which astonished readers such as G. M. Trevelyan (who proclaimed that Strachey had come to curse and stayed to bless), partly arose from Strachey's having associated the Queen with his mother. Lady Strachey, then in her eighties, had not been happy at the prospect of her son writing on Queen Victoria. 'She no doubt lays herself open to drastic treatment which is one reason I think it better left alone,' she had written to him. 'She could not help being stupid, but she tried to do her duty, and considering the period she began in, her upbringing, her early associations, and her position, this was a difficult matter and highly to her credit. She has won a place in public affection and a reputation in our history which it would be highly unpopular, and I think not quite fair, to attempt to bring down.'

Strachey's biography inaugurated a new and legendary view of the Queen—a whimsical, teasing, half-admiring, half-mocking view that found in Victoria a quaintly impressive symbol of a quaintly impressive age. The book, which was to be translated into some twenty languages, was an instantaneous success when it was published in 1921. In England the first five thousand copies were sold out within twenty-four hours and another four impressions printed within the year; in America it was even more popular and went through seventeen impressions during the 1920s. Many critics regarded it as a masterpiece of biography, a technical *tour de force*. 'To mould this vast material into a synthetic form,' wrote Harold Nicolson; 'to convey not merely unity of impression but a convincing sense of scientific reality; to maintain throughout an attitude of detachment; to preserve the exquisite poise and balance of sustained and gentle irony, and to secure these objects with no apparent effort . . . this, in all certainty, is an achievement which required the very highest gifts of intellect and imagination.' Strachey had not only recreated the Queen, he had extended the architecture of biography. 'He it was who first saw the possibilities of this new medium,' wrote Lord David Cecil. 'He it was who evolved the technical equipment for its expression. We may extend his building, but we must always construct on his foundations. He was the man who established the form.'

Strachey dedicated *Queen Victoria* to Virginia Woolf: 'my jealousy is twinged,' she admitted, by its great success. Some twenty years later, when she had attained her own success and Strachey was dead, she published her final assessment in *The Death of the Moth*. Strachey had probably done for 'the old Queen what Boswell did for the old dictionary maker,' she concluded. 'In time to come Lytton Strachey's Queen Victoria will be Queen Victoria, just as Boswell's Johnson is now Dr. Johnson. The other versions will fade and disappear. It was a prodigious feat.'

MICHAEL HOLROYD
*London, 1987*

# 1: ANTECEDENTS

ON November 6, 1817, died the Princess Charlotte, only child of the Prince Regent, and heir to the crown of England. Her short life had hardly been a happy one. By nature impulsive, capricious, and vehement, she had always longed for liberty; and she had never possessed it. She had been brought up among violent family quarrels, had been early separated from her disreputable and eccentric mother, and handed over to the care of her disreputable and selfish father. When she was seventeen, he decided to marry her off to the Prince of Orange; she, at first, acquiesced; but, suddenly falling in love with Prince Augustus of Prussia, she determined to break off the engagement. This was not her first love affair, for she had previously carried on a clandestine correspondence with a Captain Hess. Prince Augustus was already married, morganatically, but she did not know it, and he did not tell her. While she was spinning out the negotiations with the Prince of Orange, the allied sovereigns—it was June, 1814—arrived in London to celebrate their victory. Among them, in the suite of the Emperor of Russia, was the young and handsome Prince Leopold of Saxe-Coburg. He made several attempts to attract the notice of the Princess, but she, with her heart elsewhere, paid very little attention. Next month the Prince Regent, discovering that his daughter was having secret meetings with Prince Augustus, suddenly appeared upon the scene and, after dismissing her household, sentenced her to a strict seclusion in Windsor Park. 'God Almighty grant me patience!' she exclaimed, falling on her knees in an agony of agitation: then she jumped up, ran down the backstairs and out into the street, hailed a passing cab, and drove to her mother's house in Bayswater. She was discovered, pursued, and at length, yielded to the persuasions of her uncles, the Dukes of York and Sussex, of Brougham, and of the Bishop of Salisbury, she returned to Carlton House at two o'clock in the morning. She

*Victoria's five 'wicked uncles', younger brothers of George IV, in 1820. Eccentric, impecunious and often amoral, their matrimonial prospects had been blighted by the Royal Marriages Act of 1772, a misguided attempt to prevent royalty from marrying their social inferiors. Faced with diplomatic alliances, they tended to remain single, but often formed longstanding liaisons with commoners. Despite his fifteen children, in 1816 George III had only one legitimate grandchild, Princess Charlotte; her death the following year left the succession wide open. Frederick Duke of York and Ernest Duke of Cumberland were married but childless; Augustus Duke of Sussex remained faithful to his companion Lady Cecilia Underwood. Hastily the three remaining dukes sought wives. William Duke of Clarence and Adelaide lost all their children in infancy. But Edward Duke of Kent and the youngest brother Adolphus Duke of Cambridge both became fathers in 1819, with baby Alexandrina Victoria taking precedence over her cousin George.*

11

was immured at Windsor, but no more was heard of the Prince of Orange. Prince Augustus, too, disappeared. The way was at last open to Prince Leopold of Saxe-Coburg.

This Prince was clever enough to get round the Regent, to impress the Ministers, and to make friends with another of the Princess's uncles, the Duke of Kent. Through the Duke he was able to communicate privately with the Princess, who now declared that he was necessary to her happiness. When, after Waterloo, he was in Paris, the Duke's aide-de-camp carried letters backwards and forwards across the Channel. In January 1816 he was invited to England, and in May the marriage took place.

The character of Prince Leopold contrasted strangely with that of his wife. The younger son of a German princeling, he was at this time twenty-six years of age; he had served with distinction in the war against Napoleon; he had shown considerable diplomatic skill at the Congress of Vienna; and he was now to try his hand at the task of taming a tumultuous Princess. Cold and formal in manner, collected in speech, careful in action, he soon dominated the wild, impetuous, generous creature by his side. There was much in her, he found, of which he could not approve. She quizzed, she stamped, she roared with laughter; she had very little of that self-command which is especially required of princes; her manners were abominable. Of the latter he was a good judge, having moved, as he himself explained to his niece many years later, in the best society of Europe, being in fact 'what is called in French *de la fleur des pois*.' There was continual friction, but every scene ended in the same way. Standing before him like a rebellious boy in petticoats, her body pushed forward, her hands behind her back, with flaming cheeks and sparkling eyes, she would declare at last that she was ready to do whatever he wanted. 'If you wish it, I will do it,' she would say. 'I want nothing for myself,' he invariably answered; 'when I press something on you, it is from a conviction that it is for your interest and for your good.'

Among the members of the household at Claremont, near Esher, where the royal pair were established, was a young German physician, Christian Friedrich Stockmar. He was the son of a minor magistrate in Coburg, and, after taking part as a medical officer in the war, he had settled down as a doctor in his native town. Here he had met Prince Leopold, who had been struck by his ability, and, on his marriage, brought him to England as his personal physician. A curious fate awaited this young man; many were the gifts which the future held in store for him—many and various—influence, power, mystery, unhappiness, a broken heart. At Claremont his position was a very humble one; but the Princess took a fancy to him, called him 'Stocky,' and romped with him along the corridors. Dyspeptic by constitution, melancholic by temperament, he could yet be lively on occasion, and was known as a wit in Coburg. He was virtuous, too, and observed the royal *ménage* with approbation. 'My master,' he wrote in his diary, 'is the best of all husbands in all the five quarters of the globe; and his wife bears him an amount of love, the greatness of which can only be compared with the English national debt.' Before long he gave proof of another quality—a quality which was to colour the whole of his life—cautious sagacity. When, in the spring of 1817, it was known that the Princess was expecting a child,

*Princess Charlotte, only child of the disastrous union between the Prince Regent and Princess Caroline of Brunswick, married the twenty-six year old Prince Leopold of Saxe-Coburg in 1816. Eighteen months later she died in childbirth and the nation mourned: her obstetrician was so reviled that he committed suicide, and her father suffered a nervous breakdown which rendered him so uncharacteristically careless of his appearance that a malicious observer noted that, shedding his corsets, 'Prinny has let loose his belly, which now reaches to his knees.'*

the post of one of her physicians-in-ordinary was offered to him, and he had the good sense to refuse it. He perceived that his colleagues would be jealous of him, that his advice would probably not be taken, but that, if anything were to go wrong, it would be certainly the foreign doctor who would be blamed. Very soon, indeed, he came to the opinion that the low diet and constant bleedings, to which the unfortunate Princess was subjected, were an error; he drew the Prince aside, and begged him to communicate this opinion to the English doctors; but it was useless. The fashionable lowering treatment was continued for months. On November 5, at nine o'clock in the evening, after a labour of over fifty hours, the Princess was delivered of a dead boy. At midnight her exhausted strength gave way. Then, at last, Stockmar consented to see her; he went in, and found her obviously dying, while the doctors were plying her with wine. She seized his hand and pressed it. 'They have made me tipsy,' she said. After a little he left her, and was already in the next room when he heard her call out in her loud voice 'Stocky! Stocky!' As he ran back the death-rattle was in her throat. She tossed herself violently from side to side; then suddenly drew up her legs, and it was over.

The Prince, after hours of watching, had left the room for a few moments' rest; and Stockmar had now to tell him that his wife was dead. At first he could not be made to realise what had happened. On their way to her room he sank down on a chair while Stockmar knelt beside him: it was all a dream; it was impossible. At last, by the bed, he, too, knelt down and kissed the cold hands. Then rising and exclaiming, 'Now I am quite desolate. Promise me never to leave me,' he threw himself into Stockmar's arms.

## II

The tragedy at Claremont was of a most upsetting kind. The royal kaleidoscope had suddenly shifted, and nobody could tell how the new pattern would arrange itself. The succession to the throne, which had seemed so satisfactorily settled, now became a matter of urgent doubt.

George III was still living, an aged lunatic, at Windsor, completely impervious to the impressions of the outer world. Of his seven sons, the youngest was of more than middle age, and none had legitimate offspring. The outlook, therefore, was ambiguous. It seemed highly improbable that the Prince Regent, who had lately been obliged to abandon his stays, and presented a preposterous figure of debauched obesity, could ever again, even on the supposition that he divorced his wife and re-married, become the father of a family. Besides the Duke of Kent, who must be noticed separately, the other brothers, in order of seniority, were the Dukes of York, Clarence, Cumberland, Sussex, and Cambridge; their situations and prospects require a brief description. The Duke of York, whose escapades in times past with Mrs. Clarke and the army had brought him into trouble, now divided his life between London and a large, extravagantly ordered and extremely uncomfortable country house where he occupied himself with racing, whist, and improper stories. He was remarkable among the princes for one reason: he was the only one of them—so we are informed by a highly competent observer—who had the feelings of a gentleman. He had been long married to the Princess Royal of Prussia, a lady who rarely went to bed and was perpetually surrounded by vast numbers of dogs, parrots, and monkeys. They had no children. The Duke of Clarence had lived for many years in complete obscurity with Mrs. Jordan, the actress, in Bushey Park. By her he had had a large family of sons and daughters, and had appeared, in effect, to be married to her, when he suddenly separated from her and offered to marry Miss Wykeham, a crazy woman of large fortune, who, however, would have nothing to say to him. Shortly afterwards Mrs. Jordan died in distressed circumstances in Paris. The Duke of Cumberland was probably the most unpopular man in England. Hideously ugly, with a distorted eye, he was bad-tempered and vindictive in private, a violent reactionary in politics, and was subsequently suspected of murdering his valet and of having carried on an amorous intrigue of an extremely scandalous kind. He had lately married a German Princess, but there were as yet no children by the marriage. The Duke of Sussex had mildly literary tastes and collected books. He had married Lady Augusta Murray, by whom he had two children, but the marriage, under the Royal Marriages Act, was declared void. On Lady Augusta's death, he married Lady Cecilia Buggin; she changed her name to Underwood; but this marriage also was void. Of the Duke of Cambridge, the youngest of the brothers, not very much was known. He lived in Hanover, wore a blond wig, chattered and fidgeted a great deal, and was unmarried.

Besides his seven sons, George III had five surviving daughters. Of these, two—the Queen of Würtemberg and the Duchess of Gloucester—were married and childless. The three unmarried princesses—Augusta, Elizabeth, and Sophia—were all over forty.

# III

The fourth son of George III was Edward, Duke of Kent. He was now fifty years of age—a tall, stout, vigorous man, highly-coloured, with bushy eyebrows, a bald top to his head, and what hair he had carefully dyed a glossy black. His dress was extremely neat, and in his whole appearance there was a rigidity which did not belie his character. He had spent his early life in the army—at Gibraltar, in Canada, in the West Indies—and, under the influence of military training, had become at first a disciplinarian and at last a martinet. In 1802, having been sent to Gibraltar to restore order in a mutinous garrison, he was recalled for undue severity, and his active career had come to an end. Since then he had spent his life regulating his domestic arrangements with great exactitude, busying himself with the affairs of his numerous dependents, designing clocks, and struggling to restore order to his finances, for, in spite of his being, as someone said who knew him well, 'réglé comme du papier à musique,' and in spite of an income of £24,000 a year, he was hopelessly in debt. He had quarrelled with most of his brothers, particularly with the Prince Regent, and it was only natural that he should have joined the political Opposition and become a pillar of the Whigs.

What his political opinions may actually have been is open to doubt; it has often been asserted that he was a Liberal, or even a Radical; and, if we are to believe Robert Owen, he was a necessitarian Socialist. His relations with

Owen—the shrewd, gullible, high-minded, wrong-headed, illustrious and preposterous father of Socialism and Co-operation—were curious and characteristic. He talked of visiting the Mills at New Lanark; he did, in fact, preside at one of Owen's public meetings; he corresponded with him on confidential terms, and he even (so Owen assures us) returned, after his death, from 'the sphere of spirits' to give encouragement to the Owenites on earth. 'In an especial manner,' says Owen, 'I have to name the very anxious feelings of the spirit of his Royal Highness the late Duke of Kent (who early informed me there were no titles in the spiritual spheres into which he had entered), to benefit, not a class, a sect, a party, or any particular country, but the whole of the human race through futurity.' 'His whole spirit-proceeding with me has been most beautiful,' Owen adds, 'making his own appointments; and never in one instance has this spirit not been punctual to the minute he had named.' But Owen was of a sanguine temperament. He also numbered among his proselytes President Jefferson, Prince Metternich, and Napoleon; so that some uncertainty must still linger over the Duke of Kent's views. But there is no uncertainty about another circumstance: his Royal Highness borrowed from Robert Owen, on various occasions, various sums of money which were never repaid and amounted in all to several hundred pounds.

*The Utopian socialist Robert Owen (1771–1858) has been described as 'one of those intolerable bores who are the salt of the earth'. It was no doubt the influence of his ideas which led the Duke of Kent to reply to the royal toast with the words, 'I am a friend of civil and religious liberty, all the world over. I am an enemy to all religious tests. I am a supporter of a general system of education. All men are my brethren; and I hold that power is delegated only for the benefit of the people.'*

After the death of the Princess Charlotte it was clearly important, for more than one reason, that the Duke of Kent should marry. From the point of view of the nation, the lack of heirs in the reigning family seemed to make the step almost obligatory; it was also likely to be highly expedient from the point of view of the Duke. To marry as a public duty, for the sake of the royal succession, would surely deserve some recognition from a grateful country. When the Duke of York had married he had received a settlement of £25,000 a year. Why should not the Duke of Kent look forward to an equal sum? But the situation was not quite simple. There was the Duke of Clarence to be considered; he was the elder brother, and, if *he* married, would clearly have the prior claim. On the other hand, if the Duke of Kent married, it was important to remember that he would be making a serious sacrifice: a lady was involved.

The Duke, reflecting upon all these matters with careful attention, happened, about a month after his niece's death, to visit Brussels, and learnt that Mr. Creevey was staying in the town. Mr. Creevey was a close friend of the leading Whigs and an inveterate gossip; and it occured to the Duke that there could be no better channel through which to communicate his views upon the situation to political circles at home. Apparently it did not occur to him that Mr. Creevey was malicious and might keep a diary. He therefore sent for him on some trivial pretext, and a remarkable conversation ensued.

After referring to the death of the Princess, to the improbability of the Regent's seeking a divorce, to the childlessness of the Duke of York, and to the possibility of the Duke of Clarence marrying, the Duke adverted to his own position. 'Should the Duke of Clarence not marry,' he said, 'the next prince in succession is myself, and although I trust I shall be at all times ready to obey any call my country may make upon me, God only knows the sacrifice it will be to make, whenever I shall think it my duty to become a married man. It is now seven-and-twenty years that Madame St. Laurent and I have lived together: we are of the same age, and have been in all climates, and in all difficulties together, and you may well imagine, Mr. Creevey, the pang it will occasion me to part with her. I put it to your own feelings—in the event of any separation between you and Mrs. Creevey. . . . As for Madame St. Laurent herself, I protest I don't know what is to become of her if a marriage is to be forced upon me; her feelings are already so agitated upon the subject.' The duke went on to describe how, one morning, a day or two after the Princess Charlotte's death, a paragraph had appeared in the *Morning Chronicle*, alluding to the possibility of his marriage. He had received the newspaper at breakfast together with his letters, and 'I did as is my constant practice, I threw the newspaper across the table to Madame St. Laurent, and began to open and read my letters. I had not done so but a very short time, when my attention was called to an extraordinary noise and a strong convulsive movement in Madame St. Laurent's throat. For a short time I entertained serious apprehensions for her safety; and when, upon her recovery, I enquired into the occasion of this attack, she pointed to the article in the *Morning Chronicle*.'

The Duke then returned to the subject of the Duke of Clarence. 'My brother the Duke of Clarence is the elder brother, and has certainly the right to marry if he chooses, and I would not interfere with him on any account. If he wishes to be king—to be married and have children, poor man—God help him! let him do so. For myself—I am a man of no ambition, and wish only to remain as I am. . . . Easter, you know, falls very early this year—the 22nd of March. If the Duke of Clarence does not take any step before that time, I must find some pretext to reconcile Madame St. Laurent to my going to England for a short time. When once there, it will be easy for me to consult with my friends as to the proper steps to be taken. Should the Duke of Clarence do nothing before that time as to marrying it will become my duty, no doubt, to take some measures upon the subject myself.' Two names, the Duke said, had been mentioned in this connection—those of the Princess of Baden and the Princess of Saxe-Coburg. The latter, he thought, would perhaps be the better of the two, from the circumstance of Prince Leopold being so popular with the nation; but before any other steps were taken, he hoped and expected to see justice done to Madame St. Laurent. 'She is,' he explained, 'of very good family, and has never been an actress, and I am the first and only person who ever lived with her. Her disinterestedness, too, has been equal to her fidelity. When she first came to me it was upon £100 a year. That sum was afterwards raised to £400, and finally to £1000; but when my debts made it necessary for me to sacrifice a great part of my income, Madame St. Laurent insisted upon again returning to her income of £400 a year. If Madame St. Laurent is to return to live amongst her friends, it must be in such a state of independence as to command their respect. I shall not require very much, but a certain number of servants and a carriage are essentials.' As to his own settlement, the Duke observed that he would expect the Duke of York's marriage to be considered the precedent. 'That,' he said, 'was a marriage for the succession, and £25,000 for income was settled, in addition to all his other income, purely on that account. I shall be contented with the

*Edward, Duke of Kent, was the fourth son of George III and Queen Charlotte. 'From all what I heard', Queen Victoria wrote somewhat ungrammatically of the father she never knew, 'he was the best of all' the royal dukes—not a particularly glowing compliment in view of the undistinguished careers of all George III's fifteen children. Edward joined the army but was retired in 1803 'on a charge of disciplinary fanaticism amounting to brutality' and was soon deeply in debt. His life in exile in Quebec and Brussels was shared by the charming Julie, Madame St. Laurent, his companion for twenty-eight years; the chance discovery by the widowed Princess of Leiningen of his plans to marry her sent her temporarily into a Paris convent.*

same arrangement, without making any demands grounded on the difference of the value of money in 1792 and at present. As for the payment of my debts,' the Duke concluded, 'I don't call them great. The nation, on the contrary, is greatly my debtor.' Here a clock struck, and seemed to remind the Duke that he had an appointment; he rose, and Mr. Creevey left him.

Who could keep such a communication secret? Certainly not Mr. Creevey. He hurried off to tell the Duke of Wellington, who was very much amused, and he wrote a long account of it to Lord Sefton, who received the letter 'very apropos,' while a surgeon was sounding his bladder to ascertain whether he had a stone. 'I never saw a fellow more astonished than he was,' wrote Lord Sefton in his reply, 'at seeing me laugh as soon as the operation was over. Nothing could be more first-rate than the royal Edward's ingenuousness. One does not know which to admire most—the delicacy of his attachment to Madame St. Laurent, the refinement of his sentiments towards the Duke of Clarence, or his own perfect disinterestedness in pecuniary matters.'

As it turned out, both the brothers decided to marry. The Duke of Kent, selecting the Princess of Saxe-Coburg in preference to the Princess of Baden, was united to her on May 29, 1818. On June 11, the Duke of Clarence followed suit with a daughter of the Duke of Saxe-Meiningen. But they were disappointed in their financial expectations; for though the Government brought forward proposals to increase their allowances, together with that of the Duke of Cumberland, the motions were defeated in the House of Commons. At this the Duke of Wellington was not surprised. 'By God!' he said, 'there is a great deal to be said about that. They are the damnedest millstones about the necks of any Government that can be imagined. They have insulted—*personally* insulted—two-thirds of the gentlemen of England, and how can it be wondered at that they take their revenge upon them in the House of Commons? It is their only opportunity, and I think, by God! they are quite right to use it.' Eventually, however, Parliament increased the Duke of Kent's annuity by £6000.

The subsequent history of Madame St. Laurent has not transpired.

# IV

The new Duchess of Kent, Victoria Mary Louisa, was a daughter of Francis, Duke of Saxe-Coburg-Saalfeld, and a sister of Prince Leopold. The family was an ancient one, being a branch of the great House of Wettin, which since the eleventh century had ruled over the March of Meissen on the Elbe. In the fifteenth century the whole possessions of the House had been divided between the Albertine and Ernestine branches: from the former descended the electors and kings of Saxony; the latter, ruling over Thuringia, became further subdivided into five branches, of which the duchy of Saxe-Coburg was one. This principality was very small, containing about 60,000 inhabitants, but it enjoyed independent and sovereign rights. During the disturbed years which followed the French Revolution, its affairs became terribly involved. The Duke was extravagant, and kept open house for the swarms of refugees, who fled eastward over Germany as the French power advanced. Among

*Queen Victoria's mother was born Victoria of Saxe-Coburg-Saalfeld in 1786. When her first husband, Emich Charles, Prince of Leiningen, died in 1814, she lived with her two children (Charles, born 1804 and Feodora, born 1807) in the remote castle of Wald-Leiningen near Amorbach. The suggestion that she marry Edward Duke of Kent came from her younger brother Leopold, at that time married to the Princess Charlotte, heir apparent to the British throne. After Charlotte's death the race for the succession made the Duke press the attractive widow for a 'positive' answer, and in January 1818 she replied, 'Je quitte une situation indépendente et agréable dans l'espoir que votre amitié m'en dédommagera [I am giving up an independent and agreeable situation in the hope that your affection will compensate me].'*

these was the Prince of Leiningen, an elderly beau, whose domains on the Moselle had been seized by the French, but who was granted in compensation the territory of Amorbach in Lower Franconia. In 1803 he married the Princess Victoria, at that time seventeen years of age. Three years later Duke Francis died a ruined man. The Napoleonic harrow passed over Saxe-Coburg. The duchy was seized by the French, and the ducal family were reduced to beggary, almost to starvation. At the same time the little principality of Amorbach was devastated by the French, Russian, and Austrian armies, marching and counter-marching across it. For years there was hardly a cow in the country, nor enough grass to feed a flock a geese. Such was the desperate plight of the family which, a generation later, was to have gained a foothold in half the reigning Houses of Europe. The Napoleonic harrow had indeed done its work; the seed was planted; and the crop would have surprised Napoleon. Prince Leopold, thrown upon his own resources at fifteen, made a career for himself and married the heiress of England. The Princess of Leiningen, struggling at Amorbach with poverty, military requisitions, and a futile husband, developed an independence of character and a tenacity of purpose which were to prove useful in very different circumstances. In 1814, her husband died, leaving her with two children and the regency of the principality. After her brother's marriage with the Princess Charlotte, it was proposed that she should marry the Duke of Kent; but she declined, on the ground that the guardianship of her children and the management of her domains made other ties undesirable. The Princess Charlotte's death, however, altered the case; and when the Duke of Kent renewed his offer, she accepted it. She was thirty-two years old—short, stout, with brown eyes and hair, and rosy cheeks, cheerful and voluble, and gorgeously attired in rustling silks and bright velvets.

She was certainly fortunate in her contented disposition; for she was fated, all through her life, to have much to put up with. Her second marriage, with its dubious prospects, seemed at first to be chiefly a source of difficulties and discomforts. The Duke, declaring that he was still too poor to live in England, moved about with uneasy precision through Belgium and Germany, attending parades and inspecting barracks in a neat military cap, while the English notabilities looked askance, and the Duke of Wellington dubbed him the Corporal. 'God damme!' he exclaimed to Mr. Creevey, 'd'ye know what his sisters call him? By God! they call him Joseph Surface!' At Valenciennes, where there was a review and a great dinner, the Duchess arrived with an old and ugly lady-in-waiting, and the Duke of Wellington found himself in a difficulty. 'Who the devil is to take out the maid of honour?' he kept asking; but at last he thought of a solution. 'Damme, Freemantle, find out the mayor and let him do it.' So the Mayor of Valenciennes was brought up for the purpose, and—so we learn from Mr. Creevey—'a capital figure he was.' A few days later, at Brussels, Mr. Creevey himself had an unfortunate experience. A military school was to be inspected—before breakfast. The company assembled; everything was highly satisfactory; but the Duke of Kent continued for so long examining every detail and asking meticulous question after meticulous question, that Mr. Creevey at last could bear it no longer, and whispered to his neighbour that he was damned hungry. The Duke of

Wellington heard him, and was delighted. 'I recommend you,' he said, 'whenever you start with the royal family in a morning, and particularly with *the Corporal*, always to breakfast first.' He and his staff, it turned out, had taken that precaution, and the great man amused himself, while the stream of royal inquiries poured on, by pointing at Mr. Creevey from time to time with the remark, 'Voilà le monsieur qui n'a pas déjeuné!'

Settled down at last at Amorbach, the time hung heavily on the Duke's hands. The establishment was small, the country was impoverished; even clock-making grew tedious at last. He brooded—for in spite of his piety the Duke was not without a vein of superstition—over the prophecy of a gipsy at Gibraltar who had told him that he was to have many losses and crosses, that he was to die in happiness, and that his only child was to be a great queen. Before long it became clear that a child was to be expected: the Duke decided that it should be born in England. Funds were lacking for the journey, but his determination was not be set aside. Come what might, he declared, his child must be English-born. A carriage was hired, and the Duke himself mounted the box. Inside were the Duchess, her daughter Feodora, a girl of fourteen, with maids, nurses, lap-dogs, and canaries. Off they drove—through Germany, through France: bad roads, cheap inns, were nothing to the rigorous Duke and the equable, abundant Duchess. The Channel was crossed, London was reached in safety. The authorities provided a set of rooms in Kensington Palace; and there, on May 24, 1819, a female infant was born.

*The west front of Kensington Palace, 'the poor old Palace', as Queen Victoria described the home of her lonely childhood. Originally the country seat of William and Mary, the red-brick building, situated in an unfashionably suburban area, had become the rather dilapidated home of various lesser members of the royal family when the Duke and Duchess of Kent were granted accommodation there in 1819.*

19

# 2: CHILDHOOD

THE child who, in these not very impressive circumstances, appeared in the world, received but scant attention. There was small reason to foresee her destiny. The Duchess of Clarence, two months before, had given birth to a daughter; this infant, indeed, had died almost immediately; but it seemed highly probable that the Duchess would again become a mother; and so it actually fell out. More than this, the Duchess of Kent was young, and the Duke was strong; there was every likelihood that before long a brother would follow, to snatch her faint chance of the succession from the little princess.

Nevertheless, the Duke had other views: there were prophecies. . . . At any rate, he would christen the child Elizabeth, a name of happy augury. In this, however, he reckoned without the Regent, who, seeing a chance of annoying his brother, suddenly announced that he himself would be present at the baptism, and signified at the same time that one of the godfathers was to be the Emperor Alexander of Russia. And so when the ceremony took place, and the Archbishop of Canterbury asked by what name he was to baptise the child, the Regent replied 'Alexandrina.' At this the Duke ventured to suggest that another name might be added. 'Certainly,' said the Regent; 'Georgina?' 'Or Elizabeth?' said the Duke. There was a pause, during which the Archbishop, with the baby in his lawn sleeves, looked with some uneasiness from one Prince to the other. 'Very well, then,' said the Regent at last, 'call her after her mother. But Alexandrina must come first.' Thus, to the disgust of her father, the child was christened Alexandrina Victoria.

The Duke had other subjects of disgust. The meagre grant of the Commons had by no means put an end to his financial distresses. It was to be feared that his services were not appreciated by the nation. His debts continued to grow. For many years he had lived upon £7000 a year; but now his expenses were

*Queen Victoria aged four, from a painting by S. P. Denning. 'Up to my 5th year I had been very much indulged by everyone and set pretty well all at defiance,' admitted the Queen. 'All worshipped the poor little fatherless child whose future was still very uncertain. . . . I was not fond of learning as a little child and baffled every attempt to teach me my letters up to five years old.' At four she could trace the word 'Victoria' over a series of dots and gradually left behind the baby names of 'Drina' and 'Vickelchen'. Though brought up in 'a very simple, plain manner', the little Princess was soon made aware of her regal status: 'Bow your head, Princess,' said her nurse as gentlemen touched their hats to the tiny child riding on the donkey given to her by her uncle the Duke of York.*

exactly doubled; he could make no further reductions; as it was, there was not a single servant in his establishment who was idle for a moment from morning to night. He poured out his griefs in a long letter to Robert Owen, whose sympathy had the great merit of being practical. 'I now candidly state,' he wrote, 'that, after viewing the subject in every possible way, I am satisfied that, to continue to live in England, even in the quiet way in which we are going on, *without splendour*, and *without show*, *nothing short of doubling the seven thousand pounds will do*, REDUCTION BEING IMPOSSIBLE.' It was clear that he would be obliged to sell his house for £51,300: if that failed, he would go and live on the Continent. 'If my services are useful to my country, it surely becomes *those who have the power* to support me in substantiating those just claims I have for the very extensive losses and privations I have experienced, during the very long period of my professional servitude in the Colonies; and if this is not attainable, *it is a clear proof to me that they are not appreciated*; and under that impression I shall not scruple, in *due* time, to resume my retirement abroad, when the Duchess and myself shall have fulfilled our duties in establishing the *English* birth of my child, and giving it maternal nutriment on the soil of Old England; and which we shall certainly repeat, if Providence destines to give us any further increase of family.'

In the meantime, he decided to spend the winter at Sidmouth, 'in order,' he told Owen, 'that the Duchess may have the benefit of tepid sea bathing, and our infant that of sea air, on the fine coast of Devonshire, during the months of the year that are so odious in London.' In December the move was made. With the new year, the Duke remembered another prophecy. In 1820, a fortune-teller had told him, two members of the Royal Family would die. Who would they be? He speculated on the various possibilities: the King, it was plain, could not live much longer; and the Duchess of York had been attacked by a mortal disease. Probably it would be the King and the Duchess of York; or perhaps the King and the Duke of York; or the King and the Regent. He himself was one of the healthiest men in England. 'My brothers,' he declared, 'are not so strong as I am; I have lived a regular life. I shall outlive them all. The crown will come to me and my children.' He went out for a walk, and got his feet wet. On coming home, he neglected to change his stockings. He caught cold, inflammation of the lungs set in, and on January 22 he was a dying man. By a curious chance, young Dr. Stockmar was staying in the house at the time; two years before, he had stood by the death-bed of the Princess Charlotte; and now he was watching the Duke of Kent in his agony. On Stockmar's advice, a will was hastily prepared. The Duke's earthly possessions were of a negative character; but it was important that the guardianship of the unwitting child, whose fortunes were now so strangely changing, should be assured to the Duchess. The Duke was just able to understand the document, and to append his signature. Having inquired whether his writing was perfectly clear, he became unconscious, and breathed his last on the following morning. Six days later came the fulfilment of the second half of the gipsy's prophecy. The long, unhappy, and inglorious life of George the Third of England was ended.

## II

Such was the confusion of affairs at Sidmouth, that the Duchess found herself without the means of returning to London. Prince Leopold hurried down, and himself conducted his sister and her family, by slow and bitter stages, to Kensington. The widowed lady, in her voluminous blacks, needed all her equanimity to support her. Her prospects were more dubious than ever. She had £6000 a year of her own; but her husband's debts loomed before her like a mountain. Soon she learnt that the Duchess of Clarence was once more expecting a child. What had she to look forward to in England? Why should she remain in a foreign country, among strangers, whose language she could not speak, whose customs she could not understand? Surely it would be best to return to Amorbach, and there, among her own people, bring up her daughters in economical obscurity. But she was an inveterate optimist; she had spent her life in struggles, and would not be daunted now. And besides, she adored her baby. 'C'est mon bonheur, mes délices, mon existence,' she declared; the darling should be brought up as an English princess, whatever lot awaited her. Prince Leopold came forward nobly with an offer of an additional £3000 a year; and the Duchess remained at Kensington.

The child herself was extremely fat, and bore a remarkable resemblance to her grandfather. 'C'est l'image du feu Roi!' exclaimed the Duchess. 'C'est le Roi Georges en jupons,' echoed the surrounding ladies, as the little creature waddled with difficulty from one to the other.

Before long, the world began to be slightly interested in the nursery at Kensington. When, early in 1821, the Duchess of Clarence's second child, the Princess Elizabeth, died within three months of its birth, the interest increased. Great forces and fierce antagonisms seemed to be moving, obscurely, about the royal cradle. It was a time of faction and anger, of violent repression and profound discontent. A powerful movement, which had for long been checked by adverse circumstances, was now spreading throughout the country. New passions, new desires, were abroad; or rather, old passions and old desires, reincarnated with a new potency: love of freedom, hatred of injustice, hope for the future of man. The mighty still sat proudly in their seats, dispensing their ancient tyranny; but a storm was gathering out of the darkness, and already there was lightning in the sky. But the vastest forces must needs operate through frail human instruments; and it seemed for many years as if the great cause of English liberalism hung upon the life of the little girl at Kensington. She alone stood between the country and her terrible uncle, the Duke of Cumberland, the hideous embodiment of reaction. Inevitably, the Duchess of Kent threw in her lot with her husband's party; Whig leaders, Radical agitators, rallied round her; she was intimate with the bold Lord Durham, she was on friendly terms with the redoubtable O'Connell himself. She received Wilberforce—though, to be sure, she did not ask him to sit down. She declared in public that she put her faith in 'the liberties of the People.' It was certain that the young Princess would be brought up in the way that she should go; yet there, close behind the throne, waiting, sinister, was the Duke of Cumberland. Brougham, looking forward into the future in his scurrilous fashion, hinted at dreadful possibilities.

*This miniature of H.R.H. The Princess Victoria in 1827, by Plant after Stewart, shows a strong will behind the conventional prettiness. On her left shoulder she wears a miniature of George IV set in diamonds, worn as an order on a blue ribbon. It was given to her by the 'large and gouty' King in 1826, and she was very proud of it.*

*An artist's reconstruction of the scene as the widowed Duchess of Kent, holding the baby Victoria, receives an address of condolence from the House of Commons. The Duke of Kent had died of pneumonia on 22 January 1820, leaving his wife, who spoke little English, in a strange country with vast debts and a child of eight months old.*

'I never prayed so heartily for a Prince before,' he wrote, on hearing that George IV had been attacked by illness. 'If he had gone, all the troubles of these villains [the Tory Ministers] went with him, and they had Fred. I [the Duke of York] their own man for his life. . . . He (Fred. I) won't live long either; that Prince of Blackguards, "Brother William," is as bad a life, so we come in the course of nature to be *assassinated* by King Ernest I or Regent Ernest [the Duke of Cumberland].' Such thoughts were not peculiar to Brougham; in the seething state of public feeling, they constantly leapt to the surface; and, even so late as the year previous to her accession, the Radical newspapers were full of suggestions that the Princess Victoria was in danger from the machinations of her wicked uncle.

But no echo of these conflicts and forebodings reached the little Drina— for so she was called in the family circle—as she played with her dolls, or scampered down the passages, or rode on the donkey her uncle York had given her along the avenues of Kensington Gardens. The fair-haired, blue-eyed child was idolised by her nurses, and her mother's ladies, and her sister Feodora; and for a few years there was a danger, in spite of her mother's strictness, of her being spoilt. From time to time, she would fly into a violent passion, stamp her little foot, and set everyone at defiance; whatever they might say, she would not learn her letters—no, she *would not*; afterwards, she was very sorry, and burst into tears; but her letters remained unlearnt. When she was five years old, however, a change came, with the appearance of Fräulein Lehzen. This lady, who was the daughter of a Hanoverian clergyman and had previously been the Princess Feodora's governess, soon succeeded in instilling a new spirit into her charge. At first, indeed, she was appalled by the little Princess's outbursts of temper; never in her life, she declared, had she seen such a passionate and naughty child. Then she observed something else; the child was extraordinarily truthful; whatever punishment might follow, she never told a lie. Firm, very firm, the new governess yet had the sense to see that all the firmness in the world would be useless, unless she could win her way into little Drina's heart. She did so, and there were no more difficulties. Drina learnt her letters like an angel; and she learnt other things as well. The Baroness de Späth taught her how to make little cardboard boxes and decorate them with tinsel and painted flowers; her mother taught her religion. Sitting in the pew every Sunday morning, the child of six was seen listening in wrapt attention to the clergyman's endless sermon, for she was to be examined upon it in the afternoon. The Duchess was determined that her daughter, from the earliest possible moment, should be prepared for her high station in a way that would commend itself to the most respectable; her good, plain, thrifty German mind recoiled with horror and amazement from the shameless junketings at Carlton House; Drina should never be allowed to forget for a moment the virtues of simplicity, regularity, propriety, and devotion. The little girl, however, was really in small need of such lessons, for she was naturally simple and orderly, she was pious without difficulty, and her sense of propriety was keen. She understood very well the niceties of her own position. When, a child of six, Lady Jane Ellice was taken by her grandmother to Kensington Palace, she was put to play with the Princess Victoria, who was the same age as herself. The young visitor, ignorant of etiquette, began to make free with the toys on the floor, in a way which was a little too familiar; but 'You must not touch those,' she was quickly told, 'they are mine; and I may call you Jane, but you must not call me Victoria.' The Princess's most constant playmate was Victoire, the daughter of Sir John Conroy, the Duchess's major-domo. The two girls were very fond of one another; they would walk hand in hand together in Kensington Gardens. But little Drina was perfectly aware for which of them it was that they were followed, at a respectful distance, by a gigantic scarlet flunkey.

Warm-hearted, responsive, she loved her dear Lehzen, and she loved her dear Feodora, and her dear Victoire, and her dear Madame de Späth. And her dear Mamma . . . of course, she loved her too; it was her duty; and yet—she could not tell why it was—she was always happier when she was staying with her Uncle Leopold at Claremont. There old Mrs. Louis, who, years ago, had waited on her cousin Charlotte, petted her to her heart's content; and her uncle himself was wonderfully kind to her, talking to her seriously and gently, almost as if she were a grown-up person. She and Feodora invariably wept when the too short visit was over, and they were obliged to return to the dutiful monotony and the affectionate supervision of Kensington. But sometimes when her mother had to stay at home, she was allowed to go out driving all alone with her dear Feodora and her dear Lehzen, and she could talk and look as she liked, and it was very delightful.

The visits to Claremont were frequent enough; but one day, on a special occasion, she paid one of a rarer and more exciting kind. When she was seven years old, she and her mother and sister were asked by the King to go down to Windsor. George IV, who had transferred his fraternal ill-temper to his sister-in-law and her family, had at last grown tired of sulking, and decided to be agreeable. The old rip, bewigged and gouty, ornate and enormous, with his jewelled mistress by his side and his flaunting court about him, received the tiny creature who was one day to hold in those same halls a very different state. 'Give me your little paw,' he said; and two ages touched. Next morning, driving in his phaeton with the Duchess of Gloucester, he met the Duchess of Kent and her child in the Park. 'Pop her in,' were his orders, which, to the terror of the mother and the delight of the daughter, were immediately obeyed. Off they dashed to Virginia Water, where there was a great barge, full of lords and ladies fishing, and another barge with a band; and the King ogled Feodora, and praised her manners, and then turned to his own small niece. 'What is your favourite tune? The band shall play it.' 'God save the King, sir,' was the instant answer. The Princess's reply has been praised as an early example of a tact which was afterwards famous. But she was a very truthful child, and perhaps it was her genuine opinion.

# III

In 1827 the Duke of York, who had found some consolation for the loss of his wife in the sympathy of the Duchess of Rutland, died, leaving behind him the unfinished immensity of Stafford House and £200,000 worth of debts. Three years later George IV also disappeared, and the Duke of Clarence reigned in his stead. The new Queen, it was now clear, would in all probability never again be a mother; the Princess Victoria, therefore, was recognised by Parliament as heir-presumptive; and the Duchess of Kent, whose annuity had been doubled five years previously, was now given an additional £10,000 for the maintenance of the Princess, and was appointed regent, in case of the death of the King before the majority of her daughter. At the same time a great convulsion took place in the consitution of the State. The power of the Tories, who had dominated England for more than forty years, suddenly began to crumble. In the tremendous struggle that followed, it seemed for a moment as if the tradition of generations might be snapped, as if the blind tenacity of the reactionaries and the determined fury of their enemies could have no other issue than revolution. But the forces of compromise triumphed: the Reform Bill was passed. The centre of gravity in the constitution was shifted towards the middle clases; the Whigs came into power; and the complexion of the Government assumed a Liberal tinge. One of the results of this new state of affairs was a change in the position of the Duchess of Kent and her daughter. From being the *protégées* of an opposition clique, they became assets of the official majority of the nation. The Princess Victoria was henceforward the living symbol of the victory of the middle classes.

The Duke of Cumberland, on the other hand, suffered a corresponding eclipse: his claws had been pared by the Reform Act. He grew insignificant and almost harmless, though his ugliness remained; he was the wicked uncle still—but only of a story.

The Duchess's own liberalism was not very profound. She followed naturally in the footsteps of her husband, repeating with conviction the catchwords of her husband's clever friends and the generalisations of her clever brother Leopold. She herself had no pretensions to cleverness; she did not understand very much about the Poor Law and the Slave Trade and

'An racehorse' from Princess Victoria's first sketchbook conveys the eight-year-old artist's verve and enthusiasm. She was soon to develop more technical skill under the direction of Richard Westall, who became her drawing-master at about this time. Riding was one of her chief pleasures as a girl and a young woman, with the best of her horses and her most 'delicious rides' duly recorded in her journal.

Political Economy; but she hoped that she did her duty; and she hoped—she ardently hoped—that the same might be said of Victoria. Her educational conceptions were those of Dr. Arnold, whose views were just then beginning to permeate society. Dr. Arnold's object was, first and foremost, to make his pupils 'in the highest and truest sense of the words, Christian gentlemen'; intellectual refinements might follow. The Duchess felt convinced that it was her supreme duty in life to make quite sure that her daughter should grow up into a Christian queen. To this task she bent all her energies; and, as the child developed, she flattered herself that her efforts were not unsuccessful. When the Princess was eleven, she desired the Bishops of London and Lincoln to submit her daughter to an examination, and report upon the progress that had been made. 'I feel the time to be now come,' the Duchess explained, in a letter obviously drawn up by her own hand, 'that what has been done should be put to some test, that if anything has been done in error of judgment it may be corrected, and that the plan for the future should be open to consideration and revision. . . . I attend almost always myself every lesson, or a part; and as the lady about the Princess is a competent person, she assists Her in preparing Her lessons, for the various masters, as I resolved to act in that manner so as to be Her governess myself. . . . When she was at a proper age she commenced attending Divine Service regularly with me, and I have every feeling that she has religion at Her heart, that she is morally impressed with it to that degree, that she is less liable to error by its application to her feelings as a Child capable of reflection.' 'The general bent of Her character,' added the Duchess, 'is strength of intellect, capable of receiving with ease, information, and with a peculiar readiness in coming to a very just and benignant decision on any point Her opinion is asked on. Her adherence to truth is of so marked a character that I feel no apprehension of that Bulwark being broken down by any circumstances.' The Bishops attended at the Palace, and the result of their examination was all that could be wished. 'In answering a great variety of questions proposed to her,' they reported, 'the Princess displayed an accurate knowledge of the most important features of Scripture History, and of the leading truths and precepts of the Christian Religion as taught by the Church of England, as well as an acquaintance with the Chronology and principal facts of English History remarkable in so young a person. To questions in Geography, the use of the Globes, Arithmetic, and Latin Grammar, the answers which the Princess returned were equally satisfactory.' They did not believe that the Duchess's plan of education was susceptible of any improvement; and the Archbishop of Canterbury, who was also consulted, came to the same gratifying conclusion.

One important step, however, remained to be taken. So far, as the Duchess explained to the Bishops, the Princess had been kept in ignorance of the station that she was likely to fill. 'She is aware of its duties, and that a Sovereign should live for others; so that when Her innocent mind receives the impression of Her future fate, she receives it with a mind formed to be sensible of what is to be expected from Her, and it is to be hoped, she will be too well grounded in Her principles to be dazzled with the station she is to look to.' In the following year it was decided that she should be enlightened on this point. The well-known scene followed: the history lesson, the genealogical table of the Kings of England slipped beforehand by the governess into the book, the Princess's surprise, her inquiries, her final realisation of the facts. When the child at last understood, she was silent for a moment, and then she spoke: 'I will be good,' she said. The words were something more than a conventional protestation, something more than the expression of a superimposed desire; they were, in their limitation and their intensity, their egotism and their humility, an instinctive summary of the dominating qualities of a life. 'I cried much on learning it,' her Majesty noted long afterwards. No doubt, while the others were present, even her dear Lehzen, the little girl kept up her self-command; and then crept away somewhere to ease her heart of an inward, unfamiliar agitation, with a handkerchief, out of her mother's sight.

But her mother's sight was by no means an easy thing to escape. Morning and evening, day and night, there was no relaxation of the maternal vigilance. The child grew into the girl, the girl into the young woman; but still she slept in her mother's bedroom; still she had no place allowed her where she might sit or work by herself. An extraordinary watchfulness surrounded her every step: up to the day of her accession, she never went downstairs without someone beside her holding her hand. Plainness and regularity ruled the household. The hours, the days, the years passed slowly and methodically by. The dolls—the innumerable dolls, each one so neatly dressed, each one with its name so punctiliously entered in the catalogue— were laid aside, and a little music and a little dancing took their place. Taglioni came, to give grace and dignity to the figure, and Lablache, to train the piping treble upon his own rich bass. The Dean of Chester, the official preceptor, continued his endless instruction in Scripture history, while the Duchess of Northumberland, the official governess, presided over every lesson with becoming solemnity. Without doubt, the Princess's main achievement during her schooldays was linguistic. German was naturally the

*Sir George Hayter's pencil drawing of Princess Victoria with the Duchess of Kent suggests an affectionate relationship between mother and daughter. In reality, however, the Princess's unexpectedly strong will made her rebel against the 'Kensington system' of education, designed to subject her to the influence of her mother and Sir John Conroy. Later Queen Victoria looked back on her childhood with bitterness, recalling 'Ma never was very fond of me.'*

first language with which she was familiar; but English and French quickly followed; and she became virtually trilingual, though her mastery of English grammar remained incomplete. At the same time, she acquired a working knowledge of Italian and some smattering of Latin. Nevertheless, she did not read very much. It was not an occupation that she cared for; partly, perhaps, because the books that were given her were all either sermons, which were very dull, or poetry, which was incomprehensible. Novels were strictly forbidden. Lord Durham persuaded her mother to get her some of Miss Martineau's tales, illustrating the truths of Political Economy, and they delighted her; but it is to be feared that it was the unaccustomed pleasure of the story that filled her mind, and that she never really mastered the theory of exchanges or the nature of rent.

It was her misfortune that the mental atmosphere which surrounded her during these years of adolescence was almost entirely feminine. No father, no brother, was there to break in upon the gentle monotony of the daily round with impetuosity, with rudeness, with careless laughter and wafts of freedom from the outside world. The Princess was never called by a voice that was loud and growling; never felt, as a matter of course, a hard rough cheek on her own soft one; never climbed a wall with a boy. The visits to Claremont— delicious little escapes into male society—came to an end when she was eleven years old and Prince Leopold left England to be King of the Belgians. She loved him still; he was still 'il mio secondo padre—or, rather, *solo* padre, for he is indeed like my real father, as I have none'; but his fatherliness now came to her dimly and indirectly, through the cold channel of correspondence. Henceforward female duty, female elegance, female enthusiasm, hemmed her completely in; and her spirit, amid the enclosing folds, was hardly reached by those two great influences, without which no growing life can truly prosper—humour and imagination. The Baroness Lehzen—for she had been raised to that rank in the Hanoverian nobility by George IV before he died—was the real centre of the Princess's world. When Feodora married, when uncle Leopold went to Belgium, the Baroness was left without a competitor. The Princess gave her mother her dutiful regards; but Lehzen had her heart. The voluble, shrewd daughter of the pastor in Hanover, lavishing her devotion on her royal charge, had reaped her reward in an unbounded confidence and a passionate adoration. The girl would have gone through fire for her '*precious* Lehzen,' the 'best and truest friend,' she declared, that she had had since her birth. Her journal, begun when she was thirteen, where she registered day by day the small succession of her doings and her sentiments, bears on every page of it the traces of the Baroness and her circumambient influence. The young creature that one sees there, self-depicted in ingenuous clarity, with her sincerity, her simplicity, her quick affections and pious resolutions, might almost have been the daughter of a German pastor herself. Her enjoyments, her admirations, her *engouements* were of the kind that clothed themselves naturally in underlinings and exclamation marks. 'It was a *delightful* ride. We cantered a good deal. SWEET LITTLE ROSY WENT BEAUTIFULLY!! We came home at a $\frac{1}{4}$ past 1. . . . At 20 minutes to 7 we went out to the Opera. . . . Rubini came on and sang a song out of "Anna Boulena" *quite beautifully*. We came home at $\frac{1}{2}$ past 11.'

In her comments on her readings, the mind of the Baroness is clearly revealed. One day, by some mistake, she was allowed to take up a volume of memoirs by Fanny Kemble. 'It is certainly very pertly and oddly written. One would imagine by the style that the authoress must be very pert, and not well bred; for there are so many vulgar expressions in it. It is a great pity that a person endowed with so much talent, as Mrs. Butler really is, should turn it to so little account and publish a book which is so full of trash and nonsense which can only do her harm. I stayed up till 20 minutes past 9.' Madame de Sévigné's letters, which the Baroness read aloud, met with more approval. 'How truly elegant and natural her style is! It is so full of *naïveté*, cleverness, and grace.' But her highest admiration was reserved for the Bishop of Chester's 'Exposition of the Gospel of St. Matthew.' 'It is a very fine book indeed. Just the sort of one I like; which is just plain and comprehensible and full of truth and good feeling. It is not one of those learned books in which you have to cavil at almost every paragraph. Lehzen gave it me on the Sunday that I took the Sacrament.' A few weeks previously she had been confirmed, and she described the event as follows: 'I felt that my confirmation was one of the most solemn and important events and acts in my life; and that I trusted that it might have a salutary effect on my mind. I felt deeply repentant for all what I had done which was wrong and trusted in God Almighty to strengthen my heart and mind; and to forsake all that is bad and follow all that is virtuous and right. I went with the firm determination to become a true Christian, to try and comfort my dear Mamma in all her griefs, trials, and anxieties, and to become a dutiful and affectionate daughter to her. Also to be obedient to *dear* Lehzen, who has done so much for me. I was dressed in a white lace dress, with a white crape bonnet with a wreath of white roses round it. I went in the chariot with my dear Mamma and the others followed in another carriage.' One seems to hold in one's hand a small smooth crystal pebble, without a flaw and without a scintillation, and so transparent that one can see through it at a glance.

Yet perhaps, after all, to the discerning eye, the purity would not be absolute. The careful searcher might detect, in the virgin soil, the first faint traces of an unexpected vein. In the conventual existence visits were exciting events; and, as the Duchess had many relatives, they were not infrequent; aunts and uncles would often appear from Germany, and cousins too. When the Princess was fourteen she was delighted by the arrival of a couple of boys from Würtemberg, the Princes Alexander and Ernst, sons of her mother's sister and the reigning duke. 'They are both *extremely tall*,' she noted; 'Alexander is *very handsome*, and Ernst has a *very kind expression*. They are both EXTREMELY *amiable*.' And their departure filled her with corresponding regrets. 'We saw them get into the barge, and watched them sailing away for some time on the beach. They were so amiable and so pleasant to have in the house; they were *always satisfied, always good-humoured*; Alexander took such care of me in getting out of the boat, and rode next to me; so did Ernst.' Two years later, two other cousins arrived, the Princes Ferdinand and Augustus. 'Dear Ferdinand,' the Princess wrote, 'has elicited universal admiration from all parties. . . . He is so very unaffected, and has such a very distinguished appearance and carriage. They are both very dear and charming young men.

Augustus is very amiable too, and, when known, shows much good sense.' On another occasion, 'Dear Ferdinand came and sat near me and talked so dearly and sensibly. I do *so* love him. Dear Augustus sat near me and talked with me, and he is also a dear good young man, and is very handsome.' She could not quite decide which was the handsomer of the two. On the whole, she concluded, 'I think Ferdinand handsomer than Augustus, his eyes are so beautiful, and he has such a lively clever expression; *both* have such a sweet expression; Ferdinand has something *quite beautiful* in his expression when he speaks and smiles, and he is *so* good.' However, it was perhaps best to say that they were 'both very handsome and *very dear*.' But shortly afterwards two more cousins arrived, who threw all the rest into the shade. These were the Princes Ernest and Albert, sons of her mother's eldest brother, the Duke of Saxe-Coburg. This time the Princess was more particular in her observations. 'Ernest,' she remarked, 'is as tall as Ferdinand and Augustus; he has dark hair, and fine dark eyes and eyebrows, but the nose and mouth are not good; he has a most kind, honest and intelligent expression in his countenance, and has a very good figure. Albert, who is just as tall as Ernest but stouter, is extremely handsome; his hair is about the same colour as mine; his eyes are large and blue, and he has a beautiful nose and a very sweet mouth with fine teeth; but the charm of his countenance is his expression, which is most delightful; *c'est à la fois* full of goodness and sweetness, and very clever and intelligent.' 'Both my cousins,' she added, 'are so kind and good; they are much more *formés* and men of the world than Augustus; they speak English very well, and I speak it with them. Ernest will be 18 years old on the 21st of June, and Albert 17 on the 26th of August. Dear Uncle Ernest made me the present of a most delightful *Lory*, which is so tame that it remains on your hand and you may put your finger into its beak, or do anything with it, without its ever attempting to bite. It is larger than Mamma's grey parrot.' A little later, 'I sat between my dear cousins on the sofa and we looked at drawings. They both draw very well, particularly Albert, and are both exceedingly fond of music; they play very nicely on the piano. The more I see them the more I am delighted with them, and the more I love them. . . . It is delightful to be with them; they are so fond of being occupied too; they are quite an example for any young person.' When, after a stay of three weeks, the time came for the young men and their father to return to Germany, the moment of parting was a melancholy one. 'It was our last HAPPY HAPPY breakfast, with this dear Uncle and those *dearest* beloved cousins, whom I *do* love so VERY VERY dearly; *much more dearly* than any other cousins in the *world*. Dearly as I love Ferdinand, and also good Augustus, I love Ernest and Albert *more* than them, oh yes, MUCH *more*. . . . They have both learnt a good deal, and are very clever, naturally clever, particularly Albert, who is the most reflecting of the two, and they like very much talking about serious and instructive things and yet are so *very very* merry and gay and happy, like young people ought to be; Albert always used to have some fun and some clever witty answer at breakfast and everywhere; he used to play and fondle Dash so funnily too. . . . Dearest Albert was playing on the piano when I came down. At 11 dear Uncle, my *dearest beloved* cousins, and Charles, left us, accompanied by Count Kolowrat. I embraced both my dearest cousins most warmly, as also

*'It was with some emotion that I beheld Albert—who is Beautiful,' wrote the young Queen in 1839. 'He really is quite charming, and so excessively handsome; such beautiful blue eyes, an exquisite nose, and such a pretty mouth with delicate mustachios and slight but very slight whiskers; a beautiful figure, broad in the shoulders and a fine waist; my heart is quite going . . .'*

my dear Uncle. I cried bitterly, very bitterly.' The Princes shared her ecstasies and her italics between them; but it is clear enough where her secret preference lay. 'Particularly Albert'! She was just seventeen; and deep was the impression left upon that budding organism by the young man's charm and goodness and accomplishments, and his large blue eyes and beautiful nose, and his sweet mouth and fine teeth.

# IV

*Princess Adelaide, daughter of the widowed Duchess of the tiny state of Saxe-Meiningen, was twenty-six when she married the Duke of Clarence in 1818. Her primary duty was the production of an heir to the throne, but she and her husband (who had already fathered ten healthy illegitimate children during his liaison with Mrs. Jordan) were cruelly disappointed. She suffered a premature birth and two miscarriages—one of twins—and lost her only surviving infant, the Princess Elizabeth, at the age of three months. 'I want words to express my feelings at these repeated misfortunes to this beloved and superior woman,' wrote the Duke. 'I am quite broken hearted.' As King and Queen William and Adelaide were genuinely fond of their niece and heir Victoria; Adelaide once wrote touchingly to the Duchess of Kent, 'My children are dead but your child lives, and she is mine too.'*

King William could not away with his sister-in-law, and the Duchess fully returned his antipathy. Without considerable tact and considerable forbearance their relative positions were well calculated to cause ill-feeling; and there was very little tact in the composition of the Duchess, and no forbearance at all in that of his Majesty. A bursting, bubbling old gentleman, with quarter-deck gestures, round rolling eyes, and a head like a pineapple, his sudden elevation to the throne after fifty-six years of utter insignificance had almost sent him crazy. His natural exuberance completely got the better of him; he rushed about doing preposterous things in an extraordinary manner, spreading amusement and terror in every direction, and talking all the time. His tongue was decidedly Hanoverian, with its repetitions, its catchwords—'That's quite another thing! That's quite another thing!'—its rattling indomitability, its loud indiscreetness. His speeches, made repeatedly at the most inopportune junctures, and filled pell-mell with all the fancies and furies that happened at the moment to be whisking about in his head, were the consternation of Ministers. He was one part blackguard, people said, and three parts buffoon; but those who knew him better could not help liking him—he meant well; and he was really good-humoured and kind-hearted, if you took him the right way. If you took him the wrong way, however, you must look out for squalls, as the Duchess of Kent discovered.

She had no notion of how to deal with him—could not understand him in the least. Occupied with her own position, her own responsibilities, her duty, and her daughter, she had no attention to spare for the peppery susceptibilities of a foolish, disreputable old man. She was the mother of the heiress of England; and it was for him to recognise the fact—to put her at once upon a proper footing—to give her the precedence of a dowager Princess of Wales, with a large annuity from the privy purse. It did not occur to her that such pretensions might be galling to a king who had no legitimate child of his own, and who yet had not altogether abandoned the hope of having one. She pressed on, with bulky vigour, along the course she had laid out. Sir John Conroy, an Irishman with no judgment and a great deal of self-importance, was her intimate counsellor, and egged her on. It was advisable that Victoria should become acquainted with the various districts of England, and through several summers a succession of tours—in the West, in the Midlands, in Wales—were arranged for her. The intention of the plan was excellent, but its execution was unfortunate. The journeys, advertised in the Press, attracting enthusiastic crowds, and involving official receptions, took on the air of royal progresses. Addresses were presented by loyal citizens; the delighted Duchess, swelling in sweeping feathers and almost obliterating the diminutive Princess, read aloud, in her German accent, gracious replies prepared beforehand by Sir John, who, bustling and ridiculous, seemed to be mingling the rôles of major-domo and Prime Minister. Naturally the King fumed over his newspaper at Windsor. 'That woman is a nuisance! That woman is a nuisance!' he exclaimed. Poor Queen Adelaide, amiable though disappointed, did her best to smooth things down, changed the subject, and wrote affectionate letters to Victoria; but it was useless. News arrived that the Duchess of Kent, sailing in the Solent, had insisted that whenever her yacht appeared it should be received by royal salutes from all the men-of-war and all the forts. The King declared that these continual poppings must cease; the Premier and the First Lord of the Admiralty were consulted; and they wrote privately to the Duchess, begging her to waive her rights. But she would not hear of it; Sir John Conroy was adamant. 'As her Royal Highness's *confidential adviser*,' he said, 'I cannot recommend her to give way on this point.' Eventually the King, in a great state of excitement, issued a special Order in Council, prohibiting the firing of royal salutes to any ships except those which carried the reigning sovereign or his consort on board.

When King William quarrelled with his Whig Ministers the situation grew still more embittered, for now the Duchess, in addition to her other shortcomings, was the political partisan of his enemies. In 1836 he made an attempt to prepare the ground for a match between the Princess Victoria and one of the sons of the Prince of Orange, and at the same time did his best to prevent the visit of the young Coburg princes to Kensington. He failed in both these objects; and the only result of his efforts was to raise the anger of the King of the Belgians, who, forgetting for a moment his royal reserve, addressed an indignant letter on the subject to his niece. 'I am really *astonished*,' he wrote, 'at the conduct of your old Uncle the King; this invitation of the Prince of Orange and his sons, this forcing him on others, is very extraordinary. . . . Not later than yesterday I got a half-official communication from England, insinuating that it would be *highly* desirable that the visit of *your* relatives *should not take place this year*—qu'en dites-vous? The relations of the Queen and the King, therefore, to the God-knows-what degree, are to come in shoals and rule the land, when *your relations* are to be *forbidden* the country, and that when, as you know, the whole of your relations have ever been very dutiful and kind to the King. Really and truly I never heard or saw anything like it, and I hope it will a *little rouse your spirit*; now that slavery is even abolished in the British Colonies, I do not comprehend *why your lot alone should be to be kept a white little slavey in England*, for the pleasure of the Court, who never bought you, as I am not aware of their ever having gone to any expense on that head, or the King's ever having *spent a sixpence for your existence*. . . . Oh, consistency and political or *other honesty*, where must one look for you!'

Shortly afterwards King Leopold came to England himself, and his reception was as cold at Windsor as it was warm at Kensington. 'To hear dear Uncle speak on any subject,' the Princess wrote in her diary, 'is like reading a highly instructive book; his conversation is so enlightened, so clear. He is universally admitted to be one of the first politicians now extant. He speaks so mildly, yet firmly and impartially, about politics. Uncle tells me that

*Born in 1765, William Duke of Clarence was the third son of George III and his queen, Charlotte of Mecklenburg-Strelitz. Nicknamed 'Sailor Bill', he found a career in the navy and domestic happiness with Dorothy Jordan, a lively and kind-hearted comedy actress. After 1817 a series of royal deaths brought the bluff, tactless Duke close to the throne and in 1830, now married to Adelaide of Saxe-Meiningen, he succeeded his elder brother George IV. 'Poor man, he was always very kind to me and he meant it well I know,' wrote his niece Queen Victoria when she succeeded him in 1837. 'I am grateful for it and shall ever remember his kindness with gratitude. He was odd, very odd, and singular, but his intentions were often ill-interpreted.'*

Belgium is quite a pattern for its organisation, its industry, and prosperity; the finances are in the greatest perfection. Uncle is so beloved and revered by his Belgian subjects, that it must be a great compensation for all his extreme trouble.' But her other uncle by no means shared her sentiments. He could not, he said, put up with a water-drinker; and King Leopold would touch no wine. 'What's that you're drinking, sir?' he asked him one day at dinner. 'Water, sir.' 'God damn it, sir!' was the rejoinder. 'Why don't you drink wine? I never allow anybody to drink water at my table.'

It was clear that before very long there would be a great explosion; and in the hot days of August it came. The Duchess and the Princess had gone down to stay at Windsor for the King's birthday party, and the King himself, who was in London for the day to prorogue Parliament, paid a visit at Kensington Palace in their absence. There he found that the Duchess had just appropriated, against his express orders, a suite of seventeen apartments for her own use. He was extremely angry, and, when he returned to Windsor, after greeting the Princess with affection, he publicly rebuked the Duchess for what she had done. But this was little to what followed. On the next day was the birthday banquet; there were a hundred guests; the Duchess of Kent sat on the King's right hand, and the Princess Victoria opposite. At the end of the dinner, in reply to the toast of the King's health, he rose, and, in a long, loud, passionate speech, poured out the vials of his wrath upon the Duchess. She had, he declared, insulted him—grossly and continually; she had kept the Princess away from him in the most improper manner; she was surrounded by evil advisers, and was incompetent to act with propriety in the high station which she filled; but he would bear it no longer; he would have her to know he was King; he was determined that his authority should be respected; henceforward the Princess should attend at every Court function with the utmost regularity; and he hoped to God that his life might be spared for six months longer, so that the calamity of a regency might be avoided, and the functions of the Crown pass directly to the heiress-presumptive instead of into the hands of the 'person now near him,' upon whose conduct and capacity no reliance whatever could be placed. The flood of vituperation rushed on for what seemed an interminable period, while the Queen blushed scarlet, the Princess burst into tears, and the hundred guests sat aghast. The Duchess said not a word until the tirade was over and the company had retired; then in a tornado of rage and mortification, she called for her carriage and announced her immediate return to Kensington. It was only with the utmost difficulty that some show of a reconciliation was patched up, and the outraged lady was prevailed upon to put off her departure till the morrow.

Her troubles, however, were not over when she had shaken the dust of Windsor from her feet. In her own household she was pursued by bitterness and vexation of spirit. The apartments at Kensington were seething with subdued disaffection, with jealousies and animosities virulently intensified by long years of propinquity and spite.

There was a deadly feud between Sir John Conroy and Baroness Lehzen. But that was not all. The Duchess had grown too fond of her major-domo. There were familiarities, and one day the Princess Victoria discovered the fact. She confided what she had seen to the Baroness, and to the Baroness's

*Baroness Lehzen, aged about forty-nine, was sketched by her adoring pupil in 1833. Described by Greville as 'a clever agreeable woman', the Baroness had known Princess Victoria since babyhood; when the nurse, Mrs. Brock, left in 1824 she took over the daily supervision of the Princess, training her character, planning her education and supporting her in the struggle against Sir John Conroy.*

beloved ally, Madame de Späth. Unfortunately, Madame de Späth could not hold her tongue, and was actually foolish enough to reprove the Duchess; whereupon she was instantly dismissed. It was not so easy to get rid of the Baroness. That lady, prudent and reserved, maintained an irreproachable demeanour. Her position was strongly entrenched; she had managed to secure the support of the King; and Sir John found that he could do nothing against her. But henceforward the household was divided into two camps. The Duchess supported Sir John with all the amplitude of her authority; but the Baroness, too, had an adherent who could not be neglected. The Princess Victoria said nothing, but she had been much attached to Madame de Späth, and she adored her Lehzen. The Duchess knew only too well that in this horrid embroilment her daughter was against her. Chagrin, annoyance, moral reprobation, tossed her to and fro. She did her best to console herself with Sir John's affectionate loquacity, or with the sharp remarks of Lady Flora Hastings, one of her maids of honour, who had no love for the Baroness. The subject lent itself to satire; for the pastor's daughter, with all her airs of stiff superiority, had habits which betrayed her origin. Her passion for caraway seeds, for instance, was uncontrollable. Little bags of them came over to her from Hanover, and she sprinkled them on her bread and butter, her cabbage, and even her roast beef. Lady Flora could not resist a caustic observation; it was repeated to the Baroness, who pursed her lips in fury; and so the mischief grew.

## V

The King had prayed that he might live till his niece was of age; and a few days before her eighteenth birthday—the date of her legal majority—a sudden attack of illness very nearly carried him off. He recovered, however, and the Princess was able to go through her birthday festivities—a state ball and a drawing-room—with unperturbed enjoyment. 'Count Zichy,' she noted in her diary, 'is very good-looking in uniform, but not in plain clothes. Count Waldstein looks remarkably well in his pretty Hungarian uniform.' With the latter young gentleman she wished to dance, but there was an insurmountable difficulty. 'He could not dance quadrilles, and, as in my station I unfortunately cannot valse and galop, I could not dance with him.' Her birthday present from the King was of a pleasing nature, but it led to a painful domestic scene. In spite of the anger of her Belgian uncle, she had remained upon good terms with her English one. He had always been very kind to her, and the fact that he had quarrelled with her mother did not appear to be a reason for disliking him. He was, she said, 'odd, very odd and singular,' but, 'his intentions were often ill interpreted.' He now wrote her a letter, offering her an allowance of £10,000 a year, which he proposed should be at her own disposal, and independent of her mother. Lord Conyngham, the Lord Chamberlain, was instructed to deliver the letter into the Princess's own hands. When he arrived at Kensington, he was ushered into the presence of the Duchess and the Princess, and, when he produced the letter, the Duchess put out her hand to take it. Lord Conyngham begged her Royal Highness's pardon, and repeated the King's commands. Thereupon the

*'The Monster and Demon Incarnate' was Queen Victoria's description of Sir John Conroy, equerry to her father the Duke of Kent and later Comptroller of the Duchess of Kent's household. Hard-up and ambitious, Sir John was a handsome Irishman who soon made the pliant Duchess completely dependent on him; he saw her as regent for her young daughter and himself as the power behind the throne. Fortunately for the Princess, whose strong will resisted his attempts at domination, her uncle King William IV managed to live until she was old enough to rule in her own right.*

Duchess drew back, and the Princess took the letter. She immediately wrote to her uncle, accepting his kind proposal. The Duchess was much displeased; £4000 a year, she said, would be quite enough for Victoria; as for the remaining £6000, it would be only proper that she should have that herself.

King William had thrown off his illness, and returned to his normal life. Once more the royal circle at Windsor—their Majesties, the elder Princesses, and some unfortunate Ambassadress or Minister's wife—might be seen ranged for hours round a mahogany table, while the Queen netted a purse, and the King slept, occasionally waking from his slumbers to observe 'Exactly so, ma'am, exactly so!' But this recovery was of short duration. The old man suddenly collapsed; with no specific symptoms besides an extreme weakness, he yet showed no power of rallying; and it was clear to everyone that his death was now close at hand.

All eyes, all thoughts, turned towards the Princess Victoria; but she still remained, shut away in the seclusion of Kensington, a small, unknown figure, lost in the large shadow of her mother's domination. The preceding year had in fact been an important one in her development. The soft tendrils of her mind had for the first time begun to stretch out towards unchildish things. In this King Leopold encouraged her. After his return to Brussels, he had resumed his correspondence in a more serious strain; he discussed the details of foreign politics; he laid down the duties of kingship; he pointed out the iniquitous foolishness of the newspaper press. On the latter subject, indeed, he wrote with some asperity. 'If all the editors,' he said, 'of the papers in the countries where the liberty of the press exists were to be assembled, we should have a *crew* to which you would *not* confide a dog that you would value, still less your honour and reputation.' On the functions of a monarch, his views were unexceptionable. 'The business of the highest in a State,' he wrote, 'is certainly, in my opinion, to act with great impartiality and a spirit of justice for the good of all.' At the same time the Princess's tastes were opening out. Though she was still passionately devoted to riding and dancing, she now began to have a genuine love of music as well, and to drink in the roulades and arias of the Italian opera with high enthusiasm. She even enjoyed reading poetry—at any rate, the poetry of Sir Walter Scott.

When King Leopold learnt that King William's death was approaching, he wrote several long letters of excellent advice to his niece. 'In every letter I shall write to you,' he said, 'I mean to repeat to you, as a *fundamental rule, to be courageous, firm, and honest, as you have been till now.*' For the rest, in the crisis that was approaching, she was not to be alarmed, but to trust in her 'good natural sense and the *truth*' of her character; she was to do nothing in a hurry; to hurt no one's *amour-propre*, and to continue her confidence in the Whig administration. Not content with letters, however, King Leopold determined that the Princess should not lack personal guidance, and sent over to her aid the trusted friend whom, twenty years before, he had taken to his heart by the death-bed at Claremont. Thus, once again, as if in accordance with some preordained destiny, the figure of Stockmar is discernible—inevitably present at a momentous hour.

On June 18, the King was visibly sinking. The Archbishop of Canterbury was by his side, with all the comforts of the church. Nor did the holy words fall upon a rebellious spirit; for many years his Majesty had been a devout believer. 'When I was a young man,' he once explained at a public banquet, 'as well as I can remember, I believed in nothing but pleasure and folly—nothing at all. But when I went to sea, got into a gale, and saw the wonders of the mighty deep, then I believed; and I have been a sincere Christian ever since.' It was the anniversary of the Battle of Waterloo, and the dying man remembered it. He should be glad to live, he said, over that day; he would never see another sunset. 'I hope your Majesty may live to see many,' said Dr. Chambers. 'Oh! that's quite another thing, that's quite another thing,' was the answer. One other sunset he did live to see; and he died in the early hours of the following morning. It was June 20, 1837.

When all was over, the Archbishop and the Lord Chamberlain ordered a carriage, and drove post-haste from Windsor to Kensington. They arrived at the Palace at five o'clock, and it was only with considerable difficulty that they gained admittance. At six the Duchess woke up her daughter, and told her that the Archbishop of Canterbury and Lord Conyngham were there, and wished to see her. She got out of bed, put on her dressing-gown, and went, alone, into the room where the messengers were standing. Lord Conyngham fell on his knees, and officially announced the death of the King; the Archbishop added some personal details. Looking at the bending, murmuring dignitaries before her, she knew that she was Queen of England. 'Since it has pleased Providence,' she wrote that day in her journal, 'to place me in this station, I shall do my utmost to fulfil my duty towards my country; I am very young, and perhaps in many, though not in all things, inexperienced, but I am sure, that very few have more real good will and more real desire to do what is fit and right than I have.' But there was scant time for resolutions and reflections. At once, affairs were thick upon her. Stockmar came to breakfast, and gave some good advice. She wrote a letter to her uncle Leopold, and a hurried note to her sister Feodora. A letter came from the Prime Minister, Lord Melbourne, announcing his approaching arrival. He came at nine, in full court dress, and kissed her hand. She saw him alone, and repeated to him the lesson which, no doubt, the faithful Stockmar had taught her at breakfast, 'It has long been my intention to retain your Lordship and the rest of the present Ministry at the head of affairs'; whereupon Lord Melbourne again kissed her hand and shortly after left her. She then wrote a letter of condolence to Queen Adelaide. At eleven, Lord Melbourne came again; and at half past eleven she went downstairs into the red saloon to hold her first Council. The great assembly of lords and notables, bishops, generals, and Ministers of State, saw the doors thrown open and a very short, very slim girl in deep plain mourning come into the room alone and move forward to her seat with extraordinary dignity and grace; they saw a countenance, not beautiful, but prepossessing—fair hair, blue prominent eyes, a small curved nose, an open mouth revealing the upper teeth, a tiny chin, a clear complexion, and, over all, the strangely mingled signs of innocence, of gravity, of youth, and of composure; they heard a high unwavering voice reading aloud with perfect clarity; and then, the ceremony over, they saw the small figure rise and, with the same consummate grace, the same amazing dignity, pass out from among them, as she had come in, alone.

*In this sketch, Sir Edwin Landseer captured the charm of Victoria at twenty. As the Tory politician John Wilson Croker noted, 'Her eye was bright and calm, neither bold nor downcast, but firm and soft. There was a blush on her cheek and certainly she did look as interesting and handsome as any young lady I ever saw'.*

# 3: LORD MELBOURNE

THE new queen was almost entirely unknown to her subjects. In her public appearances her mother had invariably dominated the scene. Her private life had been that of a novice in a convent: hardly a human being from the outside world had ever spoken to her; and no human being at all, except her mother and the Baroness Lehzen, had ever been alone with her in a room. Thus it was not only the public at large that was in ignorance of everything concerning her; the inner circles of statesmen and officials and high-born ladies were equally in the dark. When she suddenly emerged from this deep obscurity, the impression that she created was immediate and profound. Her bearing at her first Council filled the whole gathering with astonishment and admiration; the Duke of Wellington, Sir Robert Peel, even the savage Croker, even the cold and caustic Greville—all were completely carried away. Everything that was reported of her subsequent proceedings seemed to be of no less happy augury. Her perceptions were quick, her decisions were sensible, her language was discreet; she performed her royal duties with extraordinary facility. Among the outside public there was a great wave of enthusiasm. Sentiment and romance were coming into fashion; and the spectacle of the little girl-queen, innocent, modest, with fair hair and pink cheeks, driving through her capital, filled the hearts of the beholders with raptures of affectionate loyalty. What, above all, struck everybody with overwhelming force was the contrast between Queen Victoria and her uncles. The nasty old men, debauched and selfish, pig-headed and ridiculous, with their perpetual burden of debts, confusions, and disreputabilities—they had vanished like the snows of winter, and here at last, crowned and radiant, was the spring. Lord John Russell, in an elaborate oration, gave voice to the general sentiment. He hoped that Victoria might prove an Elizabeth without her tyranny, an Anne without her weakness. He

*A crowd of about 400,000 people gathered outside Westminster Abbey for the young Queen Victoria's coronation ceremony. She wrote, 'Their good humour and excessive loyalty was beyond everything, and I really cannot say how proud I feel to be the Queen of such a Nation.' After the supreme moments of the crowning and the homage of the peers, the Queen descended from the throne, took off her crown 'very prettily' and humbly received the sacrament. Lord Melbourne stands by, burdened with the heavy sword of state which, according to the young Disraeli, he carried 'like a butcher'.*

asked England to pray that the illustrious Princess who had just ascended the throne with the purest intentions and the justest desires might see slavery abolished, crime diminished, and education improved. He trusted that her people would henceforward derive their strength, their conduct, and their loyalty from enlightened religious and moral principles, and that, so fortified, the reign of Victoria might prove celebrated to posterity and to all the nations of the earth.

Very soon, however, there were signs that the future might turn out to be not quite so simple and roseate as a delighted public dreamed. The 'illustrious Princess' might perhaps, after all, have something within her which squared ill with the easy vision of a well-conducted heroine in an edifying story-book. The purest intentions and the justest desires? No doubt; but was that all? To those who watched closely, for instance, there might be something ominous in the curious contour of that little mouth. When, after her first Council, she crossed the ante-room and found her mother waiting for her, she said, 'And now, Mamma, am I really and truly Queen?' 'You see, my dear, that it is so.' 'Then, dear Mamma, I hope you will grant me the first request I make to you, as Queen. Let me be by myself for an hour.' For an hour she remained in solitude. Then she reappeared, and gave a significant order: her bed was to be moved out of her mother's room. It was the doom of the Duchess of Kent. The long years of waiting were over at last; the moment of a lifetime had come; her daughter was Queen of England; and that very moment brought her own annihilation. She found herself, absolutely and irretrievably, shut off from every vestige of influence, of confidence, of power. She was surrounded, indeed, by all the outward signs of respect and consideration; but that made the inward truth of her position only the more intolerable. Through the mingled formalities of Court etiquette and filial duty, she could never penetrate to Victoria. She was unable to conceal her disappointment and her rage. 'Il n'y a plus d'avenir pour moi,' she exclaimed to Madame de Lieven; 'je ne suis plus rien.' For eighteen years, she said, this child had been the sole object of her existence, of her thoughts, her hopes, and now—no! she would not be comforted, she had lost everything, she was to the last degree unhappy. Sailing, so gallantly and so pertinaciously, through the buffeting storms of life, the stately vessel, with sails still swelling and pennons flying, had put into harbour at last; to find there nothing—a land of bleak desolation.

Within a month of the accession, the realities of the new situation assumed a visible shape. The whole royal household moved from Kensington to Buckingham Palace, and, in the new abode, the Duchess of Kent was given a suite of apartments entirely separate from the Queen's. By Victoria herself the change was welcomed, though, at the moment of departure, she could afford to be sentimental. 'Though I rejoice to *go* into B.P. for many reasons,' she wrote in her diary, 'it is not without feelings of regret that I shall bid adieu *for ever* to this my birthplace, where I have been born and bred, and to which I am really attached!' Her memory lingered for a moment over visions of the past: her sister's wedding, pleasant balls and *delicious* concerts . . . and there were other recollections. 'I have gone through painful and disagreeable scenes here, 'tis true,' she concluded, 'but still I am

*The Duchess of Kent, photographed here towards the end of her life.*

fond of the poor old palace.'

At the same time she took another decided step. She had determined that she would see no more of Sir John Conroy. She rewarded his past services with liberality: he was given a baronetcy and a pension of £3000 a year; he remained a member of the Duchess's household, but his personal intercourse with the Queen came to an abrupt conclusion.

## II

It was clear that these interior changes—whatever else they might betoken—marked the triumph of one person—the Baroness Lehzen. The pastor's daughter observed the ruin of her enemies. Discreet and victorious, she remained in possession of the field. More closely than ever did she cleave to the side of her mistress, her pupil, and her friend; and in the recesses of the palace her mysterious figure was at once invisible and omnipresent. When the Queeen's Ministers came in at one door, the Baroness went out by another; when they retired, she immediately returned. Nobody knew—nobody ever will know—the precise extent and the precise nature of her influence. She herself declared that she never discussed public affairs with the Queen, that she was concerned with private matters only—with private letters and the details of private life. Certainly her hand is everywhere discernible in Victoria's early correspondence. The Journal is written in the style of a child; the Letters are not so simple; they are the work of a child, rearranged—with the minimum of alteration, no doubt, and yet perceptibly—by a governess. And the governess was no fool: narrow, jealous, provincial, she might be; but she was an acute and vigorous woman, who had gained, by a peculiar insight, a peculiar ascendancy. That ascendancy she meant to keep. No doubt it was true that technically she took no part in public business; but the distinction between what is public and what is private is always a subtle one; and in the case of a reigning sovereign—as the next few years were to show—it is often imaginary. Considering all things—the characters of the persons, and the character of the times—it was something more than a mere matter of private interest that the bedroom of Baroness Lehzen at Buckingham Palace should have been next door to the bedroom of the Queen.

But the influence wielded by the Baroness, supreme as it seemed within its own sphere, was not unlimited; there were other forces at work. For one thing, the faithful Stockmar had taken up his residence in the palace. During the twenty years which had elapsed since the death of the Princess Charlotte, his experiences had been varied and remarkable. The unknown counsellor of a disappointed princeling had gradually risen to a position of European importance. His devotion to his master had been not only whole-hearted but cautious and wise. It was Stockmar's advice that had kept Prince Leopold in England during the critical years which followed his wife's death, and had thus secured to him the essential requisite of a *point d'appui* in the country of his adoption. It was Stockmar's discretion which had smoothed over the embarrassments surrounding the Prince's acceptance and rejection of the Greek crown. It was Stockmar who had induced the Prince to become the

*Christian Friedrich Stockmar (1787–1863) was born in Coburg, trained as a doctor and became personal physician to Prince Leopold in 1816. As friend and counsellor to the Prince, later King of the Belgians, he advised on the education of the young Prince Albert, helped to arrange the marriage between Albert and Victoria and finally acted as the Prince Consort's political confidant. There was genuine affection between Albert and his mentor. In his last illness the Prince asked repeatedly for Stockmar, who greeted his death with the words, 'Here do I see crumble before my eyes that edifice which I have devoted twenty years to construct, prompted by a desire to accomplish something great and good.'*

constitutional Sovereign of Belgium. Above all, it was Stockmar's tact, honesty, and diplomatic skill which, through a long series of arduous and complicated negotiations, had led to the guarantee of Belgian neutrality by the Great Powers. His labours had been rewarded by a German barony and by the complete confidence of King Leopold. Nor was it only in Brussels that he was treated with respect and listened to with attention. The statesmen who governed England—Lord Grey, Sir Robert Peel, Lord Palmerston, Lord Melbourne—had learnt to put a high value upon his probity and his intelligence. 'He is one of the cleverest fellows I ever saw,' said Lord Melbourne—'the most discreet man, the most well-judging, and most cool man.' And Lord Palmerston cited Baron Stockmar as the only absolutely disinterested man he had come across in life. At last he was able to retire to Coburg, and to enjoy for a few years the society of the wife and children whom his labours in the service of his master had hitherto only allowed him to visit at long intervals for a month or two at a time. But in 1836 he had been again entrusted with an important negotiation, which he had brought to a successful conclusion in the marriage of Prince Ferdinand of Saxe-Coburg, a nephew of King Leopold's, with Queen Maria II of Portugal. The House of Coburg was beginning to spread over Europe; and the establishment of the Baron at Buckingham Palace in 1837 was to be the prelude of another and a more momentous advance.

King Leopold and his counsellor provide in their careers an example of the curious diversity of human ambitions. The desires of man are wonderfully various; but no less various are the means by which those desires may reach satisfaction: and so the work of the world gets done. The correct mind of Leopold craved for the whole apparatus of royalty. Mere power would have held no attractions for him; he must be an actual king—the crowned head of a people. It was not enough to do; it was essential also to be recognised; anything else would not be fitting. The greatness that he dreamt of was surrounded by every appropriate circumstance. To be a Majesty, to be a cousin of Sovereigns, to marry a Bourbon for diplomatic ends, to correspond with the Queen of England, to be very stiff and very punctual, to found a dynasty, to bore ambassadresses into fits, to live, on the highest pinnacle, an exemplary life devoted to the public service—such were his objects, and such, in fact, were his achievements. The 'Marquis Peu-à-peu,' as George IV called him, had what he wanted. But this would never have been the case if it had not happened that the ambition of Stockmar took a form exactly complementary to his own. The sovereignty that the Baron sought for was by no means obvious. The satisfaction of his essential being lay in obscurity, in invisibility—in passing, unobserved, through a hidden entrance, into the very central chamber of power, and in sitting there, quietly, pulling the subtle strings that set the wheels of the whole world in motion. A very few people, in very high places, and exceptionally well-informed, knew that Baron Stockmar was a most important person: that was enough. The fortunes of the master and the servant, intimately interacting, rose together. The Baron's secret skill had given Leopold his unexceptionable kingdom; and Leopold, in his turn, as time went on, was able to furnish the Baron with more and more keys to more and more back doors.

Stockmar took up his abode in the Palace partly as the emissary of King Leopold, but more particularly as the friend and adviser of a queen who was almost a child, and who, no doubt, would be much in need of advice and friendship. For it would be a mistake to suppose that either of these two men was actuated by a vulgar selfishness. The King, indeed, was very well aware on which side his bread was buttered; during an adventurous and chequered life he had acquired a shrewd knowledge of the world's workings; and he was ready enough to use the knowledge to strengthen his position and to spread his influence. But then, the firmer his position and the wider his influence, the better for Europe; of that he was quite certain. And besides, he was a constitutional monarch; and it would be highly indecorous in a constitutional monarch to have any aims that were low or personal. As for Stockmar, the disinterestedness which Palmerston had noted was undoubtedly a basic element in his character. The ordinary schemer is always an optimist; and Stockmar, racked by dyspepsia and haunted by gloomy forebodings, was a constitutionally melancholy man. A schemer, no doubt, he was; but he schemed distrustfully, splenetically, to do good. To do good! What nobler end could a man scheme for? Yet it is perilous to scheme at all.

With Lehzen to supervise every detail of her conduct, with Stockmar in the next room, so full of wisdom and experience of affairs, with her Uncle Leopold's letters, too, pouring out so constantly their stream of encouragements, general reflections, and highly valuable tips, Victoria, even had she been without other guidance, would have stood in no lack of private counsellors. But other guidance she had; for all these influences paled before a new star, of the first magnitude, which, rising suddenly upon her horizon, immediately dominated her life.

# III

William Lamb, Viscount Melbourne, was fifty-eight years of age, and had been for the last three years Prime Minister of England. In every outward respect he was one of the most fortunate of mankind. He had been born into the midst of riches, brilliance, and power. His mother, fascinating and intelligent, had been a great Whig hostess, and he had been bred up as a member of that radiant society which, during the last quarter of the eighteenth century, concentrated within itself the ultimate perfections of a hundred years of triumphant aristocracy. Nature had given him beauty and brains; the unexpected death of an elder brother brought him wealth, a peerage, and the possibility of high advancement. Within that charmed circle, whatever one's personal disabilities, it was difficult to fail; and to him, with all his advantages, success was well-nigh unavoidable. With little effort, he attained political eminence. On the triumph of the Whigs he became one of the leading members of the Government; and when Lord Grey retired from the premiership he quietly stepped into the vacant place. Nor was it only in the visible signs of fortune that Fate had been kind to him. Bound to succeed, and to succeed easily, he was gifted with so fine a nature that his success became him. His mind, at once supple and copious, his temperament, at once calm and sensitive, enabled him not merely to work but to live with

*Lord Melbourne (1779–1848), from a portrait by Sir Edwin Landseer. His friendship with the young Queen was sympathetically described by Greville: 'I have no doubt he is passionately fond of her as he might be of his daughter if he had one; and the more because he is a man with a capacity for loving without having anything in the world to love. It is become his province to educate, instruct and form the most interesting mind and character in the world.' The Duke of Wellington took a less favourable view of his influence: 'I'm afraid he jokes too much with her, and makes her treat things too lightly, which are very serious.'*

43

perfect facility and with the grace of strength. In society he was a notable talker, a captivating companion, a charming man. If one looked deeper, one saw at once that he was not ordinary, that the piquancies of his conversation and his manner—his free-and-easy vaguenesses, his abrupt questions, his lollings and loungings, his innumerable oaths—were something more than an amusing ornament, were the outward manifestation of an individuality peculiar to the core.

The precise nature of this individuality was very difficult to gauge: it was dubious, complex, perhaps self-contradictory. Certainly there was an ironical discordance between the inner history of the man and his apparent fortunes. He owed all he had to his birth, and his birth was shameful; it was known well enough that his mother had passionately loved Lord Egremont, and that Lord Melbourne was not his father. His marriage, which had seemed to be the crown of his youthful ardours, was a long, miserable, desperate failure: the incredible Lady Caroline,

> . . . 'with pleasures too refined to please,
> With too much spirit to be e'er at ease,
> With too much quickness to be ever taught,
> With too much thinking to have common thought,'

was very nearly the destruction of his life. When at last he emerged from the anguish and confusion of her folly, her extravagance, her rage, her despair, and her devotion, he was left alone with endless memories of intermingled farce and tragedy, and an only son who was an imbecile. But there was something else that he owed to Lady Caroline. While she whirled with Byron in a hectic frenzy of love and fashion, he had stayed at home in an indulgence bordering on cynicism, and occupied his solitude with reading. It was thus that he had acquired those habits of study, that love of learning, and that wide and accurate knowledge of ancient and modern literature, which formed so unexpected a part of his mental equipment. His passion for reading never deserted him; even when he was Prime Minister he found time to master every new important book. With an incongruousness that was characteristic, his favourite study was theology. An accomplished classical scholar, he was deeply read in the Fathers of the Church; heavy volumes of commentary and exegesis he examined with scrupulous diligence; and at any odd moment he might be found turning over the pages of the Bible. * To the ladies whom he most liked he would lend some learned work on the Revelation, crammed with marginal notes in his own hand, or Dr. Lardner's 'Observations upon the Jewish Errors with respect to the Conversion of Mary Magdalene.' The more pious among them had high hopes that these studies would lead him into the right way; but of this there were no symptoms in his after-dinner conversation.

The paradox of his political career was no less curious. By temperament an aristocrat, by conviction a conservative, he came to power as the leader of the popular party, the party of change. He had profoundly disliked the Reform Bill, which he had only accepted at last as a necessary evil; and the Reform Bill lay at the root of the very existence, of the very meaning, of his government. He was far too sceptical to believe in progress of any kind.

Things were best as they were—or rather, they were least bad. 'You'd better try to do no good,' was one of his dictums, 'and then you'll get into no scrapes.' Education at best was futile; education of the poor was positively dangerous. The factory children? 'Oh, if you'd only have the goodness to leave them alone!' Free Trade was a delusion; the ballot was nonsense; and there was no such thing as a democracy. Nevertheless, he was not a reactionary; he was simply an opportunist. The whole duty of government, he said, was 'to prevent crime and to preserve contracts.' All one could really hope to do was to carry on. He himself carried on in a remarkable manner— with perpetual compromises, with fluctuations and contradictions, with every kind of weakness, and yet with shrewdness, with gentleness, even with conscientiousness, and a light and airy mastery of men and of events. He conducted the transactions of business with extraordinary nonchalance. Important persons, ushered up for some grave interview, found him in a towelled bed, littered with books and papers, or vaguely shaving in a dressing-room; but, when they went downstairs again, they would realise that somehow or other they had been pumped. When he had to receive a deputation, he could hardly ever do so with becoming gravity. The worthy delegates of the tallow-chandlers, or the Society for the Abolition of Capital Punishment, were distressed and mortified when, in the midst of their speeches, the Prime Minister became absorbed in blowing a feather, or suddenly cracked an unseemly joke. How could they have guessed that he had spent the night before diligently getting up the details of their case? He hated patronage and the making of appointments—a feeling rare in Ministers. 'As for the Bishops,' he burst out, 'I positively believe they die to vex me.' But when at last the appointment was made, it was made with keen discrimination. His colleagues observed another symptom—was it of his irresponsibility or his wisdom? He went to sleep in the Cabinet.

*In 1840, attention was drawn to the plight of factory children by Frances Trollope's hard-hitting novel* Michael Armstrong, The Factory Boy, *whose hero is depicted here by A. Hervieu. The following year, Richard Henry Horne's harrowing reports of his interviews with cowed, stunted and stupefied factory children in the Wolverhampton district shocked the nation. But despite such evidence, Melbourne's bluff 'leave them alone' attitude reflected the majority view.*

Probably, if he had been born a little earlier, he would have been a simpler and a happier man. As it was, he was a child of the eighteenth century whose lot was cast in a new, difficult, unsympathetic age. He was an autumn rose. With all his gracious amenity, his humour, his happy-go-lucky ways, a deep disquietude possessed him. A sentimental cynic, a sceptical believer, he was restless and melancholy at heart. Above all, he could never harden himself; those sensitive petals shivered in every wind. Whatever else he might be, one thing was certain: Lord Melbourne was always human, supremely human— too human, perhaps.

And now, with old age upon him, his life took a sudden, new, extraordinary turn. He became, in the twinkling of an eye, the intimate adviser and the daily companion of a young girl who had stepped all at once from a nursery to a throne. His relations with women had been, like everything else about him, ambiguous. Nobody had ever been able quite to gauge the shifting, emotional complexities of his married life; Lady Caroline vanished; but his peculiar susceptibilities remained. Female society of some kind or other was necessary to him, and he did not stint himself; a great part of every day was invariably spent in it. The feminine element in him made it easy, made it natural and inevitable for him to be the friend of a great many women; but the masculine element in him was strong as well. In such circumstances it is also easy, it is even natural, perhaps it is even inevitable, to be something more than a friend. There were rumours and combustions. Lord Melbourne was twice a co-respondent in a divorce action; but on each occasion he won his suit. The lovely Lady Brandon, the unhappy and brilliant Mrs. Norton . . . the law exonerated them both. Beyond that hung an impenetrable veil. But at any rate it was clear that, with such a record, the Prime Minister's position in Buckingham Palace must be a highly delicate one. However, he was used to delicacies, and he met the situation with consummate success. His behaviour was from the first moment impeccable. His manner towards the young Queen mingled, with perfect facility, the watchfulness and the respect of a statesman and a courtier with the tender solicitude of a parent. He was at once reverential and affectionate, at once the servant and the guide. At the same time the habits of his life underwent a surprising change. His comfortable, unpunctual days became subject to the unaltering routine of a palace; no longer did he sprawl on sofas; not a single 'damn' escaped his lips. The man of the world who had been the friend of Byron and the Regent, the talker whose paradoxes had held Holland House enthralled, the cynic whose ribaldries had enlivened so many deep potations, the lover whose soft words had captivated such beauty and such passion and such wit, might now be seen, evening after evening, talking with infinite politeness to a schoolgirl, bolt upright, amid the silence and the rigidity of Court etiquette.

# IV

On her side, Victoria was instantaneously fascinated by Lord Melbourne. The good report of Stockmar had no doubt prepared the way; Lehzen was wisely propitiated; and the first highly favourable impression was never afterwards belied. She found him perfect; and perfect in her sight he remained. Her absolute and unconcealed adoration was very natural; what innocent young creature could have resisted, in any circumstances, the charm and the devotion of such a man? But, in her situation, there was a special influence which gave a peculiar glow to all she felt. After years of emptiness and dullness and suppression, she had come suddenly, in the heyday of youth, into freedom and power. She was mistress of herself, of great domains and palaces; she was Queen of England. Responsibilities and difficulties she might have, no doubt, and in heavy measure; but one feeling dominated and absorbed all others—the feeling of joy. Everything pleased her. She was in high spirits from morning till night. Mr. Creevey, grown old now, and very near his end, catching a glimpse of her at Brighton, was much amused, in his sharp fashion, by the ingenuous gaiety of 'little Vic.'—'A more homely little being you never beheld, *when she is at her ease*, and she is evidently dying to be always more so. She laughs in real earnest, opening her mouth as wide as it can go, showing not very pretty gums. . . . She eats quite as heartily as she laughs, I think I may say she gobbles. . . . She blushes and laughs every instant in so natural a way as to disarm anybody.' But it was not merely when she was laughing or gobbling that she enjoyed herself; the performance of her official duties gave her intense satisfaction. 'I really have immensely to do,' she wrote in her journal a few days after her accession; 'I receive so many communications from my Ministers, but I like it very much.' And again, a week later, 'I repeat what I said before that I have *so many* communications from the Ministers, and from me to them, and I get so many papers to sign every day, that I have always a *very great* deal to do. I *delight* in this work.' Through the girl's immaturity the vigorous predestined tastes of the woman were pushing themselves into existence with eager velocity, with delicious force.

One detail of her happy situation deserves particular mention. Apart from the splendour of her social position and the momentousness of her political one, she was a person of great wealth. As soon as Parliament met, an annuity of £385,000 was settled upon her. When the expenses of her household had been discharged, she was left with £68,000 a year of her own. She enjoyed besides the revenues of the Duchy of Lancaster, which amounted annually to over £27,000. The first use to which she put her money was characteristic: she paid off her father's debts. In money matters, no less than in other matters, she was determined to be correct. She had the instincts of a man of business; and she never could have borne to be in a positon that was financially unsound.

With youth and happiness gilding every hour, the days passed merrily enough. And each day hinged upon Lord Melbourne. Her diary shows us, with undiminished clarity, the life of the young sovereign during the early months of her reign—a life satisfactorily regular, full of delightful business, a life of simple pleasures, mostly physical—riding, eating, dancing—a quick, easy, highly unsophisticated life, sufficient unto itself. The light of the morning is upon it; and, in the rosy radiance, the figure of 'Lord M.' emerges, glorified and supreme. If she is the heroine of the story, he is the hero; but indeed they are more than hero and heroine, for there are no other characters at all. Lehzen, the Baron, Uncle Leopold, are unsubstantial shadows—the incidental supers of the piece. Her paradise was peopled by two persons, and surely that was enough. One sees them together still, a curious couple, strangly united in those artless pages, under the magical illumination of that dawn of eighty years ago: the polished high fine gentleman with the whitening hair and whiskers and the thick dark eyebrows and the mobile lips and the big expressive eyes; and beside him the tiny Queen—fair, slim, elegant, active, in her plain girl's dress and little tippet, looking up at him earnestly, adoringly, with eyes blue and projecting, and half-open mouth. So they appear upon every page of the Journal; upon every page Lord M. is present, Lord M. is speaking, Lord M. is being amusing, instructive, delightful, and affectionate at once, while Victoria drinks in the honeyed words, laughs till she shows her gums, tries hard to remember, and runs off, as soon as she is left alone, to put it all down. Their long conversations touched upon a multitude of topics. Lord M. would criticise books, throw out a remark or two on the British Constitution, make some passing reflections on human life, and tell story after story of the great people of the eighteenth century. Then there would be business—a despatch perhaps from Lord Durham in Canada, which Lord M. would read. But first he must explain a little. 'He said that I must know that Canada originally belonged to the

*Queen Victoria in 1842, aged twenty-three.*

French, and was only ceded to the English in 1790, when it was taken in an expedition under Wolfe; "a very daring enterprise," he said. Canada was then entirely French, and the British only came afterwards. . . . Lord M. explained this very clearly (and much better than I have done) and said a good deal more about it. He then read me Durham's despatch, which is a very long one and took him more than ½ an hour to read. Lord M. read it beautifully with that fine soft voice of his, and with so much expression, so that it is needless to say I was much interested by it.' And then the talk would take a more personal turn. Lord M. would describe his boyhood, and she would learn that 'he wore his hair long, as all boys then did, till he was 17; (*how* handsome he must have looked!).' Or she would find out about his queer tastes and habits—how he never carried a watch, which seemed quite extraordinary. '"I always ask the servant what o'clock it is, and then he tells me what he likes," said Lord M.' Or, as the rooks wheeled about round the trees, 'in a manner which indicated rain,' he would say that he could sit looking at them for an hour, and 'was quite surprised at my disliking them. . . . Lord M. said, "The rooks are my delight."'

The day's routine, whether in London or at Windsor, was almost invariable. The morning was devoted to business and Lord M. In the afternoon the whole Court went out riding. The Queen, in her velvet riding-habit and a top-hat with a veil draped about the brim, headed the cavalcade; and Lord M. rode beside her. The lively troupe went fast and far, to the extreme exhilaration of Her Majesty. Back in the Palace again, there was still time for a little more fun before dinner—a game of battledore and shuttlecock perhaps, or a romp along the galleries with some children. Dinner came, and the ceremonial decidedly tightened. The gentleman of highest rank sat on the right hand of the Queen; on her left—it soon became an established rule—sat Lord Melbourne. After the ladies had left the dining-room, the gentlemen were not permitted to remain behind for very

*A drawing by 'HB' (John Doyle) of the young Queen out riding between the Prime Minister Lord Melbourne, and Lord John Russell, Home Secretary and Leader of the House of Commons. Entitled 'Susannah and the Elders', it refers to a favourite subject for artists, the Old Testament story of a virtuous young woman betrayed by corrupt and powerful men.*

Above: Lord Melbourne featured prominently in the royal sketchbooks and journal during the first summer of the young Queen's reign. In this small watercolour Victoria captured the characteristic style of the urbane yet paternal aristocrat, with haircut and neckwear reminiscent of the Regency fashions of his youth.

THE QUEEN AND PRINCE ALBERT AT HOME.

Left: a portrait by Richard Westall of his eleven-year-old pupil sketching out of doors, accompanied by her dog Fanny. Although he never attained professional success, Westall was a gifted and conscientious teacher, who gave Victoria's natural ability a firm grounding in technical skill which lasted for a lifetime of sketching and painting.

Above: in this anonymous lithograph, probably dating from about 1844, doors leading 'To the Queen's Private Apartments' open to reveal 'The Queen and Prince Albert at Home'. The tender playfulness captured in this popular print was true to life. Prince Albert in particular took endless delight in his children. In 1844 the Queen could write with satisfaction that, 'they say no Sovereign was ever more loved than I am (I am bold enough to say), and this, because of our domestic home, the good example it presents.'

*Right: 'Baby Beatrice' seen from behind in a watercolour sketch done by the Queen in 1860. Aged only four when her father died, Princess Beatrice was often allowed the privileges due to the youngest of a large family, and her pert sayings enliven the widowed Queen's journals. As she grew older, Princess Beatrice developed into a Victorian 'home daughter', left to care for an ageing parent as the elder siblings married. Despite the Queen's 'most violent dislike' of 'my precious Baby marrying at all', she agreed to accept Prince Henry of Battenburg as a son-in-law in 1884, on condition that the couple should live with her so that the 'sweet Child remains with poor, old shattered me.'*

*Previous pages: a summer scene of the royal family at Osborne, painted by the Queen in 1850 at a time when she was having tuition from the watercolourist William Leighton Leitch. Seven of the royal children are shown: Vicky, the two older boys Bertie and Affie (Alfred), Alice, the two little girls Helena and Louise and, carried by his nurse, baby Arthur.*

*Left: a collection of Scottish scenes shows the Queen's real ability as a watercolourist. While in the Highlands she filled numerous small albums, from which she would later select the best specimens to be collected and bound in larger books.*

*Vicky at her Marriage. Chapel Royal Jan 25. 1858*

Above: 'All had been so brilliant, so satisfactory & now ALL was over & our dear Child gone!' wrote the Queen after the marriage of the seventeen-year-old Princess Royal to Prince Frederick William of Prussia in January 1858. Recollecting the events of the day, she later painted Vicky, 'composed and in a fine, quiet disposition' wearing her wedding dress of white moiré antique, trimmed with three flounces of Honiton lace and wreaths and sprays of orange flowers and myrtle, with veil and wreath to match.

long; indeed, the short time allowed them for their wine-drinking formed the subject—so it was rumoured—of one of the very few disputes between the Queen and her Prime Minister;* but her determination carried the day, and from that moment after-dinner drunkenness began to go out of fashion. When the company was reassembled in the drawing-room the etiquette was stiff. For a few minutes the Queen spoke in turn to each one of her guests; and during these short uneasy colloquies the aridity of royalty was apt to became painfully evident. One night Mr. Greville, the Clerk of the Privy Council, was present; his turn soon came; the middle-aged, hard-faced *viveur* was addressed by his young hostess. 'Have you been riding to-day, Mr. Greville?' asked the Queen. 'No, Madam, I have not,' replied Mr. Greville. 'It was a fine day,' continued the Queen. 'Yes, Madam, a very fine day,' said Mr. Greville. 'It was rather cold, though,' said the Queen. 'It *was* rather cold, Madam,' said Mr. Greville. 'Your sister, Lady Frances Egerton, rides, I think, doesn't she?' said the Queen. 'She does ride sometimes, Madam,' said Mr. Greville. There was a pause, after which Mr. Greville ventured to take the lead, though he did not venture to change the subject. 'Has your Majesty been riding to-day?' asked Mr. Greville. 'Oh yes, a very long ride,' answered the Queen with animation. 'Has your Majesty got a nice horse?' said Mr. Greville. 'Oh, a very nice horse,' said the Queen. It was over. Her Majesty gave a smile and an inclination of the head, Mr. Greville a profound bow, and the next conversation began with the next gentleman. When all the guests had been disposed of, the Duchess of Kent sat down to her whist, while everybody else was ranged about the round table. Lord Melbourne sat beside the Queen, and talked pertinaciously—very often à *propos* to the contents of one of the large albums of engravings with which the round table was covered—until it was half-past eleven and time to go to bed.

Occasionally, there were little diversions: the evening might be spent at the opera or at the play. Next morning the royal critic was careful to note down her impressions. 'It was Shakespeare's tragedy of *Hamlet*, and we came in at the beginning of it. Mr. Charles Kean (son of old Kean) acted the part of Hamlet, and I must say beautifully. His conception of this very difficult, and I may almost say incomprehensible, character is admirable; his delivery of all the fine long speeches quite beautiful; he is excessively graceful and all his actions and attitudes are good, though not at all good-looking in face. . . . I came away just as *Hamlet* was over.' Later on, she went to see Macready in *King Lear*. The story was new to her; she knew nothing about it, and at first she took very little interest in what was passing on the stage; she preferred to chatter and laugh with the Lord Chamberlain. But, as the play went on, her mood changed; her attention was fixed, and then she laughed no more. Yet she was puzzled; it seemed a strange, a horrible business. What did Lord M. think? Lord M. thought it was a very fine play, but to be sure, 'a rough, coarse play, written for those times, with exaggerated characters.' 'I'm glad you've seen it,' he added. But, undoubtedly, the evenings which she enjoyed most were those on which there was dancing. She was always ready enough to seize any excuse—the arrival of cousins—a birthday—a gathering of young people—to give the command for that. Then, when the band played, and the figures of the dancers swayed to the music, and she felt her own figure swaying too, with youthful spirits so close on every side— then her happiness reached its height, her eyes sparkled, she must go on and on into the small hours of the morning. For a moment Lord M. himself was forgotten.

## V

The months flew past. The summer was over: 'the pleasantest summer I EVER passed in *my life*, and I shall never forget this first summer of my reign.' With surprising rapidity, another summer was upon her. The coronation came and went—a curious dream. The antique, intricate, endless ceremonial worked itself out as best it could, like some machine of gigantic complexity which was a little out of order. The small central figure went through her gyrations. She sat; she walked; she prayed; she carried about an orb that was almost too heavy to hold; the Archbishop of Canterbury came and crushed a ring upon the wrong finger, so that she was ready to cry out with the pain; old Lord Rolle tripped up in his mantle and fell down the steps as he was doing homage; she was taken into a side chapel, where the altar was covered with a tablecloth, sandwiches, and bottles of wine; she perceived Lehzen in an upper box and exchanged a smile with her as she sat, robed and crowned, on the Confessor's throne. 'I shall ever remember this day as the *proudest* of my life,' she noted. But the pride was soon merged once more in youth and simplicity. When she returned to Buckingham Palace at last she was not tired; she ran up to her private rooms, doffed her splendours, and gave her dog Dash its evening bath.

Life flowed on again with its accustomed smoothness—though, of course, the smoothness was occasionally disturbed. For one thing, there was the distressing behaviour of Uncle Leopold. The King of the Belgians had not been able to resist attempting to make use of his family position to further his diplomatic ends. But, indeed, why should there be any question of resisting? Was not such a course of conduct, far from being a temptation, simply *selon*

*The pomp of Victoria's coronation was marred by turmoil and confusion behind the scenes. The waspish Greville recorded that, 'the different actors in the ceremonial were very imperfect in their parts, and had neglected to rehearse them. Lord John Thynne, who officiated for the Duke of Westminster, told me that nobody knew what was to be done except the Archbishop and himself (who had rehearsed), Lord Willoughby (who is experienced in these matters), and the Duke of Wellington; and consequently there was a continual difficulty and embarrassment, and the Queen never knew what she was to do next.'*

*les règles?* What were royal marriages for, if they did not enable sovereigns, in spite of the hindrances of constitutions, to control foreign politics? For the highest purposes, of course; that was understood. The Queen of England was his niece—more than that—almost his daughter; his confidential agent was living, in a position of intimate favour, at her court. Surely, in such circumstances, it would be preposterous, it would be positively incorrect, to lose the opportunity of bending to his wishes by means of personal influence, behind the backs of the English Ministers, the foreign policy of England.

He set about the task with becoming precautions. He continued in his letters his admirable advice. Within a few days of her accession, he recommended the young Queen to lay emphasis, on every possible occasion, upon her English birth; to praise the English nation; 'the Established Church I also recommend strongly; you cannot, without *pledging* yourself to anything *particular, say too much on the subject.*' And then 'before you decide on anything important I should be glad if you would consult me; this would also have the advantage of giving you time'; nothing was more injurious than to be hurried into wrong decisions unawares. His niece replied at once with all the accustomed warmth of her affection; but she wrote hurriedly—and, perhaps, a trifle vaguely too. '*Your* advice is always of the *greatest importance* to me,' she said.

Had he, possibly, gone too far? He could not be certain; perhaps Victoria *had* been hurried. In any case, he would be careful; he would draw back— *pour mieux sauter,* he added to himself with a smile. In his next letters he made no reference to his suggestions of consultations with himself; he merely pointed out the wisdom, in general, of refusing to decide upon important questions off-hand. So far, his advice was taken; and it was noticed that the Queen, when applications were made to her, rarely gave an immediate answer. Even with Lord Melbourne, it was the same; when he asked for her opinion upon any subject, she would reply that she would think it over, and tell him her conclusions next day.

King Leopold's counsels continued. The Princess de Lieven, he said, was a dangerous woman; there was reason to think that she would make attempts to pry into what did not concern her; let Victoria beware. 'A rule which I cannot sufficiently recommend is *never to permit* people to speak on subjects concerning yourself or your affairs, without you having yourself desired them to do so.' Should such a thing occur, 'change the conversation, and make the individual feel that he has made a mistake.' This piece of advice was also taken; for it fell out as the King had predicted. Madame de Lieven sought an audience, and appeared to be verging towards confidential topics; whereupon the Queen, becoming slightly embarrassed, talked of nothing but common-places. The individual felt that she had made a mistake.

The King's next warning was remarkable. Letters, he pointed out, are almost invariably read in the post. This was inconvenient, no doubt; but the fact, once properly grasped, was not without its advantages. 'I will give you an example: we are still plagued by Prussia concerning those fortresses; now to tell the Prussian Government many things, which we *should not like* to tell them officially, the Minister is going to write a despatch to our man at Berlin, sending it *by post*; the Prussians *are sure* to read it, and to learn in this way what we wish them to hear.' Analogous circumstances might very probably occur in England. 'I tell you the *trick*,' wrote His Majesty, 'that you should be able to guard against it.' Such were the subtleties of constitutional sovereignty.

It seemed that the time had come for another step. The King's next letter was full of foreign politics—the situation in Spain and Portugal, the character of Louis-Philippe; and he received a favourable answer. Victoria, it is true, began by saying that she had shown the *political part* of his letter to Lord Melbourne; but she proceeded to a discussion of foreign affairs. It appeared that she was not unwilling to exchange observations on such matters with her uncle. So far, so good. But King Leopold was still cautious; though a crisis was impending in his diplomacy, he still hung back; at last, however, he could keep silence no longer. It was of the utmost importance to him that, in his manœuvrings with France and Holland, he should have, or at any rate appear to have, English support. But the English Government appeared to adopt a neutral attitude; it was too bad; not to be for him was to be against him—could they not see that? Yet, perhaps, they were only wavering, and a little pressure upon them from Victoria might still save all. He determined to put the case before her, delicately yet forcibly—just as he saw it himself. 'All I want from your kind Majesty,' he wrote, 'is, that you will *occasionally* express to your Ministers, and particularly to good Lord Melbourne, that, as far as it is *compatible* with the interests *of your own* dominions, you do *not* wish that your Government should take the lead in such measures as might in a short time bring on the *destruction* of this country, as well as that of your uncle and his family.' The result of this appeal was unexpected: there was dead silence for more than a week. When Victoria at last wrote, she was prodigal of her affection—'it would, indeed, my dearest Uncle, be *very wrong* of you, if you thought my feelings of warm and devoted attachment to you, and of great affection for you, could be changed—*nothing* can ever change them'—but her references to foreign politics, though they were lengthy and elaborate, were non-committal in the extreme; they were almost cast in an official and diplomatic form. Her Ministers, she said, entirely shared her views upon the subject; she understood and sympathised with the difficulties of her beloved uncle's position; and he might rest assured 'that both Lord Melbourne and Lord Palmerston are most anxious at all times for the prosperity and welfare of Belgium.' That was all. The King in his reply declared himself delighted, and re-echoed the affectionate protestations of his niece. 'My dearest and most beloved Victoria,' he said, 'you have written me a *very dear* and long letter, which has given me *great pleasure and satisfaction*.' He would not admit that he had had a rebuff.

A few months later the crisis came. King Leopold determined to make a bold push, and to carry Victoria with him, this time, by a display of royal vigour and avuncular authority. In an abrupt, an almost peremptory letter, he laid his case, once more, before his niece. 'You know from experience,' he wrote, 'that I *never ask anything of you*. . . . But, as I said before, if we are not careful we may see serious consequences which may affect more or less everybody, and *this* ought to be the object of our most anxious attention. I remain, my dear Victoria, your affectionate uncle, Leopold R.' The Queen

*Victoria's 'Dearest, most Beloved Uncle' Leopold was something of a father figure to her in her youth, and she kept up a voluminous correspondence with him until his death in 1865. Born in 1790, he was the younger brother of the future Duchess of Kent, but his connection with the British royal family dated from his brief marriage to the Princess Charlotte in 1816. Nicknamed 'Monsieur Peu à Peu' by the Prince Regent, his cautious nature made him decline the offer of the Greek throne in 1831, but shortly afterwards he agreed to become King of the Belgians.*

immediately despatched this letter to Lord Melbourne, who replied with a carefully thought-out form of words, signifying nothing whatever, which, he suggested, she should send to her uncle. She did so, copying out the elaborate formula, with a liberal scattering of 'dear Uncles' interspersed; and she concluded her letter with a message of 'affectionate love to Aunt Louise and the children.' Then at last King Leopold was obliged to recognise the facts. His next letter contained no reference at all to politics. 'I am glad,' he wrote, 'to find that you like Brighton better than last year. I think Brighton very agreeable at this time of year, till the east wind sets in. The pavilion, besides, is comfortable; that cannot be denied. Before my marriage, it was there that I met the Regent. Charlotte afterwards came with old Queen Charlotte. How distant all this already, but still how present to one's memory.' Like poor Madame de Lieven, his Majesty felt that he had made a mistake.

Nevertheless, he could not quite give up all hope. Another opportunity offered, and he made another effort—but there was not very much conviction in it, and it was immediately crushed. 'My dear Uncle,' the Queen wrote, 'I have to thank you for your last letter, which I received on Sunday. Though you seem not to dislike my political sparks, I think it is better not to increase them, as they might finally take fire, particularly as I see with regret that upon this one subject we cannot agree. I shall, therefore, limit myself to my expressions of very sincere wishes for the welfare and prosperity of Belgium.' After that, it was clear that there was no more to be said. Henceforeward there is audible in the King's letters a curiously elegiac note. 'My dearest Victoria, your *delightful* little letter has just arrived and went like *an arrow to my heart.* Yes, my beloved Victoria! I *do love you tenderly.* . . . I love you *for yourself,* and I love in you the dear child whose welfare I tenderly watched.' He had gone through much; yet, if life had its disappointments, it had its satisfactions too. 'I have all the honours that can be given, and I am, politically speaking, very solidly established.' But there were other things besides politics; there were romantic yearnings in his heart. 'The only longing I still have is for the Orient, where I perhaps shall once end my life, rising in the west and setting in the east.' As for his devotion to his niece, that could never end. 'I never press my services on you, nor my councils, though I may say with some truth that from the extraordinary fate which the higher powers had ordained for me, my experience, both political and of private life, is great. I am *always ready* to be useful to you *when and where* it may be, and I repeat it, *all I want in return is some little sincere affection from you.*'

# VI

The correspondence with King Leopold was significant of much that still lay partly hidden in the character of Victoria. Her attitude towards her uncle had never wavered for a moment. To all his advances she had presented an absolutely unyielding front. The foreign policy of England was not his province; it was hers and her Ministers'; his insinuations, his entreaties, his struggles—all were quite useless; and he must understand that this was so. The rigidity of her position was the more striking owing to the respectfulness and the affection with which it was accompanied. From start to finish the unmoved Queen remained the devoted niece. Leopold himself must have envied such perfect correctitude; but what may be admirable in an elderly statesman is alarming in a maiden of nineteen. And privileged observers were not without their fears. The strange mixture of ingenuous light-heartedness and fixed determination, of frankness and reticence, of childishness and pride, seemed to augur a future perplexed and full of dangers. As time passed the less pleasant qualities in this curious composition revealed themselves more often and more seriously. There were signs of an imperious, a peremptory temper, an egotism that was strong and hard. It was noticed that the palace etiquette, far from relaxing, grew ever more and more inflexible. By some, this was attributed to Lehzen's influence; but, if that was so, Lehzen had a willing pupil; for the slightest infringements of the freezing rules of regularity and deference were invariably and immediately visited by the sharp and haughty glances of the Queen. Yet Her Majesty's eyes, crushing as they could be, were less crushing than her mouth. The self-will depicted in those small projecting teeth and that small receding chin was of a more dismaying kind than that which a powerful jaw betokens; it was a self-will imperturbable, impenetrable, unreasoning; a self-will dangerously akin to obstinacy. And the obstinacy of monarchs is not as that of other men.

Within two years of her accession, the storm-clouds which, from the first, had been dimly visible on the horizon, gathered and burst. Victoria's relations with her mother had not improved. The Duchess of Kent, still surrounded by all the galling appearances of filial consideration, remained in Buckingham Palace a discarded figure, powerless and inconsolable. Sir John Conroy, banished from the presence of the Queen, still presided over the Duchess's household, and the hostilities of Kensington continued unabated in the new surroundings. Lady Flora Hastings still cracked her malicious jokes; the animosity of the Baroness was still unappeased. One day, Lady Flora found the joke was turned against her. Early in 1839, travelling in the suite of the Duchess, she had returned from Scotland in the same carriage with Sir John. A change in her figure became the subject of an unseemly jest; tongues wagged; and the jest grew serious. It was whispered that Lady Flora was with child. The state of her health seemed to confirm the suspicion; she consulted Sir James Clark, the royal physician, and, after the consultation, Sir James let his tongue wag, too. On this, the scandal flared up sky-high. Everyone was talking; the Baroness was not surprised; the Duchess rallied tumultuously to the support of her lady; the Queen was informed. At last, the extraordinary expedient of a medical examination was resorted to, during which Sir James, according to Lady Flora, behaved with brutal rudeness, while a second doctor was extremely polite. Finally, both physicians signed a certificate entirely exculpating the lady. But this was by no means the end of the business. The Hastings family, socially a very powerful one, threw itself into the fray with all the fury of outraged pride and injured innocence; Lord Hastings insisted upon an audience of the Queen, wrote to the papers, and demanded the dismissal of Sir James Clark. The Queen expressed her regret to Lady Flora, but Sir James Clark was not dismissed. The tide of opinion turned violently against the Queen and her advisers; high society was

An assured self-portrait of the Queen at twenty-six suggests a maturing woman not averse to the exercise of power and authority.

disgusted by all this washing of dirty linen in Buckingham Palace; the public at large was indignant at the ill-treatment of Lady Flora. By the end of March, the popularity, so radiant and so abundant, with which the young Sovereign had begun her reign, had entirely disappeared.

There can be no doubt that a great lack of discretion had been shown by the Court. Ill-natured tittle-tattle, which should have been instantly nipped in the bud, had been allowed to assume disgraceful proportions; and the Throne itself had become involved in the personal malignities of the palace. A particularly awkward question had been raised by the position of Sir James Clark. The Duke of Wellington, upon whom it was customary to fall back, in cases of great difficulty in high places, had been consulted upon this question, and he had given it as his opinion that, as it would be impossible to remove Sir James without a public enquiry, Sir James must certainly stay where he was. Probably the Duke was right; but the fact that the peccant doctor continued in the Queen's service made the Hastings family irreconcilable and produced an unpleasant impression of unrepentant error upon the public mind. As for Victoria, she was very young and quite inexperienced; and she can hardly be blamed for having failed to control an extremely difficult situation. That was clearly Lord Melbourne's task; he was a man of the world, and, with vigilance and circumspection, he might have quietly put out the ugly flames while they were still smouldering. He did not do so; he was lazy and easy-going; the Baroness was persistent, and he let things slide. But doubtless his position was not an easy one; passions ran high in the palace; and Victoria was not only very young, she was very headstrong, too. Did he possess the magic bridle which would curb that fiery steed? He could not be certain. And then, suddenly, another violent crisis revealed more unmistakably than ever the nature of the mind with which he had to deal.

# VII

The Queen had for long been haunted by a terror that the day might come when she would be obliged to part with her Minister. Ever since the passage of the Reform Bill, the power of the Whig Government had steadily declined. The General Election of 1837 had left them with a very small majority in the House of Commons; since then, they had been in constant difficulties—abroad, at home, in Ireland; the Radical group had grown hostile; it became highly doubtful how much longer they could survive. The Queen watched the development of events in great anxiety. She was a Whig by birth, by upbringing, by every association, public and private; and, even if those ties had never existed, the mere fact that Lord M. was the head of the Whigs would have amply sufficed to determine her politics. The fall of the Whigs would mean a sad upset for Lord M. But it would have a still more terrible consequence: Lord M. would have to leave her; and the daily, the hourly, presence of Lord M. had become an integral part of her life. Six months after her accession she had noted in her diary 'I shall be very sorry to lose him *even* for *one* night'; and this feeling of personal dependence on her Minister steadily increased. In these circumstances it was natural that she

*A satirical comment on the Bedchamber Crisis of 1839 portrays Prime Minister Sir Robert Peel as the 'ministerial wolf' with evil designs on the patronage, perquisites, etc. in the royal Red Ridinghood's basket. With Windsor Castle in the background, he is clearly trespassing on the royal preserve; the classical reference to Mount 'Peelion' likens him to the rebellious giants of Greek mythology who piled up Mounts Pelion and Ossa in a vain attempt to scale Olympus and defeat the gods.*

should have become a Whig partisan. Of the wider significance of political questions she knew nothing; all she saw was that her friends were in office and about her, and that it would be dreadful if they ceased to be so. 'I cannot say,' she wrote when a critical division was impending, '(though I feel *confident* of *our success*) HOW *low*, HOW *sad* I feel, when I think of the POSSIBILITY of this excellent and truly kind man not *remaining* my Minister! Yet I trust fervently that *He* who has so wonderfully protected me through such manifold difficulties will not *now* desert me! I should have like to have expressed to Lord M. my anxiety, but the tears were nearer than words throughout the time I saw him, and I felt I should have choked, had I attempted to say anything.' Lord Melbourne realised clearly enough how undesirable was such a state of mind in a constitutional sovereign who might be called upon at any moment to receive as her Ministers the leaders of the opposite party; he did what he could to cool her ardour; but in vain.

With considerable lack of foresight, too, he had himself helped to bring about this unfortunate condition of affairs. From the moment of her accession, he had surrounded the Queen with ladies of his own party: the Mistress of the Robes and all the Ladies of the Bedchamber were Whigs. In the ordinary course, the Queen never saw a Tory; eventually she took pains never to see one in any circumstances. She disliked the whole tribe, and she did not conceal the fact. She particularly disliked Sir Robert Peel, who would almost certainly be the next Prime Minister. His manners were detestable, and he wanted to turn out Lord M. His supporters, without exception, were equally bad; and as for Sir James Graham, she could not bear the sight of him; he was exactly like Sir John Conroy.

The affair of Lady Flora intensified these party rumours still further. The Hastings were Tories, and Lord Melbourne and the Court were attacked by the Tory press in unmeasured language. The Queen's sectarian zeal proportionately increased. But the dreaded hour was now fast approaching. Early in May the Ministers were visibly tottering; on a vital point of policy they could only secure a majority of five in the House of Commons; they determined to resign. When Victoria heard the news she burst into tears. Was it possible, then, that all was over? Was she indeed about to see Lord M. for the last time? Lord M. came; and it is a curious fact that, even in this crowning moment of misery and agitation, the precise girl noted, to the minute, the exact time of the arrival and departure of her beloved Minister. The conversation was touching and prolonged; but it could only end in one way—the Queen must send for the Duke of Wellington. When, next morning, the Duke came, he advised her Majesty to send for Sir Robert Peel. She was in 'a state of dreadful grief,' but she swallowed down her tears, and braced herself, with royal resolution, for the odious, odious interview.

Peel was by nature reserved, proud, and shy. His manners were not perfect, and he knew it; he was easily embarrassed, and, at such moments, he grew even more stiff and formal than before, while his feet mechanically performed upon the carpet a dancing-master's measure. Anxious as he now was to win the Queen's good graces, his very anxiety to do so made the attainment of his object the more difficult. He entirely failed to make any headway whatever with the haughty hostile girl before him. She coldly noted that he appeared

## THE ROYAL RED RIDING HOOD.

### AND THE MINISTERIAL WOLF.

to be unhappy and 'put out,' and, while he stood in painful fixity, with an occasional uneasy pointing of the toe, her heart sank within her at the sight of that manner, 'oh! how different, how dreadfully different, to the frank, open, natural, and most kind warm manner of Lord Melbourne.' Nevertheless, the audience passd without disaster. Only at one point had there been some slight hint of a disagreement. Peel had decided that a change would be necessary in the composition of the royal Household: the Queen must no longer be entirely surrounded by the wives and sisters of his opponents; some, at any rate, of the Ladies of the Bedchamber should be friendly to his Government. When this matter was touched upon, the Queen had intimated that she wished her Household to remain unchanged; to which Sir Robert had replied that the question could be settled later, and shortly afterwards withdrew to arrange the details of his Cabinet. While he was present, Victoria had remained, as she herself said, 'very much collected, civil and high, and betrayed no agitation'; but as soon as she was alone she completely broke down. Then she pulled herself together to write to Lord Melbourne an account of all that had happened, and of her own wretchedness. 'She feels,' she said, 'Lord Melbourne will understand it, amongst enemies to those she most relied on and most esteemed; but what is worst of all is the being deprived of seeing Lord Melbourne as she used to do.'

Lord Melbourne replied with a very wise letter. He attempted to calm the Queen and to induce her to accept the new position gracefully; and he had nothing but good words for the Tory leaders. As for the question of the Ladies of the Household, the Queen, he said, should strongly urge what she desired, as it was a matter which concerned her personally; 'but,' he added, 'if Sir Robert is unable to concede it, it will not do to refuse and to put off the negotiation upon it.'

On this point there can be little doubt that Lord Melbourne was right. The question was a complicated and subtle one, and it had never arisen before; but subsequent constitutional practice has determined that a Queen Regnant must accede to the wishes of her Prime Minister as to the *personnel* of the female part of her Household. Lord Melbourne's wisdom, however, was wasted. The Queen would not be soothed, and still less would she take advice. It was outrageous of the Tories to want to deprive her of her Ladies, and that night she made up her mind that, whatever Sir Robert might say, she would refuse to consent to the removal of a single one of them. Accordingly, when, next morning, Peel appeared again, she was ready for action. He began by detailing the Cabinet appointments, and then he added 'Now, Ma'am, about the Ladies'—when the Queen sharply interrupted him. 'I cannot give up *any* of my Ladies,' she said. 'What, Ma'am!' said Sir Robert, 'does your Majesty mean to retain them *all*?' 'All,' said the Queen. Sir Robert's face worked strangely; he could not conceal his agitation. 'The Mistress of the Robes and the Ladies of the Bedchamber?' he brought out at last. '*All*,' replied once more Her Majesty. It was in vain that Peel pleaded and argued; in vain that he spoke, growing every moment more pompous and uneasy, of the constitution, and Queens Regnant, and the public interest; in vain that he danced his pathetic minuet. She was adamant; but he, too, through all his embarrassment, showed no sign of yielding; and when at last

'A cold, odd man,' wrote Queen Victoria of Sir Robert Peel, whose smile had been likened to 'the silver handles on a coffin'. Son of a wealthy manufacturer, Peel entered Parliament in 1809. As Home Secretary in 1829 he was responsible for the Metropolitan Police Act (hence the famous Peelers); he became Prime Minister in 1834 as the result of an election campaign during which he issued the Tamworth Manifesto, an electoral address defining the Conservative party in terms that affected politics for the rest of the century. After her initial distrust, the Queen came to accept Peel, although his career ended when personal convictions led him to go against party policy on the repeal of the corn laws. He was bitterly attacked by his fellow Tories, led by Disraeli, and resigned in 1846. He died in 1850, aged sixty-two, as the result of a fall from his horse.

he left her nothing had been decided—the whole formation of the Government was hanging in the wind. A frenzy of excitement now seized upon Victoria. Sir Robert, she believed in her fury, had tried to outwit her, to take her friends from her, to impose his will upon her own; but that was not all: she had suddenly perceived, while the poor man was moving so uneasily before her, the one thing that she was desperately longing for—a loophole of escape. She seized a pen and dashed off a note to Lord Melbourne.

'Sir Robert has behaved very ill,' she wrote; 'he insisted on my giving up my Ladies, to which I replied that I *never* would consent, and I never saw a man so frightened. . . . I was calm but very decided, and I think you would have been pleased to see my composure and great firmness; the Queen of England will not submit to such trickery. Keep yourself in readiness, for you may soon be wanted.' Hardly had she finished when the Duke of Wellington was announced. 'Well, Ma'am,' he said as he entered, 'I am very sorry to find there is a difficulty.' 'Oh!' she instantly replied, '*he* began it, not me.' She felt that only one thing now was needed: she must be firm. And firm she was. The venerable conqueror of Napoleon was outfaced by the relentless equanimity of a girl in her teens. He could not move the Queen one inch. At last, she even ventured to rally him. 'Is Sir Robert so weak,' she asked, 'that even the Ladies must be of his opinion?' On which the Duke made a brief and humble expostulation, bowed low, and departed.

Had she won? Time would show; and in the meantime she scribbled down another letter. 'Lord Melbourne must not think the Queen rash in her conduct. . . . The Queen felt this was an attempt to see whether she could be led and managed like a child.' The Tories were not only wicked but ridiculous. Peel, having, as she understood, expressed a wish to remove only those members of the Household who were in Parliament, now objected to her Ladies. 'I should like to know,' she exclaimed in triumphant scorn, 'if they mean to give the *Ladies* seats in Parliament?'

The end of the crisis was now fast approaching. Sir Robert returned, and told her that if she insisted upon retaining all her Ladies he could not form a Government. She replied that she would send him her final decision in writing. Next morning the late Whig Cabinet met. Lord Melbourne read to them the Queen's letters, and the group of elderly politicans were overcome by an extraordinary wave of enthusiasm. They knew very well that, to say the least, it was highly doubtful whether the Queen had acted in strict accordance with the constitution; that in doing what she had done she had brushed aside Lord Melbourne's advice; that, in reality, there was no public reason whatever why they should go back upon their decision to resign. But such considerations vanished before the passionate urgency of Victoria. The intensity of her determination swept them headlong down the stream of her desire. They unanimously felt that 'it was impossible to abandon such a Queen and such a woman.' Forgetting that they were no longer her Majesty's Ministers, they took the unprecedented course of advising the Queen by letter to put an end to her negotiaton with Sir Robert Peel. She did so; all was over; she had triumphed. That evening there was a ball at the Palace. Everyone was present. 'Peel and the Duke of Wellington came by looking very much put out.' She was perfectly happy; Lord M. was Prime Minister once more, and he was by her side.*

# VIII

Happiness had returned with Lord M., but it was happiness in the midst of agitation. The domestic imbroglio continued unabated, until at last the Duke, rejected as a Minister, was called in once again in his old capacity as moral physician to the family. Something was accomplished when, at last, he induced Sir John Conroy to resign his place about the Duchess of Kent and leave the Palace for ever; something more when he persuaded the Queen to write an affectionate letter to her mother. The way seemed open for a reconciliation, but the Duchess was stormy still. She didn't believe that Victoria had written that letter; it was not in her handwriting; and she sent for the Duke to tell him so. The Duke, assuring her that the letter was genuine, begged her to forget the past. But that was not so easy. 'What am I to do if Lord Melbourne comes up to me?' 'Do, ma'am? Why, receive him with civility.' Well, she would make an effort. . . . 'But what am I to do if Victoria asks me to shake hands with Lehzen?' 'Do, ma'am? Why, take her in your arms and kiss her.' 'What!' The Duchess bristled in every feather, and then she burst into a hearty laugh. 'No, ma'am, no,' said the Duke, laughing too. 'I don't mean you are to take *Lehzen* in your arms and kiss *her*, but the Queen.'

The Duke might perhaps have succeeded, had not all attempts at conciliation been rendered hopeless by a tragical event. Lady Flora, it was discovered, had been suffering from a terrible internal malady, which now grew rapidly worse. There could be little doubt that she was dying. The Queen's unpopularity reached an extraordinary height. More than once she was publicly insulted. 'Mrs. Melbourne,' was shouted at her when she appeared at her balcony; and, at Ascot, she was hissed by the Duchess of Montrose and Lady Sarah Ingestre as she passed. Lady Flora died. The whole scandal burst out again with redoubled vehemence; while, in the Palace, the two parties were henceforth divided by an impassable, a Stygian, gulf.

Nevertheless, Lord M. was back, and every trouble faded under the enchantment of his presence and his conversation. He, on his side, had gone through much; and his distresses were intensified by a consciousness of his own shortcomings. He realised clearly enough that, if he had intervened at the right moment, the Hastings scandal might have been averted; and, in the bedchamber crisis, he knew that he had allowed his judgment to be overruled and his conduct to be swayed by private feelings and the impetuosity of Victora. But he was not one to suffer too acutely from the pangs of conscience. In spite of the dullness and the formality of the Court, his relationship with the Queen had come to be the dominating interest in his life; to have been deprived of it would have been heart-rending; that dread eventuality had been—somehow—avoided; he was installed once more, in a kind of triumph; let him enjoy the fleeting hours to the full! And so, cherished of the favour of a sovereign and warmed by the adoration of a girl, the autumn rose, in those autumn months of 1839, came to a wondrous blooming. The petals expanded, beautifully, for the last time. For the last time in this unlooked-for, this incongruous, this almost incredible intercourse, the old epicure tasted the exquisiteness of romance. To watch, to teach, to restrain, to encourage the royal young creature beside him—that was much; to feel with such a constant intimacy the impact of her quick affection, her radiant vitality—that was more; most of all, perhaps, was it good to linger vaguely in humorous contemplation, in idle apostrophe, to talk disconnectedly, to make a little joke about an apple or a furbelow, to dream. The springs of his sensibility, hidden deep within him, were overflowing. Often, as he bent over her hand and kissed it, he found himself in tears.

Upon Victoria, with all her impermeability, it was inevitable that such a companionship should have produced, eventually, an effect. She was no longer the simple schoolgirl of two years since. The change was visible even in her public demeanour. Her expression, once 'ingenuous and serene,' now appeared to a shrewd observer to be 'bold and discontented.' She had learnt something of the pleasures of power and the pains of it; but that was not all. Lord Melbourne with his gentle instruction had sought to lead her into the paths of wisdom and moderation, but the whole unconscious movement of his character had swayed her in a very different direction. The hard clear pebble, subjected for so long and so constantly to that encircling and insidious fluidity, had suffered a curious corrosion; it seemed to be actually growing a little soft and a little clouded. Humanity and fallibility are infectious things; was it possible that Lehzen's prim pupil had caught them? That she was beginning to listen to siren voices? That the secret impulses of self-expression, of self-indulgence even, were mastering her life? For a moment the child of a new age looked back, and wavered towards the eighteenth century. It was the most critical moment of her career. Had those influences lasted, the development of her character, the history of her life, would have been completely changed.

And why should they not last? She, for one, was very anxious that they should. Let them last for ever! She was surrounded by Whigs, she was free to do whatever she wanted, she had Lord M.; she could not believe that she could ever be happier. Any change would be for the worse; and the worst change of all . . . no, she would not hear of it; it would be quite intolerable, it would upset everything, if she were to marry. And yet everyone seemed to want her to—the general public, the Ministers, her Saxe-Coburg relations— it was always the same story. Of course, she knew very well that there were excellent reasons for it. For one thing, if she remained childless, and were to die, her uncle Cumberland, who was now the King of Hanover, would succeed to the Throne of England. That, no doubt, would be a most unpleasant event; and she entirely sympathised with everybody who wished to avoid it. But there was no hurry; naturally, she would marry in the end— but not just yet—not for three or four years. What was tiresome was that her uncle Leopold had apparently determined, not only that she ought to marry, but that her cousin Albert ought to be her husband. That was very like her uncle Leopold, who wanted to have a finger in every pie; and it was true that

*Arthur Wellesley, first Duke of Wellington (1769–1852), soldier and statesman, defeated Napoleon at Waterloo in 1815, and was Tory Prime Minister from 1828 to 1830. Queen Victoria wrote of him: 'He was the GREATEST man this country ever produced.'*

After a 'terrible' Channel crossing lasting over five hours, the little steam-packet Ariel reaches Dover, bringing Prince Albert to England for his marriage to Queen Victoria. Everyone on board had been seasick, especially the Prince, who described himself as arriving with a face 'the colour of a wax candle'. Enthusiastic crowds braved the weather to welcome the young Queen's future husband, but malicious broadsheets greeted him rather differently:

'Here comes the bridegroom of
    Victoria's choice,
The nominee of Lehzen's vulgar
    voice;
He comes to take "for better or
    for worse"
England's fat Queen and
    England's fatter purse.'

long ago, in far-off days, before her accession even, she had written to him in a way which might well have encouraged him in such a notion. She had told him then that Albert possessed 'every quality that could be desired to render her perfectly happy,' and had begged her 'dearest uncle to take care of the health of one, now *so dear* to me, and to take him under *your special* protection,' adding, 'I hope and trust all will go on prosperously and well on this subject of so much importance to me.' But that had been years ago, when she was a mere child; perhaps, indeed, to judge from the language, the letter had been dictated by Lehzen; at any rate, her feelings, and all the circumstances, had now entirely changed. Albert hardly interested her at all.

In later life the Queen declared that she had never for a moment dreamt of marrying anyone but her cousin; her letters and diaries tell a very different story. On August 26, 1837, she wrote in her journal: 'Today is my *dearest* cousin Albert's 18th birthday, and I pray Heaven to pour its choicest blessings on his beloved head!' In the subsequent years, however, the date passes unnoticed. It had been arranged that Stockmar should accompany the Prince to Italy, and the faithful Baron left her side for that purpose. He wrote to her more than once with sympathetic descriptions of his young companion; but her mind was by this time made up. She liked and admired Albert very much, but she did not want to marry him. 'At present,' she told

70

Lord Melbourne in April 1839, 'my feeling is quite against ever marrying.' When her cousin's Italian tour came to an end, she began to grow nervous; she knew that, according to a long-standing engagement, his next journey would be to England. He would probably arrive in the autumn, and by July her uneasiness was intense. She determined to write to her uncle, in order to make her position clear. It must be understood, she said, that 'there is *no engagement* between us.' If she should like Albert, she could 'make *no final promise this year*, for, at the *very earliest*, any such event could not take place till *two or three years hence*.' She had, she said, 'a *great* repugnance' to change her present position; and, if she should not like him, she was '*very* anxious that it should be understood that she would *not* be guilty of any breach of promise, for she *never gave any*.' To Lord Melbourne she was more explicit. She told him that she 'had no great wish to see Albert, as the whole subject was an odious one'; she hated to have to decide about it; and she repeated once again that seeing Albert would be 'a disagreeable thing.' But there was no escaping the horrid business; the visit must be made, and she must see him. The summer slipped by and was over; it was the autumn already; on the evening of October 10 Albert, accompanied by his brother Ernest, arrived at Windsor.

Albert arrived; and the whole structure of her existence crumbled into nothingness like a house of cards. He was beautiful—she gasped—she knew no more. Then, in a flash, a thousand mysteries were revealed to her; the past, the present, rushed upon her with a new significance; the delusions of years were abolished, and an extraordinary, an irresistible certitude leapt into being in the light of those blue eyes, the smile of that lovely mouth. The succeeding hours passed in a rapture. She was able to observe a few more details—the 'exquisite nose,' the 'delicate moustachios and slight but very slight whiskers,' the 'beautiful figure, broad in the shoulders and a fine waist.' She rode with him, danced with him, talked with him, and it was all perfection. She had no shadow of a doubt. He had come on a Thursday evening, and on the following Sunday morning she told Lord Melbourne that she had 'a good deal changed her opinion as to marrying.' Next morning, she told him that she had made up her mind to marry Albert. The morning after that, she sent for her cousin. She received him alone, and 'after a few minutes I said to him that I thought he must be aware *why* I wished them to come here—and that it would make me *too happy* if he would consent to what I wished (to marry me).' Then 'we embraced each other, and he was *so* kind, *so* affectionate.' She said that she was quite unworthy of him, while he murmured that he would be very happy 'Das Leben mit dir zu zubringen.' They parted, and she felt 'the happiest of human beings,' when Lord M. came in. At first she beat about the bush, and talked of the weather, and indifferent subjects. Somehow or other she felt a little nervous with her old friend. At last, summoning up her courage, she said, 'I have got well through this with Albert.' 'Oh! you have,' said Lord M. *

# 4: MARRIAGE

T was decidedly a family match. Prince Francis Charles Augustus Albert Emmanuel of Saxe-Coburg-Gotha—for such was his full title— had been born just three months after his cousin Victoria, and the same midwife had assisted at the two births. The children's grandmother, the Dowager Duchess of Coburg, had from the first looked forward to their marriage; as they grew up, the Duke, the Duchess of Kent, and King Leopold came equally to desire it. The Prince, ever since the time when, as a child of three, his nurse had told him that some day 'the little English May flower' would be his wife, had never thought of marrying anyone else. When eventually Baron Stockmar himself signified his assent, the affair seemed as good as settled.

The Duke had one other child—Prince Ernest, Albert's senior by one year, and heir to the principality. The Duchess was a sprightly and beautiful woman, with fair hair and blue eyes; Albert was very like her and was her declared favourite. But in his fifth year he was parted from her for ever. The ducal court was not noted for the strictness of its morals; the Duke was a man of gallantry, and it was rumoured that the Duchess followed her husband's example. There were scandals: one of the Court Chamberlains, a charming and cultivated man of Jewish extraction, was talked of; at last there was a separation, followed by a divorce. The Duchess retired to Paris, and died unhappily in 1831. Her memory was always very dear to Albert.

He grew up a pretty, clever, and high-spirited boy. Usually well-behaved, he was, however, sometimes violent. He had a will of his own, and asserted it; his elder brother was less passionate, less purposeful, and, in their wrangles, it was Albert who came out top. The two boys, living for the most part in one or other of the Duke's country houses, among pretty hills and woods and streams, had been at a very early age—Albert was less than

*Publishers of sheet-music catered for the public interest in the young Queen's wedding. 'Society is unhinged by Her Majesty's marriage,' wrote Charles Dickens, 'and I am sorry to add that I have fallen hopelessly in love with the Queen and wander up and down with vague and dismal thoughts of running away to some uninhabited island with a maid of honour to be entrapped by conspiracy for that purpose.' In a theatrical outburst the author of Pickwick Papers declared: 'I am raving with love for the Queen'; he spoke of razors and throwing himself into the Serpentine. 'I think she will be sorry when I am gone. I should wish to be embalmed and kept (if practicable) on top of the triumphal arch at Buckingham Palace when she is in town and on the north east turrets of the Round Tower when she is at Windsor.' The 'Triumphal Arch' was the Marble Arch, which at that time stood in front of Buckingham Palace.*

73

*Portrait painter Robert Thorburn specialized in transforming his Victorian sitters into figures from a romantic past. Here he presented Prince Albert and his elder brother as knightly gallants, while succeeding in contrasting the sensitive, innocent Albert (left) with the bolder, more challenging Ernest. Although devoted to each other as children, the two young men developed on very different lines, Ernest taking after their disreputable and dissipated father.*

four—separated from their nurses and put under a tutor, in whose charge they remained until they went to the University. They were brought up in a simple and unostentatious manner, for the Duke was poor and the duchy very small and very insignificant. Before long it became evident that Albert was a model lad. Intelligent and painstaking, he had been touched by the moral earnestness of his generation; at the age of eleven he surprised his father by telling him that he hoped to make himself 'a good and useful man.' And yet he was not over-serious; though, perhaps, he had little humour, he was full of fun—of practical jokes and mimicry. He was no milksop; he rode, and shot, and fenced; above all did he delight in being out of doors, and never was he happier than in his long rambles with his brother through the wild country round his beloved Rosenau—stalking the deer, admiring the scenery, and returning laden with specimens for his natural history collection. He was, besides, passionately fond of music. In one particular it was observed that he did not take after his father: owing either to his peculiar upbringing or to a more fundamental idiosyncrasy he had a marked distaste for the opposite sex. At the age of five, at a children's dance, he screamed with disgust and anger when a little girl was led up to him for a partner; and though, later on, he grew more successful in disguising such feelings, the feelings remained.

The brothers were very popular in Coburg, and, when the time came for them to be confirmed, the preliminary examination, which, according to ancient custom, was held in public in the 'Giants' Hall' of the Castle, was attended by an enthusiastic crowd of functionaries, clergy, delegates from the villages of the duchy, and miscellaneous onlookers. There were also present, besides the Duke and the Dowager Duchess, their Serene Highnesses the Princes Alexander and Ernest of Würtemberg, Prince Leiningen, Princess Hohenlohe-Langenburg, and Princess Hohenlohe-Schillingsfürst. Dr. Jacobi, the Court chaplain, presided at an altar, simply but appropriately decorated, which had been placed at the end of the hall; and the proceedings began by the choir singing the first verse of the hymn, 'Come, Holy Ghost.' After some introductory remarks, Dr. Jacobi began the examination. 'The dignified and decorous bearing of the Princes,' we are told in a contemporary account, 'their strict attention to the questions, the frankness, decision, and correctness of their answers, produced a deep impression on the numerous assembly. Nothing was more striking in their answers than the evidence they gave of deep feeling and of inward strength of conviction. The questions put by the examiner were not such as to be met by a simple "yes" or "no." They were carefully considered in order to give the audience a clear insight into the views and feelings of the young princes. One of the most touching moments was when the examiner asked the hereditary prince whether he intended steadfastly to hold to the Evangelical Church, and the Prince answered not only "Yes!" but added in a clear and decided tone: "I and my brother are firmly resolved ever to remain faithful to the acknowledged truth."' The examination having lasted an hour, Dr. Jacobi made some concluding observations, followed by a short prayer; the second and third verses of the opening hymn were sung; and the ceremony was over. The Princes, stepping down from the altar, were embraced by the Duke and the Dowager Duchess; after which the loyal inhabitants of Coburg dispersed, well satisfied with their entertainment.

Albert's mental development now proceeded apace. In his seventeenth year he began a careful study of German literature and German philosophy. He set about, he told his tutor, 'to follow the thoughts of the great Klopstock into their depths—though in this, for the most part,' he modestly added, 'I do not succeed.' He wrote an essay on the 'Mode of Thought of the Germans, and a Sketch of the History of German Civilisation,' 'making use,' he said, 'in its general outlines, of the divisions which the treatment of the subject itself demands,' and concluding with 'a retrospect of the shortcomings of our time, with an appeal to every one to correct those shortcomings in his own case, and thus set a good example to others.' Placed for some months under the care of King Leopold at Brussels, he came under the influence of Adolphe Quetelet, a mathematical professor, who was particularly interested in the application of the laws of probability to political and moral phenomena; this line of inquiry attracted the Prince, and the friendship thus begun continued till the end of his life. From Brussels he went to the University of Bonn, where he was speedily distinguished both by his intellectual and his social activities; his energies were absorbed in metaphysics, law, political economy, music, fencing, and amateur theatricals. Thirty years later his fellow-students recalled with delight the fits of laughter into which they had been sent by Prince Albert's mimicry. The *verve* with which his Serene Highness reproduced the tones and gestures of one of the professors who used to point to a picture of a row of houses in Venice with the remark, 'That is the Ponte Realte,' and of another who fell down in a race and was obliged to look for his spectacles, was especially appreciated.

After a year at Bonn, the time had come for a foreign tour, and Baron Stockmar arrived from England to accompany the Prince on an expedition to Italy. The Baron had been already, two years previously, consulted by King Leopold as to his views upon the proposed marriage of Albert and Victoria. His reply had been remarkable. With a characteristic foresight, a characteristic absence of optimism, a characteristic sense of the moral elements in the stituation, Stockmar had pointed out what were, in his opinion, the conditions essential to make the marriage a success. Albert, he wrote, was a fine young fellow, well grown for his age, with agreeable and valuable qualities; and it was probable that in a few years he would turn out a strong, handsome man, of a kindly, simple, yet dignified demeanour. 'Thus, externally, he possesses all that pleases the sex, and at all times and in all countries must please.' Supposing, therefore, that Victoria herself was in favour of the marriage, the further question arose as to whether Albert's mental qualities were such as to fit him for the position of husband of the Queen of England. On this point, continued the Baron, one heard much to his credit; the Prince was said to be discreet and intelligent; but all such judgments were necessarily partial, and the Baron preferred to reserve his opinion until he could come to a trustworthy conclusion from personal observation. And then he added: 'But all this is not enough. The young man ought to have not merely great ability, but a *right* ambition, and great force of will as well. To pursue for a lifetime a political career so arduous demands more than energy and inclination—it demands also that earnest frame of mind which is ready of its own accord to sacrifice mere pleasure to real usefulness. If he is not satisfied hereafter with the consciousness of having achieved one of the most influential positions in Europe, how often will he feel tempted to repent his adventure! If he does not from the very outset accept it as a vocation of grave responsibility, on the efficient performance of which his honour and happiness depend, there is small likelihood of his succeeding.'

Such were the views of Stockmar on the qualifications necessary for the due fulfilment of that destiny which Albert's family had marked out for him; and he hoped, during the tour in Italy, to come to some conclusion as to how far the Prince possessed them. Albert on his side was much impressed by the Baron, whom he had previously seen but rarely; he also became acquainted, for the first time in his life, with a young Englishman, Lieut. Francis Seymour, who had been engaged to accompany him, whom he found *sehr liebenswürdig*, and with whom he struck up a warm friendship. He delighted in the galleries and scenery of Florence, though with Rome he was less impressed. 'But for some beautiful palaces,' he said, 'it might just as well be any town in Germany.' In an interview with Pope Gregory XVI, he took the opportunity of displaying his erudition. When the Pope observed that the

Greeks had taken their art from the Etruscans, Albert replied that, on the contrary, in his opinion, they had borrowed from the Egyptians: his Holiness politely acquiesced. Wherever he went he was eager to increase his knowledge, and, at a ball in Florence, he was observed paying no attention whatever to the ladies, and deep in conversation with the learned Signor Capponi. 'Voilà un prince dont nous pouvons être fiers,' said the Grand Duke of Tuscany, who was standing by: 'la belle danseuse l'attend, le savant l'occupe.'

On his return to Germany, Stockmar's observations, imparted to King Leopold, were still critical. Albert, he said, was intelligent, kind, and amiable; he was full of the best intentions and the noblest resolutions, and his judgment was in many things beyond his years. But great exertion was repugnant to him; he seemed to be too willing to spare himself, and his good resolutions too often came to nothing. It was particularly unfortunate that he took not the slightest interest in politics, and never read a newspaper. In his manners, too, there was still room for improvement. 'He will always,' said the Baron, 'have more success with men than with women, in whose society he shows too little *empressement*, and is too indifferent and retiring.' One other feature of the case was noted by the keen eye of the old physician: the Prince's constitution was not a strong one. Yet, on the whole, he was favourable to the projected marriage. But by now the chief obstacle seemed to lie in another quarter. Victoria was apparently determined to commit herself to nothing. And so it happened that when Albert went to England he had made up his mind to withdraw entirely from the affair. Nothing would induce him, he confessed to a friend, to be kept vaguely waiting; he would break it all off at once. His reception at Windsor threw an entirely new light upon the situation. The wheel of fortune turned with a sudden rapidity; and he found, in the arms of Victoria, the irrevocable assurance of his overwhelming fate.

## II

He was not in love with her. Affection, gratitude, the natural reactions to the unqualified devotion of a lively young cousin who was also a queen—such feelings possessed him, but the ardours of reciprocal passion were not his. Though he found that he liked Victoria very much, what immediately interested him in his curious position was less her than himself. Dazzled and delighted, riding, dancing, singing, laughing, amid the splendours of Windsor, he was aware of a new sensation—the stirrings of ambition in his breast. His place would indeed be a high, an enviable one! And then, on the instant, came another thought. The teaching of religion, the admonitions of Stockmar, his own inmost convictions, all spoke with the same utterance. He would not be there to please himself, but for a very different purpose—to do good. He must be 'noble, manly, and princely in all things,' he would have 'to live and to sacrifice himself for the benefit of his new country,' to 'use his powers and endeavours for a great object—that of promoting the welfare of multitudes of his fellow-men.' One serious thought led on to another. The wealth and the bustle of the English Court might be delightful for the moment, but, after all, it was Coburg that had his heart. 'While I shall be untiring,' he wrote to his grandmother, 'in my efforts and labours for the country to which I shall in future belong, and where I am called to so high a position, I shall never cease *ein treuer Deutscher, Coburger, Gothaner zu sein.*' And now he must part from Coburg for ever! Sobered and sad, he sought relief in his brother Ernest's company; the two young men would shut themselves up together, and, sitting down at the pianoforte, would escape from the present and the future in the sweet familiar gaiety of a Haydn duet.

They returned to Germany; and while Albert, for a few farewell months, enjoyed, for the last time, the happiness of home, Victoria, for the last time, resumed her old life in London and Windsor. She corresponded daily with her future husband in a mingled flow of German and English; but the accustomed routine reasserted itself; the business and the pleasures of the day would brook no interruption; Lord M. was once more constantly beside her; and the Tories were as intolerable as ever. Indeed, they were more so. For now, in these final moments, the old feud burst out with redoubled fury. The impetuous sovereign found, to her chagrin, that there might be disadvantages in being the declared enemy of one of the great parties in the State. On two occasions, the Tories directly thwarted her in a matter on which she had set her heart. She wished her husband's rank to be fixed by statute, and their opposition prevented it. She wished her husband to receive a settlement from the nation of £50,000 a year; and, again owing to the Tories, he was allowed only £30,000. It was too bad. When the question was discussed in Parliament, it had been pointed out that the bulk of the population was suffering from great poverty, and that £30,000 was the whole revenue of Coburg; but her uncle Leopold had been given £50,000, and it would be monstrous to give Albert less. Sir Robert Peel—it might have been expected—had had the effrontery to speak and vote for the smaller sum. She was very angry, and determined to revenge herself by omitting to invite a single Tory to her wedding. She would make an exception in favour of old Lord Liverpool, but even the Duke of Wellington she refused to ask. When it was represented to her that it would amount to a national scandal if the Duke were absent from her wedding, she was angrier than ever. 'What! That old rebel! I won't have him,' she was reported to have said. Eventually she was induced to send him an invitation; but she made no attempt to conceal the bitterness of her feelings, and the Duke himself was only too well aware of all that had passed.

Nor was it only against the Tories that her irritation rose. As the time for her wedding approached, her temper grew steadily sharper and more arbitrary. Queen Adelaide annoyed her. King Leopold, too, was 'ungracious' in his correspondence; 'Dear Uncle,' she told Albert, 'is given to believe that he must rule the roast everywhere. However,' she added with asperity, 'that is not a necessity.' Even Albert himself was not impeccable. Engulfed by Coburgs, he failed to appreciate the complexity of English affairs. There were difficulties about his household. He had a notion that he ought not to be surrounded by violent Whigs; very likely, but he would not understand that the only alternatives to violent Whigs were violent Tories; and it would be preposterous if his Lords and Gentlemen were to be found voting against the Queen's. He wanted to appoint his own Private Secretary. But how could he choose the right person? Lord M. was obviously best qualified to make the appointment; and Lord M. had decided that the Prince should take over his own Private Secretary—George Anson, a staunch Whig. Albert protested, but it was useless; Victoria simply announced that Anson was appointed, and instructed Lehzen to send the Prince an explanation of the details of the case. Then, again, he had written anxiously upon the necessity of maintaining unspotted the moral purity of the Court. Lord M.'s pupil considered that dear Albert was strait-laced, and, in a brisk Anglo-German missive, set forth her own views. 'I like Lady A. very much,' she told him, 'only she is a little *strict and particular,* and too severe towards others, which is not right; for I think one ought always to be indulgent towards other people, as I always think, if we had not been well taken care of, we might also have gone astray. That is always my feeling. Yet it is always right to show that one does not like to see what is obviously wrong; but it is very dangerous to be *too* severe, and I am certain that as a rule such people always greatly regret that in their youth they have not been so careful as they ought to have been. I have explained this so badly and written it so badly, that I fear you will hardly be able to make it out.'

On one other matter she was insistent. Since the affair of Lady Flora Hastings, a sad fate had overtaken Sir James Clark. His flourishing practice had quite collapsed; nobody would go to him any more. But the Queen remained faithful. She would show the world how little she cared for its disapproval, and she desired Albert to make 'poor Clark' his physician in ordinary. He did as he was told; but, as it turned out, the appointment was not a happy one.

The wedding-day was fixed, and it was time for Albert to tear himself away from his family and the scenes of his childhood. With an aching heart, he had revisited his beloved haunts—the woods and the valleys where he had spent so many happy hours shooting rabbits and collecting botanical specimens; in deep depression, he had sat through the farewell banquets in the Palace and listened to the *Freischütz* performed by the State band. It was time to go. The streets were packed as he drove through them; for a short space his eyes were gladdened by a sea of friendly German faces, and his ears by a gathering volume of good guttural sounds. He stopped to bid a last adieu to his grandmother. It was a heart-rending moment. 'Albert! Albert!' she shrieked, and fell fainting into the arms of her attendants as his carriage drove away. He was whirled rapidly to his destiny. At Calais a steamboat awaited him, and, together with his father and his brother, he stepped, dejected, on board. A little later, he was more dejected still. The crossing was a very rough one; the Duke went hurriedly below; while the two Princes, we are told, lay on either side of the cabin staircase 'in an almost helpless state.' At Dover a large crowd was collected on the pier, and 'it was by no common effort that Prince Albert, who had continued to suffer up to the last moment, got up to bow to the people.' His sense of duty triumphed. It was a curious omen: his whole life in England was foreshadowed as he landed on English ground.

Meanwhile Victoria, in growing agitation, was a prey to temper and to nerves. She grew feverish, and at last Sir James Clark pronounced that she

*Diminutive beside the tall slim Albert, Victoria on her wedding morning wore a white satin dress trimmed with Honiton lace, and a veil secured by a wreath of orange blossom. Amongst her jewellery was Albert's gift of a sapphire and diamond brooch.*

was going to have the measles. But, once again, Sir James's diagnosis was incorrect. It was not the measles that was attacking her, but a very different malady; she was suddenly prostrated by alarm, regret, and doubt. For two years she had been her own mistress—the two happiest years, by far, of her life. And now it was all to end! She was to come under an alien domination—she would have to promise that she would honour and obey . . . someone, who might, after all, thwart her, oppose her—and how dreadful that would be! Why had she embarked on this hazardous experiment? Why had she not been contented with Lord M.? No doubt, she loved Albert; but she loved power too. At any rate, one thing was certain: she might be Albert's wife, but she would always be Queen of England. He reappeared, in an exquisite uniform, and her hesitations melted in his presence like mist before the sun. On February 10, 1840, the marriage took place. The wedded pair drove down to Windsor; but they were not, of course, entirely alone. They were accompanied by their suites, and, in particular, by two persons—the Baron Stockmar and the Baroness Lehzen.

# III

Albert had foreseen that his married life would not be all plain sailing; but he had by no means realised the gravity and the complication of the difficulties which he would have to face. Politically, he was a cipher. Lord Melbourne was not only Prime Minister, he was in effect the Private Secretary of the Queen, and thus controlled the whole of the political existence of the sovereign. A queen's husband was an entity unknown to the British Constitution. In State affairs there seemed to be no place for him; nor was Victoria herself at all unwilling that this should be so. 'The English,' she had told the Prince when, during their engagement, a proposal had been made to give him a peerage, 'are very jealous of any foreigner interfering in the government of this country, and have already in some of the papers expressed a hope that you would not interfere. Now, though I know you never would, still, if you were a Peer, they would all say, the Prince meant to play a political part.' 'I know you never would!' In reality, she was not quite so certain; but she wished Albert to understand her views. He would, she hoped, make a perfect husband; but, as for governing the country, he would see that she and Lord M. between them could manage that very well, without his help.

But it was not only in politics that the Prince discovered that the part cut out for him was a negligible one. Even as a husband, he found, his functions were to be of an extremely limited kind. Over the whole of Victoria's private life the Baroness reigned supreme; and she had not the slightest intention of allowing that supremacy to be diminished by one iota. Since the accession, her power had greatly increased. Besides the undefined and enormous influence which she exercised through her management of the Queen's private correspondence, she was now the superintendent of the royal establishment and controlled the important office of Privy Purse. Albert very soon perceived that he was not master in his own house. Every detail of his own and his wife's existence was supervised by a third person: nothing could be done until the consent of Lehzen had first been obtained. And Victoria, who adored Lehzen with unabated intensity, saw nothing in all this that was wrong.

Nor was the Prince happier in his social surroundings. A shy young foreigner, awkward in ladies' company, unexpansive and self-opinionated, it was improbable that, in any circumstances, he would have been a society success. His appearance, too, was against him. Though in the eyes of Victoria he was the mirror of manly beauty, her subjects, whose eyes were of a less Teutonic cast, did not agree with her. To them—and particularly to the high-born ladies and gentlemen who naturally saw him most—what was immediately and distressingly striking in Albert's face and figure and whole demeanour was his un-English look. His features were regular, no doubt, but there was something smooth and smug about them; he was tall, but he was clumsily put together, and he walked with a slight slouch. Really, they thought, this youth was more like some kind of foreign tenor than anything else. These were serious disadvantages; but the line of conduct which the Prince adopted from the first moment of his arrival was far from calculated to dispel them. Owing partly to a natural awkwardness, partly to a fear of undue familiarity, and partly to a desire to be absolutely correct, his manners were infused with an extraordinary stiffness and formality. Whenever he appeared in company, he seemed to be surrounded by a thick hedge of prickly etiquette. He never went out into ordinary society; he never walked in the streets of London; he was invariably accompanied by an equerry when he rode or drove. He wanted to be irreproachable and, if that involved friendlessness, it could not be helped. Besides, he had no very high opinion of the English. So far as he could see, they cared for nothing but fox-hunting and Sunday observances; they oscillated between an undue frivolity and an undue gloom; if you spoke to them of friendly joyousness they stared; and they did not understand either the Laws of Thought or the wit of a German University. Since it was clear that with such people he could have very little in common, there was no reason whatever for relaxing in their favour the rules of etiquette. In strict privacy, he could be natural and charming; Seymour and Anson were devoted to him, and he returned their affection; but they were subordinates—the receivers of his confidences and the agents of his will. From the support and the solace of true companionship he was utterly cut off.

A friend, indeed, he had—or rather, a mentor. The Baron, established once more in the royal residence, was determined to work with as whole-hearted a detachment for the Prince's benefit as, more than twenty years before, he had worked for his uncle's. The situations then and now, similar in many respects, were yet full of differences. Perhaps in either case the difficulties to be encountered were equally great; but the present problem was the more complex and the more interesting. The young doctor, unknown and insignificant, whose only assets were his own wits and the friendship of an unimportant Prince, had been replaced by the accomplished confidant of kings and ministers, ripe in years, in reputation, and in the wisdom of a vast experience. It was possible for him to treat Albert with something of the affectionate authority of a father; but, on the other hand, Albert was no

*Queen Victoria constantly recorded scenes and impressions in her sketchbooks, and made this hurried sketch of herself in her wedding veil on the day after her marriage. Her blissful enjoyment of the first days with Albert is touching. On the third morning she noted in her journal: 'My dearest Albert put on my stockings for me. I went in and saw him shave; a great delight for me.'*

Leopold. As the Baron was very well aware, he had none of his uncle's rigidity of ambition, none of his overweening impulse to be personally great. He was virtuous and well-intentioned; he was clever and well-informed; but he took no interest in politics, and there were no signs that he possessed any commanding force of character. Left to himself, he would almost certainly have subsided into a high-minded nonentity, an aimless dilettante busy over culture, a palace appendage without influence or power. But he was not left to himself: Stockmar saw to that. For ever at his pupil's elbow, the hidden Baron pushed him forward, with tireless pressure, along the path which had been trod by Leopold so many years ago. But, this time, the goal at the end of it was something more than the mediocre royalty that Leopold had reached. The prize which Stockmar, with all the energy of disinterested devotion, had determined should be Albert's was a tremendous prize indeed.

The beginning of the undertaking proved to be the most arduous part of it. Albert was easily dispirited: what was the use of struggling to perform in a rôle which bored him and which, it was quite clear, nobody but the dear good Baron had any desire that he should take up? It was simpler, and it saved a great deal of trouble, to let things slide. But Stockmar would not have it. Incessantly, he harped upon two strings—Albert's sense of duty and his personal pride. Had the Prince forgotten the noble aims to which his life was to be devoted? And was he going to allow himself, his wife, his family, his whole existence, to be governed by Baroness Lehzen? The latter consideration was a potent one. Albert had never been accustomed to giving way; and now, more than ever before, it would be humiliating to do so. Not only was he constantly exasperated by the position of the Baroness in the royal household; there was another and a still more serious cause of complaint. He was, he knew very well, his wife's intellectual superior, and yet he found, to his intense annoyance, that there were parts of her mind over which he exercised no influence. When, urged on by the Baron, he attempted to discuss politics with Victoria, she eluded the subject, drifted into generalities, and then began to talk of something else. She was treating him as she had once treated their uncle Leopold. When at last he protested, she replied that her conduct was merely the result of indolence; that when she was with *him* she could not bear to bother her head with anything so dull as politics. The excuse was worse than the fault: was he the wife and she the husband? It almost seemed so. But the Baron declared that the root of the mischief was Lehzen: that it was she who encouraged the Queen to have secrets; who did worse—undermined the natural ingenuousness of Victoria, and induced her to give, unconsciously no doubt, false reasons to explain away her conduct.

Minor disagreements made matters worse. The royal couple differed in their tastes. Albert, brought up in a régime of Spartan simplicity and early hours, found the great Court functions intolerably wearisome, and was invariably observed to be nodding on the sofa at half-past ten; while the Queen's favourite form of enjoyment was to dance through the night, and then, going out into the portico of the Palace, watch the sun rise behind St. Paul's and the towers of Westminster. She loved London and he detested it. It was only in Windsor that he felt he could really breathe; but Windsor too had its terrors: though during the day there he could paint and walk and

*By 1841 the honeymoon was over, but Prince Albert had not yet discovered any worthy employment: he is depicted in Punch as a bored and bedraggled Cupid 'out of place'. But shortly after this he was given his first job, chairing the Royal Commission to select works of art to adorn the new Palace of Westminster.*

play on the piano, after dinner black tedium descended like a pall. He would have liked to summon distinguished scientific and literary men to his presence, and after ascertaining their views upon various points of art and learning, to set forth his own; but unfortunately Victoria 'had no fancy to encourage such people'; knowing that she was unequal to taking a part in their conversation, she insisted that the evening routine should remain unaltered; the regulation interchange of platitudes with official persons was followed as usual by the round table and the books of engravings, while the Prince, with three of his attendants, played game after game of double chess.

It was only natural that in so peculiar a situation, in which the elements of power, passion, and pride were so strangely apportioned, there should have been occasionally something more than mere irritation—a struggle of angry wills. Victoria, no more than Albert, was in the habit of playing second fiddle. Her arbitrary temper flashed out. Her vitality, her obstinacy, her overweening sense of her own position, might well have beaten down before them his superiorities and his rights. But she fought at a disadvantage; she

83

was, in very truth, no longer her own mistress; a profound preoccupation dominated her, seizing upon her inmost purposes for its own extraordinary ends. She was madly in love. The details of those curious battles are unknown to us; but Prince Ernest, who remained in England with his brother for some months, noted them with a friendly and startled eye. One story, indeed, survives, ill-authenticated and perhaps mythical, yet summing up, as such stories often do, the central facts of the case. When, in wrath, the Prince one day had locked himself into his room, Victoria, no less furious, knocked on the door to be admitted. 'Who is there?' he asked. 'The Queen of England,' was the answer. He did not move, and again there was a hail of knocks. The question and the answer were repeated many times; but at last there was a pause, and then a gentler knocking. 'Who is there?' came once more the relentless question. But this time the reply was different. 'Your wife, Albert.' And the door was immediately opened.

Very gradually the Prince's position changed. He began to find the study of politics less uninteresting than he had supposed; he read Blackstone, and took lessons in English Law; he was occasionally present when the Queen interviewed her Ministers; and at Lord Melbourne's suggestion he was shown all the despatches relating to Foreign Affairs. Sometimes he would commit his views to paper, and read them aloud to the Prime Minister, who, infinitely kind and courteous, listened with attention, but seldom made any reply. An important step was taken when, before the birth of the Princess Royal, the Prince, without any opposition in Parliament, was appointed Regent in case of the death of the Queen. Stockmar, owing to whose intervention with the Tories this happy result had been brought about, now felt himself at liberty to take a holiday with his family in Coburg; but his solicitude, poured out in innumerable letters, still watched over his pupil from afar. 'Dear Prince,' he wrote, 'I am satisfied with the news you have sent me. Mistakes, misunderstandings, obstructions, which come in vexatious opposition to one's views, are always to be taken for just what they are— namely, natural phenomena of life, which represent one of its sides, and that the shady one. In overcoming them with dignity, your mind has to exercise, to train, to enlighten itself; and your character to gain force, endurance, and the necessary hardness.' The Prince had done well so far; but he must continue in the right path; above all, he was 'never to relax.'—'Never to relax in putting your magnanimity to the proof; never to relax in logical separation of what is great and essential from what is trivial and of no moment; never to relax in keeping yourself up to a high standard—in the determination, daily renewed, to be consistent, patient, courageous.' It was a hard programme, perhaps, for a young man of twenty-one; and yet there was something in it which touched the very depths of Albert's soul. He sighed, but he listened—listened as to the voice of a spiritual director inspired with divine truth. 'The stars which are needful to you now,' the voice continued, 'and perhaps for some time to come, are *Love, Honesty, Truth*. All those whose minds are warped, or who are destitute of true feeling, will *be apt to mistake you*, and to persuade themselves and the world that you are not the man you are—or, at least, may become. . . . Do you, therefore, be on the alert betimes, with your eyes open in every direction. . . . I wish for my

A dachshund, drawn and etched by Prince Albert in 1840. He and the Queen were particularly fond of this breed.

Prince a great, noble, warm, and true heart, such as shall serve as the richest and surest basis for the noblest views of human nature, and the firmest resolve to give them development.'

Before long, the decisive moment came. There was a General Election, and it became certain that the Tories, at last, must come into power. The Queen disliked them as much as ever; but, with a large majority in the House of Commons, they would now be in a position to insist upon their wishes being attended to. Lord Melbourne himself was the first to realise the importance of carrying out the inevitable transition with as little friction as possible; and with his consent, the Prince, following up the *rapprochement* which had begun over the Regency Act, opened, through Anson, a negotiation with Sir Robert Peel. In a series of secret interviews, a complete understanding was reached upon the difficult and complex question of the Bedchamber. It was agreed that the constitutional point should not be raised, but that, on the formation of the Tory Government, the principal Whig ladies should retire, and their places be filled by others appointed by Sir Robert. Thus, in effect, though not in form, the Crown abandoned the claims of 1839, and they have never been subsequently put forward. The transaction was a turning-point in the Prince's career. He had conducted an important negotiation with skill and tact; he had been brought into close and friendly relations with the new Prime Minister; it was obvious that a great political future lay before him. Victoria was much impressed and deeply grateful. 'My dearest Angel,' she told King Leopold, 'is indeed a great comfort to me. He takes the greatest interest in what goes on, feeling with and for me, and yet abstaining as he ought from biassing me either way, though we talk much on the subject, and his judgment is, as you say, good and mild.' She was in need of all the comfort and assistance he could give her. Lord M. was going; and she could hardly bring herself to speak to Peel. Yes; she would discuss everything with Albert now!

Stockmar, who had returned to England, watched the departure of Lord Melbourne with satisfaction. If all went well, the Prince should now wield a supreme political influence over Victoria. But would all go well? An unexpected development put the Baron into a serious fright. When the dreadful moment finally came, and the Queen, in anguish, bade adieu to her beloved Minister, it was settled between them that, though it would be inadvisable to meet very often, they could continue to correspond. Never were the inconsistencies of Lord Melbourne's character shown more clearly than in what followed. So long as he was in office, his attitude towards Peel had been irreproachable; he had done all he could to facilitate the change of government; he had even, through more than one channel, transmitted privately to his successful rival advice as to the best means of winning the Queen's good graces. Yet, no sooner was he in opposition than his heart failed him. He could not bear the thought of surrendering altogether the privilege and the pleasure of giving counsel to Victoria—of being cut off completely from the power and the intimacy which had been his for so long and in such abundant measure. Though he had declared that he would be perfectly discreet in his letters, he could not resist taking advantage of the opening they afforded. He discussed in detail various public questions, and, in particular, gave the Queen a great deal of advice in the matter of appointments. This advice was followed. Lord Melbourne recommended that Lord Heytesbury, who, he said, was an able man, should be made Ambassador at Vienna; and a week later the Queen wrote to the Foreign Secretary urging that Lord Heytesbury, whom she believed to be a very able man, should be employed 'on some important mission.' Stockmar was very much alarmed. He wrote a memorandum, pointing out the unconstitutional nature of Lord Melbourne's proceedings and the unpleasant position in which the Queen might find herself if they were discovered by Peel; and he instructed Anson to take this memorandum to the ex-Minister. Lord Melbourne, lounging on a sofa, read it through with compressed lips. 'This is quite an apple-pie opinion,' he said. When Anson ventured to expostulate further, suggesting that it was unseemly in the leader of the Opposition to maintain an intimate relationship with the Sovereign, the old man lost his temper. 'God eternally damn it!' he exclaimed, leaping up from his sofa, and dashing about the room. 'Flesh and blood cannot stand this!' He continued to write to the Queen, as before; and two more violent bombardments from the Baron were needed before he was brought to reason. Then, gradually, his letters grew less and less frequent, with fewer and fewer references to public concerns; at last, they were entirely innocuous. The Baron smiled; Lord M. had accepted the inevitable.

The Whig ministry resigned in September, 1841; but more than a year was to elapse before another and an equally momentous change was effected—the removal of Lehzen. For, in the end, the mysterious governess was conquered. The steps are unknown by which Victoria was at last led to accept her withdrawal with composure—perhaps with relief; but it is clear that Albert's domestic position must have been greatly strengthened by the appearance of children. The birth of the Princess Royal had been followed in November 1841 by that of the Prince of Wales; and before very long another baby was expected. The Baroness, with all her affection, could have but a remote share in such family delights. She lost ground perceptibly. It was noticed as a phenomenon that, once or twice, when the Court travelled, she was left behind at Windsor. The Prince was very cautious; at the change of Ministry, Lord Melbourne had advised him to choose that moment for decisive action; but he judged it wiser to wait. Time and the pressure of inevitable circumstances were for him; every day his predominance grew more assured—and every night. At length he perceived that he need hesitate no longer—that every wish, every velleity of his had only to be expressed to be at once Victoria's. He spoke, and Lehzen vanished for ever. No more would she reign in that royal heart and those royal halls. No more, watching from a window at Windsor, would she follow her pupil and her sovereign, walking on the terrace among the obsequious multitude, with the eye of triumphant love. Returning to her native Hanover she established herself at Bückeburg in a small but comfortable house, the walls of which were entirely covered by portraits of Her Majesty. The Baron, in spite of his dyspepsia, smiled again: Albert was supreme.

# IV

The early discords had passed away completely—resolved into the absolute harmony of married life. Victoria, overcome by a new, an unimagined revelation, had surrendered her whole soul to her husband. The beauty and the charm which so suddenly had made her his at first were, she now saw, no more than the outward manifestation of the true Albert. There was an inward beauty, an inward glory which, blind that she was, she had then but dimly apprehended, but of which now she was aware in every fibre of her being—he was good—he was great! How could she ever have dreamt of setting up her will against his wisdom, her ignorance against his knowledge, her fancies against his perfect taste? Had she really once loved London and late hours and dissipation? She who now was only happy in the country, she who jumped out of bed every morning—oh, so early!—with Albert, to take a walk, before breakfast, with Albert alone! How wonderful it was to be taught by him! To be told by him which trees were which; and to learn all about the bees! And then to sit doing cross-stitch while he read aloud to her Hallam's Constitutional History of England! Or to listen to him playing on his new organ ('The organ is the first of instruments,' he said); or to sing to him a song by Mendelssohn, with a great deal of care over the time and the breathing, and only a very occasional false note! And, after dinner, too—oh, how good of him! He had given up his double chess! And so there could be round games at the round table, or everyone could spend the evening in the most amusing way imaginable—spinning counters and rings. When the babies came it was still more wonderful. Pussy was such a clever little girl ('I am not Pussy! I am the Princess Royal!' she had angrily exclaimed on one occasion); and Bertie—well, she could only pray *most* fervently that the little Prince of Wales would grow up to 'resemble his angelic dearest Father in *every*, *every* respect, both in body and mind.' Her dear Mamma, too, had been drawn once more into the family circle, for Albert had brought about a

*Pussy.*

*Before going to Bed.*

The Princess Royal being prepared for bed, drawn and etched by Queen Victoria. The Queen's eldest daughter was known as 'Pussy' until the age of about three, when she felt sufficiently grown-up to demand to be called 'Vicky'—short for Victoria Adelaide Mary Louise.

*The new illustrated papers eagerly published Christmas features like this drawing by J.L. Williams of the royal couple and their children admiring a candle-lit Christmas tree while the Duchess of Kent looks on benignly. George III's German queen, Charlotte, is credited with introducing the Christmas tree to Great Britain, but it was Prince Albert who popularized the tradition. At Windsor small trees— one for each member of the family—were placed on decorated tables and hung with cakes, sweets and toys.*

reconciliation, and the departure of Lehzen had helped to obliterate the past. In Victoria's eyes, life had become an idyll, and, if the essential elements of an idyll are happiness, love and simplicity, an idyll it was; though, indeed, it was of a kind that might have disconcerted Theocritus. 'Albert brought in dearest little Pussy,' wrote Her Majesty in her journal, 'in such a smart white merino dress trimmed with blue, which Mamma had given her, and a pretty cap, and placed her on my bed, seating himself next to her, and she was very dear and good. And as my precious, invaluable Albert sat there, and our little Love between us, I felt quite moved with happiness and gratitude to God.'

The past—the past of only three years since—when she looked back upon it, seemed a thing so remote and alien that she could explain it to herself in no other way than as some kind of delusion—an unfortunate mistake. Turning over an old volume of her diary, she came upon this sentence—'As for "the confidence of the Crown," God knows! No *Minister, no friend* EVER possessed it so entirely as this truly excellent Lord Melbourne possesses mine!' A pang shot through her—she seized a pen, and wrote upon the margin— 'Reading this again, I cannot forbear remarking what an artificial sort of happiness *mine* was *then*, and what a blessing it is I have now in my beloved Husband *real* and solid happiness, which no Politics, no worldly reverses *can* change; it could not have lasted long as it was then, for after all, kind and excellent as Lord M. is, and kind as he was to me, it was but in Society that I had amusement, and I was only living on that superficial resource, which I *then fancied* was happiness! Thank God! for *me* and others, this is changed, and I *know what* REAL *happiness* is—V.R.' How did she know? What is the distinction between happiness that is real and happiness that is felt? So a philosopher—Lord M. himself perhaps—might have inquired. But she was no philosopher, and Lord M. was a phantom, and Albert was beside her, and that was enough.

Happy, certainly, she was; and she wanted everyone to know it. Her letters to King Leopold are sprinkled thick with raptures. 'Oh! my dearest uncle, I am sure if you knew *how* happy, how blessed I feel, and how *proud* I feel in possessing *such* a perfect being as my husband . . .' such ecstasies seemed to gush from her pen unceasingly and almost of their own accord. When, one day, without thinking, Lady Lyttelton described someone to her as being 'as happy as a queen,' and then grew a little confused, 'Don't correct yourself, Lady Lyttelton,' said Her Majesty. 'A queen *is* a very happy woman.'

But this new happiness was no lotus dream. On the contrary, it was bracing, rather than relaxing. Never before had she felt so acutely the necessity for doing her duty. She worked more methodically than ever at the business of State; she watched over her children with untiring vigilance. She carried on a large correspondence; she was occupied with her farm—her dairy—a whole multitude of household avocations—from morning till night. Her active, eager little body hurrying with quick steps after the long strides of Albert down the corridors and avenues of Windsor, seemed the very expression of her spirit. Amid all the softness, the deliciousness of unmixed joy, all the liquescence, the overflowings of inexhaustible sentiment, her native rigidity remained. 'A vein of iron,' said Lady Lyttelton, who, as royal governess, had good means of observation, 'runs through her most

extraordinary character.'

Sometimes the delightful routine of domestic existence had to be interrupted. It was necessary to exchange Windsor for Buckingham Palace, to open Parliament, or to interview official personages, or, occasionally, to entertain foreign visitors at the Castle. Then the quiet Court put on a sudden magnificence, and sovereigns from over the seas—Louis Philippe, or the King of Prussia, or the King of Saxony—found at Windsor an entertainment that was indeed a royal one. Few spectacles in Europe, it was agreed, produced an effect so imposing as the great Waterloo banqueting hall, crowded with guests in sparkling diamonds and blazing uniforms, the long walls hung with the stately portraits of heroes, and the tables loaded with the gorgeous gold plate of the Kings of England. But, in that wealth of splendour, the most imposing spectacle of all was the Queen. The little *Hausfrau*, who had spent the day before walking out with her children, inspecting her livestock, practising shakes at the piano, and filling up her journal with adoring descriptions of her husband, suddenly shone forth, without art, without effort, by a spontaneous and natural transition, the very culmination of Majesty. The Tsar of Russia himself was deeply impressed. Victoria on her side viewed with secret awe the tremendous Nicholas. 'A great event and a great compliment *his* visit certainly is,' she told her uncle, 'and the people *here* are extremely flattered at it. He is certainly a *very striking* man; still very handsome. His profile is *beautiful*, and his manners *most* dignified and graceful; extremely civil—quite alarmingly so, as he is so full of attentions and *politeness*. But the expression of the *eyes* is *formidable*, and unlike anything I ever saw before.' She and Albert and 'the good King of Saxony,' who happened to be there at the same time, and whom, she said, 'we like much—he is *so* unassuming'—drew together like tame villatic fowl in the presence of that awful eagle. When he was gone, they compared notes about his face, his unhappiness, and his despotic power over millions. Well! She for her part could not help pitying him, and she thanked God she was Queen of England.

When the time came for returning some of these visits, the royal pair set forth in their yacht, much to Victoria's satisfaction. 'I do love a ship!' she exclaimed, ran up and down ladders with the greatest agility, and cracked jokes with the sailors. The Prince was more aloof. They visited Louis Philippe at the Château d'Eu; they visited King Leopold in Brussels. It happened that a still more remarkable Englishwoman was in the Belgian capital, but she was not remarked; and Queen Victoria passed unknowing before the steady gaze of one of the mistresses in M. Héger's *pensionnat*. 'A little, stout, vivacious lady, very plainly dressed—not much dignity or pretension about her,' was Charlotte Brontë's comment as the royal carriage and six flashed by her, making her wait on the pavement for a moment, and interrupting the train of her reflections. Victoria was in high spirits, and even succeeded in instilling a little cheerfulness into her uncle's sombre Court. King Leopold, indeed, was perfectly contented. His dearest hopes had been fulfilled; all his ambitions were satisfied; and for the rest of his life he had only to enjoy, in undisturbed decorum, his throne, his respectability, the table of precedence, and the punctual discharge of his irksome duties. But unfortunately the felicity of

*Coburg, in Thuringia, from a sketch by Prince Albert. A relatively small principality, Coburg lay between Bavaria and the numerous dukedoms and margravates of Franconia and the Rhineland. As children, Albert and his brother spent winter at the Ehrenburg, their father's castle in the town of Coburg, and spring and summer at their country home, the Rosenau.*

those who surrounded him was less complete. His Court, it was murmured, was as gloomy as a conventicle, and the most dismal of all the sufferers was his wife. 'Pas de plaisanteries, madame!' he had exclaimed to the unfortunate successor of the Princess Charlotte, when, in the early days of their marriage, she had attempted a feeble joke. Did she not understand that the consort of a constitutional sovereign must not be frivolous? She understood, at last, only too well; and when the startled walls of the state apartments re-echoed to the chattering and the laughter of Victoria, the poor lady found that she had almost forgotten how to smile.

Another year, Germany was visited, and Albert displayed the beauties of his home. When Victoria crossed the frontier, she was much excited—and she was astonished as well. 'To hear the people speak German,' she noted in her diary, 'and to see the German soldiers, etc., seemed to me so singular.' Having recovered from this slight shock, she found the country charming. She was fêted everywhere, crowds of the surrounding royalties swooped down to welcome her, and the prettiest groups of peasant children, dressed in their best clothes, presented her with bunches of flowers. The principality of Coburg, with its romantic scenery and its well-behaved inhabitants, particularly delighted her; and when she woke up one morning to find herself in 'dear Rosenau, my Albert's birthplace,' it was 'like a beautiful dream.' On her return home, she expatiated, in a letter to Kind Leopold, upon the pleasures of the trip, dwelling especially upon the intensity of her affection for Albert's native land. 'I have a feeling,' she said, 'for our dear little Germany, which I cannot describe. I felt it at Rosenau so much. It is a something which touches me, and which goes to my heart, and makes me inclined to cry. I never felt at any other place that sort of pensive pleasure and peace which I felt there. I fear I almost like it too much.'

V

The husband was not so happy as the wife. In spite of the great improvement in his situation, in spite of a growing family and the adoration of Victoria, Albert was still a stranger in a strange land, and the serenity of spiritual satisfaction was denied him. It was something, no doubt, to have dominated his immediate environment; but it was not enough; and, besides, in the very completeness of his success, there was a bitterness. Victoria idolised him; but it was understanding that he craved for, not idolatry; and how much did Victoria, filled to the brim though she was with him, understand him? How much does the bucket understand the well? He was lonely. He went to his organ and improvised with learned modulations until the sounds, swelling and subsiding through elaborate cadences, brought some solace to his heart. Then, with the elasticity of youth, he hurried off to play with the babies, or to design a new pigsty, or to read aloud the 'Church History of Scotland' to Victoria, or pirouette before her on one toe, like a ballet-dancer, with a fixed smile, to show her how she ought to behave when she appeared in public places. Thus did he amuse himself; but there was one distraction in which he did not indulge. He never flirted—no, not with the prettiest ladies of the Court. When, during their engagement, the Queen had remarked with pride to Lord Melbourne that the Prince paid no attention to any other woman, the cynic had answered 'No, that sort of thing is apt to come later'; upon which she had scolded him severely, and then hurried off to Stockmar to repeat what Lord M. had said. But the Baron had reassured her; though in other cases, he had replied, that might happen, he did not think it would in Albert's. And the Baron was right. Throughout their married life no rival female charms ever gave cause to Victoria for one moment's pang of jealousy.

What more and more absorbed him—bringing with it a curious comfort of its own—was his work. With the advent of Peel, he began to intervene actively in the affairs of the State. In more ways than one—in the cast of their intelligence, in their moral earnestness, even in the uneasy formalism of their manners—the two men resembled each other; there was a sympathy between them; and thus Peel was ready enough to listen to the advice of Stockmar, and to urge the Prince forward into public life. A royal commission was about to be formed to enquire whether advantage might not be taken of the rebuilding of the Houses of Parliament to encourage the Fine Arts in the United Kingdom; and Peel, with great perspicacity, asked the Prince to preside over it. The work was of a kind which precisely suited Albert: his love of art, his love of method, his love of coming into contact—close yet dignified—with distinguished men—it satisfied them all; and he threw himself into it *con amore*. Some of the members of the commission were somewhat alarmed when, in his opening speech, he pointed out the necessity of dividing the subjects to be considered into 'categories'—the word, they thought, smacked dangerously of German metaphysics; but their confidence returned when they observed His Royal Highness's extraordinary technical acquaintance with the processes of fresco-painting. When the question arose as to whether the decorations upon the walls of the new

*Prince Albert in 1851, at the age of thirty-two. 'He is, if possible, more ingenuous and sensible and gracious than ever; and he is as happy and cheerful now as he looked dull and sleepy in London. It is only that the poor man likes nothing but das Landleben [country life], and she is so complying towards him that it may lead her to like it too at last,' wrote Lady Lyttelton, the royal governess. The Prince's influence and the demands of their growing family had persuaded the Queen to exchange the delights of the social round in London for the quiet, domestic life which her husband preferred.*

buildings should, or should not, have a moral purpose, the Prince spoke strongly for the affirmative. Although many, he observed, would give but a passing glance to the works, the painter was not therefore to forget that others might view them with more thoughtful eyes. This argument convinced the commission, and it was decided that the subjects to be depicted should be of an improving nature. The frescoes were carried out in accordance with the commission's instructions, but unfortunately before very long they had become, even to the most thoughtful eyes, totally invisible. It seems that His Royal Highness's technical acquaintance with the processes of fresco-painting was incomplete.

The next task upon which the Prince embarked was a more arduous one: he determined to reform the organisation of the royal household. This reform had been long overdue. For years past the confusion, discomfort, and extravagance in the royal residences, and in Buckingham Palace particularly, had been scandalous; no reform had been practicable under the rule of the Baroness; but her functions had now devolved upon the Prince, and in 1844 he boldly attacked the problem. Three years earlier, Stockmar, after careful enquiry, had revealed in an elaborate memorandum an extraordinary state of affairs. The control of the household, it appeared, was divided in the strangest manner between a number of authorities, each independent of the other, each possessed of vague and fluctuating powers, without responsibility and without co-ordination. Of these authorities, the most prominent were the Lord Steward and the Lord Chamberlain—noblemen of high rank and political importance, who changed office with every administration, who did not reside with the Court, and had no effective representatives attached to it. The distribution of their respective functions was uncertain and peculiar. In Buckingham Palace, it was believed that the Lord Chamberlain had charge of the whole of the rooms, with the exception of the kitchen, sculleries, and pantries, which were claimed by the Lord Steward. At the same time, the outside of the Palace was under the control of neither of these functionaries—but of the Office of Woods and Forests; and thus, while the insides of the windows were cleaned by the department of the Lord Chamberlain—or possibly, in certain cases, of the Lord Steward—the Office of Woods and Forests cleaned their outsides. Of the servants, the housekeepers, the pages, and the housemaids were under the authority of the Lord Chamberlain; the clerk of the kitchen, the cooks, and the porters were under that of the Lord Steward; but the footmen, the livery-porters, and the under-butlers took their orders from yet another official—the Master of the Horse. Naturally, in these circumstances the service was extremely defective and the lack of discipline among the servants disgraceful. They absented themselves for as long as they pleased and whenever the fancy took them; 'and if,' as the Baron put it, 'smoking, drinking, and other irregularities occur in the dormitories, where footmen, etc., sleep ten and twelve in each room, no one can help it.' As for Her Majesty's guests, there was nobody to show them to their rooms, and they were often left, having utterly lost their way in the complicated passages, to wander helpless by the hour. The strange divisions of authority extended not only to persons but to things. The Queen observed that there was never a fire in the dining-room. She enquired why. The answer was, 'The

Lord Steward lays the fire, and the Lord Chamberlain lights it'; the underlings of those two great noblemen having failed to come to an accommodation, there was no help for it—the Queen must eat in the cold.

A surprising incident opened everyone's eyes to the confusion and negligence that reigned in the Palace. A fortnight after the birth of the Princess Royal the nurse heard a suspicious noise in the room next to the Queen's bedroom. She called to one of the pages, who, looking under a large sofa, perceived there a crouching figure 'with a most repulsive appearance.' It was 'the boy Jones.' This enigmatical personage, whose escapades dominated the newspapers for several ensuing months, and whose motives and character remained to the end ambiguous, was an undersized lad of seventeen, the son of a tailor, who had apparently gained admittance to the Palace by climbing over the garden wall and walking in through an open window. Two years before he had paid a similar visit in the guise of a chimney-sweep. He now declared that he had spent three days in the Palace, hiding under various beds, that he had 'helped himself to soup and other eatables,' and that he had 'sat upon the throne, seen the Queen, and heard the Princess Royal squall.' Every detail of the strange affair was eagerly canvassed. *The Times* reported that the boy Jones had 'from his infancy been fond of reading,' but that 'his countenance is exceedingly sullen.' It added: 'The sofa under which the boy Jones was discovered, we understand, is one of the most costly and magnificent material and workmanship, and ordered expressly for the accommodation of the royal and illustrious visitors who call to pay their respects to Her Majesty.' The culprit was sent for three months to the 'House of Correction.' When he emerged, he immediately returned to Buckingham Palace. He was discovered, and sent back to the 'House of Correction' for another three months, after which he was offered £4 a week by a music hall to appear upon the stage. He refused this offer, and shortly afterwards was found by the police loitering round Buckingham Palace. The authorities acted vigorously, and, without any trial or process of law, shipped the boy Jones off to sea. A year later his ship put into Portsmouth to refit, and he at once disembarked and walked to London. He was re-arrested before he reached the Palace, and sent back to his ship, the *Warspite*. On this occasion it was noticed that he had 'much improved in personal appearance and grown quite corpulent'; and so the boy Jones passed out of history, though we catch one last glimpse of him in 1844 falling overboard in the night between Tunis and Algiers. He was fished up again; but it was conjectured—as one of the *Warspite's* officers explained in a letter to *The Times*—that his fall had not been accidental, but that he had deliberately jumped into the Mediterranean in order to 'see the life-buoy light burning.' Of a boy with such a record, what else could be supposed?

But discomfort and alarm were not the only results of the mismanagement of the household; the waste, extravagance, and peculation that also flowed from it were immeasurable. There were preposterous perquisites and malpractices of every kind. It was, for instance, an ancient and immutable rule that a candle that had once been lighted should never be lighted again; what happened to the old candles nobody knew. Again, the Prince, examining the accounts, was puzzled by a weekly expenditure of thirty-five shillings on 'Red Room Wine.' He enquired into the matter, and after great difficulty discovered that in the time of George III a room in Windsor Castle with red hangings had once been used as a guard-room, and that five shillings a day had been allowed to provide wine for the officers. The guard had long since been moved elsewhere, but the payment for wine in the Red Room continued, the money being received by a half-pay officer who held the sinecure position of under-butler.

After much laborious investigation, and a stiff struggle with the multitude of vested interests which had been brought into being by long years of neglect, the Prince succeeded in effecting a complete reform. The various conflicting authorities were induced to resign their powers into the hands of a single official, the Master of the Household, who became responsible for the entire management of the royal palaces. Great economies were made, and the whole crowd of venerable abuses was swept away. Among others, the unlucky half-pay officer of the Red Room was, much to his surprise, given the choice of relinquishing his weekly emolument or of performing the duties of an under-butler. Even the irregularities among the footmen, etc., were greatly diminished. There were outcries and complaints; the Prince was accused of meddling, of injustice, and of saving candle-ends; but he held on his course, and before long the admirable administration of the royal household was recognised as a convincing proof of his perseverance and capacity.

At the same time his activity was increasing enormously in a more important sphere. He had become the Queen's Private Secretary, her confidential adviser, her second self. He was now always present at her interviews with Ministers. He took, like the Queen, a special interest in foreign policy; but there was no public question in which his influence was not felt. A double process was at work; while Victoria fell more and more absolutely under his intellectual predominance, he, simultaneously, grew more and more completely absorbed by the machinery of high politics—the incessant and multifarious business of a great State. Nobody any more could call him a dilettante; he was a worker, a public personage, a man of affairs. Stockmar noted the change with exultation. 'The Prince,' he wrote, 'has improved very much lately. He has evidently a head for politics. He has become, too, far more independent. His mental activity is constantly on the increase, and he gives the greater part of his time to business, without complaining.' 'The relations between husband and wife,' added the Baron, 'are all one could desire.'

Long before Peel's ministry came to an end, there had been a complete change in Victoria's attitude towards him. His appreciation of the Prince had softened her heart; the sincerity and warmth of his nature, which, in private intercourse with those whom he wished to please, had the power of gradually dissipating the awkwardness of his manners, did the rest. She came in time to regard him with intense feelings of respect and attachment. She spoke of 'our worthy Peel,' for whom, she said, she had 'an *extreme* admiration' and who had shown himself 'a man of unbounded *loyalty, courage,* patriotism, and *high-mindedness,* and his conduct towards me has been *chivalrous* almost, I might say.' She dreaded his removal from office almost as frantically as she had once

*In this assured sketch by her mother, 'Fat Alice', or 'Fatima' as the Queen and Prince Albert called their third child, walks with her nurse in the gardens at Buckingham Palace. Alice's first attempts at walking had led to great amusement because of her chubby physique, but when she took to 'roaring' and beating her head on the floor during violent temper tantrums her governess 'thought the case very grave'.*

dreaded that of Lord M. It would be, she declared, a *great calamity*. Six years before, what would she have said, if a prophet had told her that the day would come when she would be horrified by the triumph of the Whigs? Yet there was no escaping it; she had to face the return of her old friends. In the ministerial crises of 1845 and 1846, the Prince played a dominating part. Everybody recognised that he was the real centre of the negotiations—the actual controller of the forces and the functions of the Crown. The process by which this result was reached had been so gradual as to be almost imperceptible; but it may be said with certainty that, by the close of Peel's administration, Albert had become, in effect, the King of England.

# VI

With the final emergence of the Prince came the final extinction of Lord Melbourne. A year after his loss of office, he had been struck down by a paralytic seizure; he had apparently recovered, but his old elasticity had gone for ever. Moody, restless, and unhappy, he wandered like a ghost about the town, bursting into soliloquies in public places, or asking odd questions, suddenly, *à propos de bottes*. 'I'll be hanged if I'll do it for you, my Lord,' he was heard to say in the hall at Brooks's, standing by himself, and addressing the air after much thought. 'Don't you consider,' he abruptly asked a fellow-guest at Lady Holland's, leaning across the dinner-table in a pause of the conversation, 'that it was a most damnable act of Henri Quatre to change his religion with a view to securing the Crown?' He sat at home, brooding for hours in miserable solitude. He turned over his books—his classics and his Testaments—but they brought him no comfort at all. He longed for the return of the past, for the impossible, for he knew not what, for the devilries of Caro, for the happy platitudes of Windsor. His friends had left him, and no wonder, he said in bitterness—the fire was out. He secretly hoped for a return to power, scanning the newspapers with solicitude, and occasionally making a speech in the House of Lords. His correspondence with the Queen continued, and he appeared from time to time at Court; but he was a mere simulacrum of his former self; 'the dream,' wrote Victoria, 'is *past*.' As for his political views, they could no longer be tolerated. The Prince was an ardent Free Trader, and so, of course, was the Queen; and when, dining at Windsor at the time of the repeal of the Corn Laws, Lord Melbourne suddenly exclaimed, 'Ma'am, it's a damned dishonest act!' everyone was extremely embarrassed. Her Majesty laughed and tried to change the conversation, but without avail; Lord Melbourne returned to the charge again and again with—'I say, Ma'am, it's damned dishonest!'—until the Queen said 'Lord Melbourne, I must beg you not to say anything more on this subject now'; and then he held his tongue. She was kind to him, writing him long letters, and always remembering his birthday; but it was kindness at a distance, and he knew it. He had become 'poor Lord Melbourne.' A profound disquietude devoured him. He tried to fix his mind on the condition of agriculture and the Oxford Movement. He wrote long memoranda in utterly undecipherable handwriting. He was convinced that he had lost all his money, and could not possibly afford to be a Knight of the Garter. He had run through everything, and yet—if Peel went out, he might be sent for—why not? He was never sent for. The Whigs ignored him in their consultations, and the leadership of the party passed to Lord John Russell. When Lord John became Prime Minister, there was much politeness, but Lord Melbourne was not asked to join the Cabinet. He bore the blow with perfect amenity; but he understood, at last, that that was the end.

For two years more he lingered, sinking slowly into unconsciousness and imbecility. Sometimes, propped up in his chair, he would be heard to murmur, with unexpected appositeness, the words of Samson:—

> 'So much I feel my genial spirits droop,
> My hopes all flat, nature within me seems
> In all her functions weary of herself,
> My race of glory run, and race of shame,
> And I shall shortly be with them that rest.'

A few days before his death, Victoria, learning that there was no hope of his recovery, turned her mind for a little towards that which had once been Lord M. 'You will grieve to hear,' she told King Leopold, 'that our good, dear, old friend Melbourne is dying. . . . One cannot forget how good and kind and amiable he was, and it brings back so many recollections to my mind, though, God knows! I never wish that time back again.'

She was in little danger. The tide of circumstance was flowing now with irresistible fullness towards a very different consummation. The seriousness of Albert, the claims of her children, her own inmost inclinations; and the movement of the whole surrounding world, combined to urge her forward along the narrow way of public and domestic duty. Her family steadily increased. Within eighteen months of the birth of the Prince of Wales the Princess Alice appeared, and a year later the Prince Alfred, and then the Princess Helena, and, two years afterwards, the Princess Louise; and still there were signs that the pretty row of royal infants was not complete. The parents, more and more involved in family cares and family happiness, found the pomp of Windsor galling, and longed for some more intimate and remote

W. Kohler's cartoon 'Tender Annuals' makes fun of the rapidly expanding royal family. John Bull chides Albert with the words, 'Hollo! Hollo! Young fellow, come, come. I shall have such a stock of them sort o' plants on my hands I sha'nt know what to do with them.' A street ballad echoing the same thought has Victoria resolving 'Albert, dear Albert, we'll do it no more,' to the Prince Consort's consternation.

retreat. On the advice of Peel they purchased the estate of Osborne, in the Isle of Wight. Their skill and economy in financial matters enabled them to lay aside a substantial sum of money; and they could afford, out of their savings, not merely to buy the property but to build a new house for themselves and to furnish it at a cost of £200,000. At Osborne, by the sea-shore, and among the woods, which Albert, with memories of Rosenau in his mind, had so carefully planted, the royal family spent every hour that could be snatched from Windsor and London—delightful hours of deep retirement and peaceful work. The public looked on with approval. A few aristocrats might sniff or titter; but with the nation at large the Queen was now once more extremely popular. The middle-classes, in particular, were pleased. They liked a love-match; they liked a household which combined the advantages of royalty and virtue, and in which they seemed to see, reflected as in some resplendent looking-glass, the ideal image of the very lives they led themselves. Their own existences, less exalted, but oh! so soothingly similar, acquired an added excellence, an added succulence, from the early hours, the regularity, the plain tuckers, the round games, the roast beef and Yorkshire pudding of Osborne. It was indeed a model Court. Not only were its central personages the patterns of propriety, but no breath of scandal, no shadow of indecorum, might approach its utmost boundaries. For Victoria, with all the zeal of a convert, upheld now the standard of moral purity with an inflexibility surpassing, if that were possible, Albert's own. She blushed to think how she had once believed—how she had once actually told *him*—that one might be too strict and particular in such matters, and that one ought to be indulgent towards other people's dreadful sins. But she was no longer Lord M.'s pupil: she was Albert's wife. She was more—the embodiment, the living apex of a new era in the generations of mankind. The last vestige of the eighteenth century had disappeared; cynicism and subtlety were shrivelled into powder; and duty, industry, morality, and domesticity triumphed over them. Even the very chairs and tables had assumed, with a singular responsiveness, the forms of prim solidity. The Victorian Age was in full swing.

*Queen Victoria's etching of a favourite niece, Adelaide Hohenlohe, daughter of her half-sister Feodora.*

# VII

Only one thing more was needed: material expression must be given to the new ideals and the new forces, so that they might stand revealed in visible glory before the eyes of an astonished world. It was for Albert to supply this want. He mused, and was inspired: the Great Exhibition came into his head.

Without consulting anyone, he thought out the details of his conception with the minutest care. There had been exhibitions before in the world, but this should surpass them all. It should contain specimens of what every country could produce in raw materials, in machinery and mechanical inventions, in manufactures, and in the applied and plastic arts. It should not be merely useful and ornamental; it should teach a high moral lesson. It should be an international monument to those supreme blessings of civilisation—peace, progress, and prosperity. For some time past the Prince had been devoting much of his attention to the problems of commerce and industry. He had a taste for machinery of every kind, and his sharp eye had more than once detected, with the precision of an expert, a missing cogwheel in some vast and complicated engine. A visit to Liverpool, where he opened the Albert Dock, impressed upon his mind the immensity of modern industrial forces, though in a letter to Victoria describing his experiences, he was careful to retain his customary lightness of touch. 'As I write,' he playfully remarked, 'you will be making your evening toilette, and not be ready in time for dinner. I must set about the same task, and not, let me hope, with the same result. . . . The loyalty and enthusiasm of the inhabitants are great; but the heat is greater still. I am satisfied that if the population of Liverpool had been weighed this morning, and were to be weighed again now, they would be found many degrees lighter. The docks are wonderful, and the mass of shipping incredible.' In art and science he had been deeply interested since boyhood; his reform of the household had put his talent for organisation beyond a doubt; and thus from every point of view the Prince was well qualified for his task. Having matured his plans, he summoned a small committee and laid an outline of his scheme before it. The committee approved, and the great undertaking was set on foot without delay.

Two years, however, passed before it was completed. For two years the Prince laboured with extraordinary and incessant energy. At first all went smoothly. The leading manufacturers warmly took up the idea; the colonies and the East India Company were sympathetic; the great foreign nations were eager to send in their contributions; the powerful support of Sir Robert Peel was obtained, and the use of a site in Hyde Park, selected by the Prince, was sanctioned by the Government. Out of 234 plans for the Exhibition building, the Prince chose that of Joseph Paxton, famous as a designer of gigantic conservatories; and the work was on the point of being put in hand when a series of unexpected difficulties arose. Opposition to the whole scheme, which had long been smouldering in various quarters, suddenly burst forth. There was an outcry, headed by *The Times*, against the use of the Park for the Exhibition; for a moment it seemed as if the building would be relegated to a suburb; but, after a fierce debate in the House, the supporters of the site in the Park won the day. Then it appeared that the project lacked a sufficient financial backing; but this obstacle, too, was surmounted, and eventually £200,000 was subscribed as a guarantee fund. The enormous glass edifice rose higher and higher, covering acres and enclosing towering elm trees beneath its roof: and then the fury of its enemies reached a climax. The fashionable, the cautious, the Protectionists, the pious, all joined in the hue and cry. It was pointed out that the Exhibition would serve as a rallying point for all the ruffians in England, for all the malcontents in Europe; and that on the day of its opening there would certainly be a riot and probably a revolution. It was asserted that the glass roof was porous, and that the droppings of fifty million sparrows would utterly destroy every object beneath it. Agitated Nonconformists declared that the Exhibition was an arrogant and wicked enterprise which would infallibly bring down God's punishment upon the nation. Colonel Sibthorpe, in the debate on the Address, prayed that hail and lightning might descend from heaven on the accursed thing. The Prince,

*Another child study etched by the Queen soon after her marriage. She and Albert learned this hobby together, on one occasion summoning Sir Edwin Landseer and his brother Tom to Buckingham Palace to advise on technique.*

99

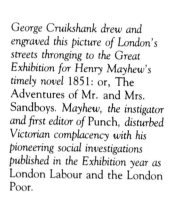

*George Cruikshank drew and engraved this picture of London's streets thronging to the Great Exhibition for Henry Mayhew's timely novel 1851: or, The Adventures of Mr. and Mrs. Sandboys. Mayhew, the instigator and first editor of* Punch, *disturbed Victorian complacency with his pioneering social investigations published in the Exhibition year as* London Labour and the London Poor.

with unyielding perseverance and infinite patience, pressed on to his goal. His health was seriously affected; he suffered from constant sleeplessness; his strength was almost worn out. But he remembered the injunctions of Stockmar and never relaxed. The volume of his labours grew more prodigious every day; he toiled at committees, presided over public meetings, made speeches, and carried on communications with every corner of the civilised world—and his efforts were rewarded. On May 1, 1851, the Great Exhibition was opened by the Queen before an enormous concourse of persons, amid scenes of dazzling brilliancy and triumphant enthusiasm.

Victoria herself was in a state of excitement which bordered on delirium. She performed her duties in a trance of joy, gratitude, and amazement, and, when it was all over, her feelings poured themselves out into her journal in a torrential flood. The day had been nothing but an endless succession of glories—or rather, one vast glory—one vast radiation of Albert. Everything she had seen, everything she had felt or heard, had been so beautiful, so wonderful, that even the royal underlinings broke down under the burden of emphasis, while her remembering pen rushed on, regardless, from splendour to splendour—the huge crowds, so well-behaved and loyal—flags of all the nations floating—the inside of the building, so immense, with myriads of people and the sun shining through the roof—a little side-room, where we left our shawls—palm-trees and machinery—dear Albert—the place so big that we could hardly hear the organ—thankfulness to God—a curious assemblage of political and distinguished men—the March from 'Athalie'—God bless my dearest Albert, God bless my dearest country!—a glass fountain—the Duke and Lord Anglesey walking arm in arm—a beautiful Amazon, in bronze, by Kiss—Mr. Paxton, who might be justly proud, and rose from being a common gardener's boy—Sir George Grey in tears, and everybody astonished and delighted.

A striking incident occurred when, after a short prayer by the Archbishop of Canterbury, the choir of 600 voices burst into the 'Hallelujah Chorus.' At that moment a Chinaman, dressed in full national costume, stepped out into the middle of the central nave, and, advancing slowly towards the royal group, did obeisance to Her Majesty. The Queen, much impressed, had no doubt that he was an eminent mandarin; and, when the final procession was formed, orders were given that, as no representative of the Celestial Empire was present, he should be included in the diplomatic cortège. He accordingly, with the utmost gravity, followed immediately behind the Ambassadors. He subsequently disappeared, and it was rumoured, among ill-natured people, that, far from being a mandarin, the fellow was a mere imposter. But nobody ever really discovered the nature of the comments that had been lurking behind the matchless impassivity of that yellow face.

A few days later Victoria poured out her heart to her uncle. The first of May, she said, was 'the *greatest* day in our history, the most *beautiful* and *imposing* and *touching* spectacle ever seen, and the triumph of my beloved Albert. . . . It was the *happiest*, *proudest* day in my life, and I can think of nothing else. Albert's dearest name is immortalised with this *great* conception, *his* own, and my *own* dear country *showed* she was *worthy* of it. The triumph is *immense*.'

It was. The enthusiasm was universal; even the bitterest scoffers were converted, and joined in the chorus of praise. Congratulations from public bodies poured in; the City of Paris gave a great *fête* to the Exhibition committee; and the Queen and the Prince made a triumphal progress through the North of England. The financial results were equally remarkable. The total profit made by the Exhibition amounted to a sum of £165,000, which was employed in the purchase of land for the erection of a permanent National Museum in South Kensington. During the six months of its existence in Hyde Park over six million persons visited it, and not a single accident occurred. But there is an end to all things; and the time had come for the Crystal Palace to be removed to the salubrious seclusion of Sydenham. Victoria, sad but resigned, paid her final visit. 'It looked so beautiful,' she said, 'I could not believe it was the last time I was to see it. An organ, accompanied by a fine and powerful wind instrument called the sommerophone, was being played, and it nearly upset me. The canvas is very dirty, the red curtains are faded and many things are very much soiled, still the effect is fresh and new as ever and most beautiful. The glass fountain was already removed. . . . and the sappers and miners were rolling about the little boxes just as they did at the beginning. It made us all very melancholy.' But more cheerful thoughts followed. When all was over, she expressed her boundless satisfaction in a dithyrambic letter to the Prime Minister. Her beloved husband's name, she said, was for ever immortalised, and that this was universally recognised by the country was a source to her of immense happiness and gratitude. 'She feels grateful to Providence,' her Majesty concluded, 'to have permitted her to be united to so great, so noble, so excellent a Prince, and this year will ever remain the proudest and happiest of her life. The day of the closing of the Exhibition (which the Queen regretted much she could not witness), was the twelfth anniversary of her betrothal to the Prince, which is a curious coincidence.'

# 5: LORD PALMERSTON

I͡N 1851 the Prince's fortunes reached their highwater mark. The success of the Great Exhibition enormously increased his reputation and seemed to assure him henceforward a leading place in the national life. But before the year was out another triumph, in a very different sphere of action, was also his. This triumph, big with fateful consequences, was itself the outcome of a series of complicated circumstances which had been gathering to a climax for many years.

The unpopularity of Albert in high society had not diminished with time. Aristocratic persons continued to regard him with disfavour; and he on his side withdrew further and further into a contemptuous reserve. For a moment, indeed, it appeared as if the dislike of the upper classes was about to be suddenly converted into cordiality; for they learnt with amazement that the Prince, during a country visit, had ridden to hounds and acquitted himself remarkably well. They had always taken it for granted that his horsemanship was of some second-rate foreign quality, and here he was jumping five-barred gates and tearing after the fox as if he had been born and bred in Leicestershire. They could hardly believe it; was it possible that they had made a mistake, and that Albert was a good fellow after all? Had he wished to be thought so he would certainly have seized this opportunity, purchased several hunters, and used them constantly. But he had no such desire; hunting bored him, and made Victoria nervous. He continued, as before, to ride, as he himself put it, for exercise or convenience, not for amusement; and it was agreed that though the Prince, no doubt, could keep in his saddle well enough, he was no sportsman.

This was a serious matter. It was not merely that Albert was laughed at by fine ladies and sneered at by fine gentlemen; it was not merely that Victoria, who before her marriage had cut some figure in society, had, under her

George Cruikshank's etching 'The British Beehive' was designed in 1840 and revised in 1867. In this symbolic representation of British society the 'Queen Bee' presides over her aristocracy and carefully stratified ranks of workers, while the whole edifice rests on the bank of the 'richest country in the world', the Army and the Navy. Cruikshank's light-hearted vision illustrates Victorian England's thriving industry, rigid class system, respect for tradition and belief in liberal concepts like an 'honest and indcpendent free press' and 'freedom to all religious denominations'.

103

*The Prime Minister Lord Palmerston (1784–1865), photographed in 1864, the year when he celebrated a successful debate in the Commons by ascending nimbly to the Ladies' Gallery to embrace his wife. This impressed even the critical Disraeli, who wrote: 'what pluck to mount those dreadful stairs at three o'clock in the morning and at eighty years of age. . . . It was a great moment.' Nine years earlier, Disraeli had panned him mercilessly: 'At the best only ginger beer and not champaign, and now an old painted Pantaloon, very deaf, very blind, and with false teeth, which would fall out of his mouth when speaking, if he did not hesitate and halt so in his talk.' But 'Pam' remained a popular and effective leader for another decade, who brought his country through the Crimean War and continued to voice the principles of liberal nationalism shared by many of his countrymen. Like other aristocrats brought up in the urbane and sophisticated pre-Victorian world, Palmerston did not always observe mid-century moral conventions. At the age of seventy-nine, he was threatened with court action for improper relations with a Mrs. Cane, and London society wondered, 'though she was Cain, was he Abel?'*

husband's influence, almost completely given it up. Since Charles the Second the sovereigns of England had, with a single exception, always been unfashionable; and the fact that the exception was George the Fourth seemed to give an added significance to the rule. What was grave was not the lack of fashion, but the lack of other and more important qualities. The hostility of the upper classes was symptomatic of an antagonism more profound than one of manners or even of tastes. The Prince, in a word, was un-English. What that word precisely meant it was difficult to say; but the fact was patent to every eye. Lord Palmerston, also, was not fashionable; the great Whig aristocrats looked askance at him, and tolerated him only as an unpleasant necessity thrust upon them by fate. But Lord Palmerston was English through and through; there was something in him that expressed, with extraordinary vigour, the fundamental qualities of the English race. And he was the very antithesis of the Prince. By a curious chance it so happened that this typical Englishman was brought into closer contact than any other of his countrymen with the alien from over the sea. It thus fell out that differences which, in more fortunate circumstances, might have been smoothed away and obliterated, became accentuated to the highest pitch. All the mysterious forces in Albert's soul leapt out to do battle with his adversary, and, in the long and violent conflict that followed, it almost seemed as if he was struggling with England herself.

Palmerston's whole life had been spent in the government of the country. At twenty-two he had been a Minister; at twenty-five he had been offered the Chancellorship of the Exchequer, which, with that prudence which formed so unexpected a part of his character, he had declined to accept. His first spell of office had lasted uninterruptedly for twenty-one years. When Lord Grey came into power he received the Foreign Secretaryship, a post which he continued to occupy, with two intervals, for another twenty-one years. Throughout this period his reputation with the public had steadily grown, and when, in 1846, he became Foreign Secretary for the third time, his position in the country was almost, if not quite, on an equality with that of the Prime Minister, Lord John Russell. He was a tall, big man of sixty-two, with a jaunty air, a large face, dyed whiskers, and a long, sardonic upper lip. His private life was far from respectable, but he had greatly strengthened his position in society by marrying, late in life, Lady Cowper, the sister of Lord Melbourne, and one of the most influential of the Whig hostesses. Powerful, experienced, and supremely self-confident, he naturally paid very little attention to Albert. Why should he? The Prince was interested in foreign affairs? Very well, then; let the Prince pay attention to *him*—to him, who had been a Cabinet Minister when Albert was in the cradle, who was the chosen leader of a great nation, and who had never failed in anything he had undertaken in the whole course of his life. Not that he wanted the Prince's attention—far from it: so far as he could see, Albert was merely a young foreigner, who suffered from having no vices, and whose only claim to distinction was that he had happened to marry the Queen of England. This estimate, as he found out to his cost, was a mistaken one. Albert was by no means insignificant, and, behind Albert, there was another figure by no means insignificant either—there was Stockmar.

But Palmerston, busy with his plans, his ambitions, and the management of a great department, brushed all such considerations on one side; it was his favourite method of action. He lived by instinct—by a quick eye and a strong hand, a dexterous management of every crisis as it arose, a half-unconscious sense of the vital elements in a situation. He was very bold; and nothing gave him more exhilaration than to steer the ship of state in a high wind, on a rough sea, with every stitch of canvas on her that she could carry. But there is a point beyond which boldness becomes rashness—a point perceptible only to intuition and not to reason; and beyond that point Palmerston never went. When he saw that the case demanded it, he could go slow—very slow indeed; in fact, his whole career, so full of vigorous adventure, was nevertheless a masterly example of the proverb, 'Tout vient à point à qui sait attendre.' But when he decided to go quick, nobody went quicker. One day, returning from Osborne, he found that he had missed the train to London; he ordered a special, but the station-master told him that to put a special train upon the line at that time of day would be dangerous, and he could not allow it. Palmerston insisted, declaring that he had important business in London, which could not wait. The station-master, supported by all the officials, continued to demur; the company, he said, could not possibly take the responsibility. 'On *my* responsibility, then!' said Palmerston, in his off-hand, peremptory way; whereupon the station-master ordered up the train, and the Foreign Secretary reached London in time for his work, without an accident. The story is typical of the happy valiance with which he conducted both his

*Prowess on the hunting field at Belvoir in 1843 did wonders for the Prince's popularity; 'We had a capital run, and the Prince rode admirably to the amazement of most,' commented a fellow horseman. The Queen wrote to King Leopold, 'One can scarcely credit the absurdity of people here. Albert's riding so boldly and hard has made such a sensation that it has been written all over the country, and they make much more of it than if he had done some great act!'*

own affairs and those of the nation. 'England,' he used to say, 'is strong enough to brave consequences.' Apparently, under Palmerston's guidance, she was. While the officials protested and shook in their shoes, he would wave them away with his airy 'My responsibility!' and carry the country swiftly along the line of his choice, to a triumphant destination,—without an accident. His immense popularity was the result partly of his diplomatic successes, partly of his extraordinary personal affability, but chiefly of the genuine intensity with which he responded to the feelings and supported the interests of his countrymen. The public knew that it had in Lord Palmerston not only a high-mettled master, but also a devoted servant—that he was, in every sense of the word, a public man. When he was Prime Minister, he noticed that iron hurdles had been put up on the grass in the Green Park; he immediately wrote to the Minister responsible, ordering, in the severest language, their instant removal, declaring that they were 'an intolerable nuisance,' and that the purpose of the grass was 'to be walked upon freely and without restraint by the people, old and young, for whose enjoyment the parks are maintained.' It was in this spirit that, as Foreign Secretary, he watched over the interests of Englishmen abroad. Nothing could be more agreeable for Englishmen; but foreign governments were less pleased. They found Lord Palmerston interfering, exasperating, and alarming. In Paris they spoke with bated breath of 'ce terrible milord Palmerston'; and in Germany they made a little song about him—

> 'Hat der Teufel einen Sohn,
> So ist er sicher Palmerston.'

But their complaints, their threats, and their agitations were all in vain. Palmerston, with his upper lip sardonically curving, braved consequences, and held on his course.

The first diplomatic crisis which arose after his return to office, though the Prince and the Queen were closely concerned with it, passed off without serious disagreement between the Court and the Minister. For some years past a curious problem had been perplexing the chanceries of Europe. Spain, ever since the time of Napoleon a prey to civil convulsions, had settled down for a short interval to a state of comparative quiet under the rule of Christina, the Queen Mother, and her daughter Isabella, the young Queen. In 1846, the question of Isabella's marriage, which had for long been the subject of diplomatic speculations, suddenly became acute. Various candidates for her hand were proposed—among others, two cousins of her own, another Spanish prince, and Prince Leopold of Saxe-Coburg, a first cousin of Victoria's and Albert's; for different reasons, however, none of these young men seemed altogether satisfactory. Isabella was not yet sixteen; and it might have been supposed that her marriage could be put off for a few years more; but this was considered to be out of the question. 'Vous ne savez pas,' said a high authority, 'ce que c'est que ces princesses espagnoles; elles ont le diable au corps, et on a toujours dit que si nous ne nous hâtions pas, l'héritier viendrait avant le mari.' It might also have been supposed that the young Queen's marriage was a matter to be settled by herself, her mother, and the Spanish Government; but this again was far from being the case. It had become, by one of those periodical reversions to the ways of the eighteenth century, which, it is rumoured, are still not unknown in diplomacy, a question of dominating importance in the foreign policies both of France and England. For several years, Louis Philippe and his Prime Minister Guizot had been privately maturing a very subtle plan. It was the object of the French King to repeat the glorious *coup* of Louis XIV, and to abolish the Pyrenees by placing one of his grandsons on the throne of Spain. In order to bring this about, he did not venture to suggest that his younger son, the Duc de Montpensier, should marry Isabella; that would have been too obvious a move, which would have raised immediate and insurmountable opposition. He therefore proposed that Isabella should marry her cousin, the Duke of Cadiz, while Montpensier married Isabella's younger sister, the Infanta Fernanda; and pray, what possible objection could there be to that? The wily old King whispered into the chaste ears of Guizot the key to the secret; he had good reason to believe that the Duke of Cadiz was incapable of having children, and therefore the offspring of Fernanda would inherit the Spanish crown. Guizot rubbed his hands, and began at once to set the necessary springs in motion; but, of course, the whole scheme was very soon divulged and understood. The English Government took an extremely serious view of the matter; the balance of power was clearly at stake, and the French intrigue must be frustrated at all hazards. A diplomatic struggle of great intensity followed; and it occasionally appeared that a second War of the Spanish Succession was about to break out. This was avoided, but the consequences of this strange imbroglio were far-reaching and completely different from what any of the parties concerned could have guessed.

In the course of the long and intricate negotiations there was one point upon which Louis Philippe laid a special stress—the candidature of Prince Leopold of Saxe-Coburg. The prospect of a marriage between a Coburg Prince and the Queen of Spain was, he declared, at least as threatening to the balance of power in Europe as that of a marriage between the Duc de Montpensier and the Infanta; and, indeed, there was much to be said for his contention. The ruin which had fallen upon the House of Coburg during the Napoleonic wars had apparently served only to multiply its vitality, for that princely family had by now extended itself over Europe in an extraordinary manner. King Leopold was firmly fixed in Belgium; his niece was Queen of England; one of his nephews was the husband of the Queen of England, and another the husband of the Queen of Portugal; yet another was Duke of Würtemberg. Where was this to end? There seemed to be a Coburg Trust ready to send out one of its members at any moment to fill up any vacant place among the ruling families of Europe. And even beyond Europe there were signs of this infection spreading. An American who had arrived in Brussels had assured King Leopold that there was a strong feeling in the United States in favour of monarchy instead of the misrule of mobs, and had suggested, to the delight of His Majesty, that some branch of the Coburg family might be available for the position. That danger might, perhaps, be remote; but the Spanish danger was close at hand; and if Prince Leopold were to marry Queen Isabella the position of France would be one of humiliation, if not of positive danger. Such were the asseverations of Louis Philippe. The

English Government had no wish to support Prince Leopold, and, though Albert and Victoria had had some hankerings for the match, the wisdom of Stockmar had induced them to give up all thoughts of it. The way thus seemed open for a settlement: England would be reasonable about Leopold, if France would be reasonable about Montpensier. At the Château d'Eu, the agreement was made, in a series of conversations between the King and Guizot on the one side, and the Queen, the Prince, and Lord Aberdeen on the other. Aberdeen, as Foreign Minister, declared that England would neither recognise nor support Prince Leopold as a candidate for the hand of the Queen of Spain; while Louis Philippe solemnly promised, both to Aberdeen and to Victoria, that the Duc de Montpensier should not marry the Infanta Fernanda until after the Queen was married and had issue. All went well, and the crisis seemed to be over, when the whole question was suddenly reopened by Palmerston, who had succeeded Aberdeen at the Foreign Office. In a despatch to the English Minister at Madrid, he mentioned, in a list of possible candidates for Queen Isabella's hand, Prince Leopold of Coburg; and at the same time he took occasion to denounce in violent language the tyranny and incompetence of the Spanish Government. This despatch, indiscreet in any case, was rendered infinitely more so by being communicated to Guizot. Louis Philippe saw his opportunity and pounced on it. Though there was nothing in Palmerston's language to show that he either recognised or supported Prince Leopold, the King at once assumed that the English had broken their engagement, and that he was therefore free to do likewise. He then sent the despatch to the Queen Mother, declared that the English were intriguing for the Coburg marriage, bade her mark the animosity of Palmerston against the Spanish Government, and urged her to escape from her difficulties and ensure the friendship of France by marrying Isabella to the Duke of Cadiz and Fernanda to Montpensier. The Queen Mother, alarmed and furious, was easily convinced. There was only one difficulty: Isabella loathed the very sight of her cousin. But this was soon surmounted; there was a wild supper-party at the Palace, and in the course of it the young girl was induced to consent to anything that was asked of her. Shortly after, and on the same day, both the marriages took place.

The news burst like a bomb on the English Government, who saw with rage and mortification that they had been completely outmanoeuvred by the crafty King. Victoria, in particular, was outraged. Not only had she been the personal recipient of Louis Philippe's pledge, but he had won his way to her heart by presenting the Prince of Wales with a box of soldiers and sending the Princess Royal a beautiful Parisian doll with eyes that opened and shut. And now insult was added to injury. The Queen of the French wrote her a formal letter, calmly announcing, as a family event in which she was sure Victoria would be interested, the marriage of her son, Montpensier—'qui ajoutera à notre bonheur intérieur, le seul vrai dans ce monde, et que vous, madame, savez si bien apprécier.' But the English Queen had not long to wait for her revenge. Within eighteen months the monarchy of Louis Philippe, discredited, unpopular, and fatally weakened by the withdrawal of English support, was swept into limbo, while he and his family threw themselves as suppliant fugitives at the feet of Victoria.

# II

In this affair both the Queen and the Prince had been too much occupied with the delinquencies of Louis Philippe to have any wrath to spare for those of Palmerston; and, indeed, on the main issue, Palmerston's attitude and their own had been in complete agreement. But in this the case was unique. In every other foreign complication—and they were many and serious—during the ensuing years, the differences between the royal couple and the Foreign Secretary were constant and profound. There was a sharp quarrel over Portugal, where violently hostile parties were flying at each other's throats. The royal sympathy was naturally enlisted on behalf of the Queen and her Coburg husband, while Palmerston gave his support to the progressive elements in the country. It was not until 1848, however, that the strain became really serious. In that year of revolutions, when, in all directions and with alarming frequency, crowns kept rolling off royal heads, Albert and Victoria were appalled to find that the policy of England was persistently directed—in Germany, in Switzerland, in Austria, in Italy, in Sicily—so as to favour the insurgent forces. The situation, indeed, was just such an one as the soul of Palmerston loved. There was danger and excitement, the necessity of decision, the opportunity for action, on every hand. A disciple of Canning, with an English gentleman's contempt and dislike of foreign potentates deep in his heart, the spectacle of the popular uprisings, and of the oppressors bundled ignominiously out of the palaces they had disgraced, gave him unbounded pleasure, and he was determined that there should be no doubt whatever, all over the Continent, on which side in the great struggle England stood. It was not that he had the slightest tincture in him of philosophical radicalism; he had no philosophical tinctures of any kind; he was quite content to be inconsistent—to be a Conservative at home and a Liberal abroad. There were very good reasons for keeping the Irish in their places; but what had that to do with it? The point was this—when any decent man read an account of the political prisons in Naples his gorge rose. He did not want war; but he saw that without war a skilful and determined use of England's power might do much to further the cause of the Liberals in Europe. It was a difficult and a hazardous game to play, but he set about playing it with delighted alacrity. And then, to his intense annoyance, just as he needed all his nerve and all possible freedom of action, he found himself being hampered and distracted at every turn by . . . those people at Osborne. He saw what it was; the opposition was systematic and informed, and the Queen alone would have been incapable of it; the Prince was at the bottom of the whole thing. It was exceedingly vexatious; but Palmerston was in a hurry, and could not wait; the Prince, if he would insist upon interfering, must be brushed on one side.

Albert was very angry. He highly disapproved both of Palmerston's policy and of his methods of action. He was opposed to absolutism; but in his opinion Palmerston's proceedings were simply calculated to substitute for absolutism, all over Europe, something no better and very possibly worse—the anarchy of faction and mob violence. The dangers of this revolutionary

*George Hamilton-Gordon, fourth Earl of Aberdeen, held various posts in Tory administrations before heading a coalition government in 1852. Accused by Disraeli of 'antiquated imbecility', Aberdeen was a pacifist who strongly opposed Britain's entry into the Crimean War in 1854: 'I'm all for patching up, if we can,' he told the Queen. Early in 1855 Aberdeen's ministry fell 'with a whack', as Gladstone put it, over the mismanagement of army supplies. Aberdeen retired from politics, and died in 1860, aged seventy-six.*

ferment were grave; even in England Chartism was rampant—a sinister movement, which might at any moment upset the Constitution and abolish the Monarchy. Surely, with such dangers at home, this was a very bad time to choose for encouraging lawlessness abroad. He naturally took a particular interest in Germany. His instincts, his affections, his prepossessions, were ineradicably German; Stockmar was deeply involved in German politics; and he had a multitude of relatives among the ruling German families, who, from the midst of the hurly-burly of revolution, wrote him long and agitated letters once a week. Having considered the question of Germany's future from every point of view, he came to the conclusion, under Stockmar's guidance, that the great aim for every lover of Germany should be her unification under the sovereignty of Prussia. The intricacy of the situation was extreme, and the possibilities of good or evil which every hour might bring forth were incalculable; yet he saw with horror that Palmerston neither understood nor cared to understand the niceties of this momentous problem, but rushed on blindly, dealing blows to right and left, quite—so far as he could see—without system, and even without motive—except, indeed, a totally unreasonable distrust of the Prussian State.

But his disagreement with the details of Palmerston's policy was in reality merely a symptom of the fundamental differences between the characters of the two men. In Albert's eyes Palmerston was a coarse, reckless egotist, whose combined arrogance and ignorance must inevitably have their issue in folly and disaster. Nothing could be more antipathetic to him than a mind so strangely lacking in patience, in reflection, in principle, and in the habits of ratiocination. For to him it was intolerable to think in a hurry, to jump to slapdash decisions, to act on instincts that could not be explained. Everything must be done in due order, with careful premeditation; the premises of the position must first be firmly established; and he must reach the correct conclusion by a regular series of rational steps. In complicated questions—and what questions, rightly looked at, were not complicated?—to commit one's thoughts to paper was the wisest course, and it was the course which Albert, laborious though it might be, invariably adopted. It was as well, too, to draw up a reasoned statement after an event, as well as before it; and accordingly, whatever happened, it was always found that the Prince had made a memorandum. On one occasion he reduced to six pages of foolscap the substance of a confidential conversation with Sir Robert Peel, and, having read them aloud to him, asked him to append his signature; Sir Robert, who never liked to commit himself, became extremely uneasy; upon which the Prince, understanding that it was necessary to humour the singular susceptibilities of Englishmen, with great tact dropped that particular memorandum into the fire. But as for Palmerston, he never even gave one so much as a chance to read him a memorandum; he positively seemed to dislike discussion; and, before one knew where one was, without any warning whatever, he would plunge into some harebrained, violent project, which, as likely as not, would logically involve a European war. Closely connected, too, with this cautious, painstaking reasonableness of Albert's, was his desire to examine questions thoroughly from every point of view, to go down to the roots of things, and to act in strict accordance with some well-defined principle. Under Stockmar's tutelage he was constantly engaged in enlarging his outlook and in endeavouring to envisage vital problems both theoretically and practically—both with precision and with depth. To one whose mind was thus habitually occupied, the empirical activities of Palmerston, who had no notion what a principle meant, resembled the incoherent vagaries of a tiresome child. What did Palmerston know of economics, of science, of history? What did he care for morality and education? How much consideration had he devoted in the whole course of his life to the improvement of the condition of the working-classes and to the general amelioration of the human race? The answers to such questions were all too obvious; and yet it is easy to imagine, also, what might have been Palmerston's jaunty comment. 'Ah! your Royal Highness is busy with fine schemes and beneficent calculations—exactly! Well, as for me, I must say I'm quite satisfied with my morning's work—I've had the iron hurdles taken out of the Green Park.'

The exasperating man, however, preferred to make no comment, and to proceed in smiling silence on his inexcusable way. The process of 'brushing on one side' very soon came into operation. Important Foreign Office despatches were either submitted to the Queen so late that there was no time to correct them, or they were not submitted to her at all; or, having been submitted, and some passage in them being objected to and an alteration suggested, they were after all sent off in their original form. The Queen complained; the Prince complained; both complained together. It was quite useless. Palmerston was most apologetic—could not understand how it had occurred—must give the clerks a wigging—certainly Her Majesty's wishes should be attended to, and such a thing should never happen again. But, of course, it very soon happened again, and the royal remonstrances redoubled. Victoria, her partisan passions thoroughly aroused, imported into her protests a personal vehemence which those of Albert lacked. Did Lord Palmerston forget that she was Queen of England? How could she tolerate a state of affairs in which despatches written in her name were sent abroad without her approval or even her knowledge? What could be more derogatory to her position than to be obliged to receive indignant letters from the crowned heads to whom those despatches were addressed—letters which she did not know how to answer, since she so thoroughly agreed with them? She addressed herself to the Prime Minister. 'No remonstrance has any effect with Lord Palmerston,' she said. 'Lord Palmerston,' she told him on another occasion, 'has as usual pretended not to have had time to submit the draft to the Queen before he had sent it off.' She summoned Lord John to her presence, poured out her indignation, and afterwards, on the advice of Albert, noted down what had passed in a memorandum: 'I said that I thought that Lord Palmerston often endangered the honour of England by taking a very prejudiced and one-sided view of a question; that his writings were always as bitter as gall and did great harm, which Lord John entirely assented to, and that I often felt quite ill from anxiety.' Then she turned to her uncle. 'The state of Germany,' she wrote in a comprehensive and despairing review of the European situation, 'is dreadful, and one does feel quite ashamed about that once really so peaceful and happy country. That there are still good

*Prince Albert was inaugurated as Chancellor of Cambridge University in March 1847. Immediately he set about what has been described as 'a discreet programme of reform', introducing new subjects into the largely classical university curriculum. During the 1850s he supported the Royal Commission which gave a modern constitution to the two older universities, establishing new schools of study, extending university control over individual colleges and endowing new professorships. The Prince, who showed considerable tact in his dealings with the academic world, gradually won admiration and respect in university circles.*

people there I am sure, but they allow themselves to be worked upon in a frightful and shameful way. In France a crisis seems at hand. *What* a very bad figure we cut in this mediation! Really it is quite immoral, with Ireland quivering in our grasp and ready to throw off her allegiance at any moment, for us to force Austria to give up her lawful possessions. What shall we say if Canada, Malta, etc., begin to trouble us? It hurts me terribly.' But what did Lord Palmerston care?

Lord John's position grew more and more irksome. He did not approve of his colleague's treatment of the Queen. When he begged him to be more careful, he was met with the reply that 28,000 despatches passed through the Foreign Office in a single year, that, if every one of these were to be subjected to the royal criticism, the delay would be most serious, that, as it was, the waste of time and the worry involved in submitting drafts to the meticulous examination of Prince Albert was almost too much for an overworked Minister, and that, as a matter of fact, the postponement of important decisions owing to this cause had already produced very unpleasant diplomatic consequences. These excuses would have impressed Lord John more favourably if he had not himself had to suffer from a similar neglect. As often as not Palmerston failed to communicate even to him the most important despatches. The Foreign Secretary was becoming an almost independent power, acting on his own initiative, and swaying the policy of England on his own responsibility. On one occasion, in 1847, he had actually been upon the point of threatening to break off diplomatic relations with France without consulting either the Cabinet or the Prime Minister. And such incidents were constantly recurring. When this became known to the Prince, he saw that his opportunity had come. If he could only drive in to the utmost the wedge between the two statesmen, if he could only secure the alliance of Lord John, then the suppression or the removal of Lord Palmerston would be almost certain to follow. He set about the business with all the pertinacity of his nature. Both he and the Queen put every kind of pressure upon the Prime Minister. They wrote, they harangued, they relapsed into awful silence. It occurred to them that Lord Clarendon, an important member of the Cabinet, would be a useful channel for their griefs. They commanded him to dine at the Palace, and, directly the meal was over, 'the Queen,' as he described it afterwards, 'exploded, and went with the utmost vehemence and bitterness into the whole of Palmerston's conduct, all the effects produced all over the world, and all her own feelings and sentiments about it.' When she had finished, the Prince took up the tale, with less excitement, but with equal force. Lord Clarendon found himself in an awkward situation; he disliked Palmerston's policy, but he was his colleague, and he disapproved of the attitude of his royal hosts. In his opinion, they were 'wrong in wishing that courtiers rather than Ministers should conduct the affairs of the country,' and he thought that they 'laboured under the curious mistake that the Foreign Office was their peculiar department, and that they had the right to control, if not to direct, the foreign policy of England.' He, therefore, with extreme politeness, gave it to be understood that he would not commit himself in any way. But Lord John, in reality, needed no pressure. Attacked by his Sovereign, ignored by his Foreign

*Lord John Russell (1792–1878), third son of the sixth Duke of Bedford, was a small, thin man with a rather high, squeaky voice; cartoonists often portrayed him as a schoolboy or page. A Whig, Russell pursued the idea of Parliamentary reform for much of his political career, which began in 1813 and ended in 1866. He was twice Prime Minister but never condescended to seek popular support:*

*'Like or dislike, he does not care a jot;*

*He wants your vote, but your affections not,*

*Yet human hearts need sun as well as oats,*

*So cold a climate plays the deuce with votes.'*

Secretary, he led a miserable life. With the advent of the dreadful Schleswig-Holstein question—the most complex in the whole diplomatic history of Europe—his position, crushed between the upper and the nether millstones, grew positively unbearable. He became anxious above all things to get Palmerston out of the Foreign Office. But then—supposing Palmerston refused to go?

In a memorandum made by the Prince, at about this time, of an interview between himself, the Queen, and the Prime Minister, we catch a curious glimpse of the state of mind of those three high personages—the anxiety and irritation of Lord John, the vehement acrimony of Victoria, and the reasonable animosity of Albert—drawn together, as it were, under the shadow of an unseen Presence, the cause of that celestial anger—the gay, portentous Palmerston. At one point in the conversation Lord John observed that he believed the Foreign Secretary would consent to a change of offices; Lord Palmerston, he said, realised that he had lost the Queen's confidence—though only on public, and not on personal, grounds. But on that, the Prince noted, 'the Queen interrupted Lord John by remarking that she distrusted him on *personal* grounds also, but I remarked that Lord Palmerston had so far at least seen rightly; that he had become disagreeable to the Queen, not on account of his person, but of his political doings—to which the Queen assented.' Then the Prince suggested that there was a danger of the Cabinet breaking up, and of Lord Palmerston returning to office as Prime Minister. But on that point Lord John was reassuring: he 'thought Lord Palmerston too old to do much in the future (having passed his sixty-fifth year).' Eventually it was decided that nothing could be done for the present, but that the *utmost secrecy* must be observed; and so the conclave ended.

At last, in 1850, deliverance seemed to be at hand. There were signs that the public were growing weary of the alarums and excursions of Palmerston's diplomacy; and when his support of Don Pacifico, a British subject, in a quarrel with the Greek Government, seemed to be upon the point of involving the country in a war not only with Greece but also with France, and possibly with Russia into the bargain, a heavy cloud of distrust and displeasure appeared to be gathering and about to burst over his head. A motion directed against him in the House of Lords was passed by a substantial majority. The question was next to be discussed in the House of Commons, where another adverse vote was not improbable, and would seal the doom of the Minister. Palmerston received the attack with complete nonchalance, and then, at the last possible moment, he struck. In a speech of over four hours, in which exposition, invective, argument, declamation, plain talk and resounding eloquence were mingled together with consummate art and extraordinary felicity, he annihilated his enemies. The hostile motion was defeated, and Palmerston was once more the hero of the hour. Simultaneously, Atropos herself conspired to favour him. Sir Robert Peel was thrown from his horse and killed. By this tragic chance, Palmerston saw the one rival great enough to cope with him removed from his path. He judged—and judged rightly—that he was the most popular man in England; and when Lord John revived the project of his exchanging the Foreign Office for some other position in the Cabinet, he absolutely refused to stir.

Great was the disappointment of Albert; great was the indignation of Victoria. 'The House of Commons,' she wrote, 'is becoming very unmanageable and troublesome.' The Prince, perceiving that Palmerston was more firmly fixed in the saddle than ever, decided that something drastic must be done. Five months before, the prescient Baron had drawn up, in case of emergency, a memorandum, which had been carefully docketed, and placed in a pigeon-hole ready to hand. The emergency had now arisen, and the memorandum must be used. The Queen copied out the words of Stockmar, and sent them to the Prime Minister, requesting him to show her letter to Palmerston. 'She thinks it right,' she wrote, 'in order *to prevent any mistake* for the *future*, shortly to explain *what it is she expects from her Foreign Secretary.* She requires: (1) That he will distinctly state what he proposes in a given case, in order that the Queen may know as distinctly to *what* she has given her Royal sanction; (2) Having *once given* her sanction to a measure, that it be not arbitrarily altered or modified by the Minister; such an act she must consider as failing in sincerity towards the Crown, and justly to be visited by the exercise of her Constitutional right of dismissing that Minister.' Lord John Russell did as he was bid, and forwarded the Queen's letter to Lord Palmerston. This transaction, which was of grave constitutional significance, was entirely unknown to the outside world.

If Palmerston had been a sensitive man, he would probably have resigned on the receipt of the Queen's missive. But he was far from sensitive; he loved power, and his power was greater than ever; an unerring instinct told him that this was not the time to go. Nevertheless, he was seriously perturbed. He understood at last that he was struggling with a formidable adversary, whose skill and strength, unless they were mollified, might do irreparable injury to his career. He therefore wrote to Lord John, briefly acquiescing in the Queen's requirements—'I have taken a copy of this memorandum of the Queen and will not fail to attend to the directions which it contains'—and at the same time, he asked for an interview with the Prince. Albert at once summoned him to the Palace, and was astonished to observe, as he noted in a memorandum, that when Palmerston entered the room 'he was very much agitated, shook, and had tears in his eyes, so as quite to move me, who never under any circumstances had known him otherwise than with a bland smile on his face.' The old statesman was profuse in protestations and excuses; the young one was coldly polite. At last, after a long and inconclusive conversation, the Prince, drawing himself up, said that, in order to give Lord Palmerston 'an example of what the Queen wanted,' he would 'ask him a question point-blank.' Lord Palmerston waited in respectful silence, while the Prince proceeded as follows:—'You are aware that the Queen has objected to the Protocol about Schleswig, and of the grounds on which she has done so. Her opinion has been overruled, the Protocol stating the desire of the Great Powers to see the integrity of the Danish monarchy preserved has been signed, and upon this the King of Denmark has invaded Schleswig, where the war is raging. If Holstein is attacked also, which is likely, the Germans will not be restrained from flying to her assistance, and Russia has menaced to interfere with arms, if the Schleswigers are successful. What will you do, if this emergency arises (provoking most likely an European war), and which will arise very probably when we shall be at Balmoral and Lord John in another part of Scotland? The Queen expects from your foresight that you have contemplated this possibility, and requires a categorical answer as to what you would do in the event supposed.' Strangely enough, to this point-blank question, the Foreign Secretary appeared to be unable to reply. The whole matter, he said, was extremely complicated, and the contingencies mentioned by His Royal Highness were very unlikely to arise. The Prince persisted; but it was useless; for a full hour he struggled to extract a categorical answer, until at length Palmerston bowed himself out of the room. Albert threw up his hands in shocked amazement: what could one do with such a man?

What indeed? For, in spite of all his apologies and all his promises, within a few weeks the incorrigible reprobate was at his tricks again. The Austrian General Haynau, notorious as a rigorous suppressor of rebellion in Hungary and Italy, and in particular as a flogger of women, came to England and took it into his head to pay a visit to Messrs. Barclay and Perkins's brewery. The features of 'General Hyæna,' as he was everywhere called—his grim thin face, his enormous pepper-and-salt moustaches—had gained a horrid celebrity; and it so happened that among the clerks at the brewery there was a refugee from Vienna, who had given his fellow-workers a first-hand account of the General's characteristics. The Austrian Ambassador, scenting danger, begged his friend not to appear in public, or, if he must do so, to cut off his moustaches first. But the General would take no advice. He went to the brewery, was immediately recognised, surrounded by a crowd of angry draymen, pushed about, shouted at, punched in the ribs, and pulled by the moustaches until, bolting down an alley with the mob at his heels brandishing brooms and roaring 'Hyæna!' he managed to take refuge in a public-house, whence he was removed under the protection of several policemen. The Austrian Government was angry and demanded explanations. Palmerston, who, of course, was privately delighted by the incident,

'Butcher Haynau' received a very hostile press, which exulted in 'Haynau's taste of Barclay and Perkins's Entire'. The 'women-whipper' was derided for hiding in The George public house, kept by a Mrs. Benfield, 'taking shelter from chastisement beneath a woman's petticoat'. When rescued by the police galley, the proud Marshal certainly presented a sorry bedraggled figure, 'the clothes having been actually torn off his back, besides several very severe blows having been inflicted on him.'

replied regretting what had occurred, but adding that in his opinion the General had 'evinced a want of propriety in coming to England at the present moment'; and he delivered his note to the Ambassador without having previously submitted it to the Queen or to the Prime Minister. Naturally, when this was discovered, there was a serious storm. The Prince was especially indignant; the conduct of the draymen he regarded, with disgust and alarm, as 'a slight foretaste of what an unregulated mass of illiterate people is capable'; and Palmerston was requested by Lord John to withdraw his note, and to substitute for it another from which all censure of the General had been omitted. On this the Foreign Secretary threatened resignation, but the Prime Minister was firm. For a moment the royal hopes rose high, only to be dashed to the ground again by the cruel compliance of the enemy. Palmerston, suddenly lamb-like, agreed to everything; the note was withdrawn and altered, and peace was patched up once more.

It lasted for a year, and then, in October 1851, the arrival of Kossuth in England brought on another crisis. Palmerston's desire to receive the Hungarian patriot at his house in London was vetoed by Lord John; once more there was a sharp struggle; once more Palmerston, after threatening resignation, yielded. But still the insubordinate man could not keep quiet. A few weeks later a deputation of Radicals from Finsbury and Islington waited on him at the Foreign Office and presented him with an address, in which the Emperors of Austria and Russia were stigmatised as 'odious and detestable assassins' and 'merciless tyrants and despots.' The Foreign Secretary in his reply, while mildly deprecating these expressions, allowed his real sentiments to appear with a most undiplomatic *insouciance*. There was an immediate scandal, and the Court flowed over with rage and vituperation. 'I think,' said the Baron, 'the man has been for some time insane.' Victoria, in an agitated letter, urged Lord John to assert his authority. But Lord John perceived that on this matter the Foreign Secretary had the support of public opinion, and he judged it wiser to bide his time.

He had not long to wait. The culmination of the long series of conflicts, threats, and exacerbations came before the year was out. On December 2, Louis Napoleon's *coup d'état* took place in Paris; and on the following day Palmerston, without consulting anybody, expressed in a conversation with the French Ambassador his approval of Napoleon's act. Two days later, he was instructed by the Prime Minister, in accordance with a letter from the Queen, that it was the policy of the English Government to maintain an attitude of strict neutrality towards the affairs of France. Nevertheless, in an official despatch to the British Ambassador in Paris, he repeated the approval of the *coup d'état* which he had already given verbally to the French Ambassador in London. This despatch was submitted neither to the Queen nor to the Prime Minister. Lord John's patience, as he himself said, 'was drained to the last drop.' He dismissed Lord Palmerston.

Victoria was in ecstasies; and Albert knew that the triumph was his even more than Lord John's. It was his wish that Lord Granville, a young man whom he believed to be pliant to his influence, should be Palmerston's successor; and Lord Granville was appointed. Henceforward, it seemed that the Prince would have his way in foreign affairs. After years of struggle and mortification, success greeted him on every hand. In his family, he was an adored master; in the country, the Great Exhibition had brought him respect and glory; and now in the secret seats of power he had gained a new supremacy. He had wrestled with the terrible Lord Palmerston, the embodiment of all that was most hostile to him in the spirit of England, and his redoubtable opponent had been overthrown. Was England herself at his feet? It might be so; and yet . . . it is said that the sons of England have a certain tiresome quality: they never know when they are beaten. It was odd, but Palmerston was positively still jaunty. Was it possible? Could he believe, in his blind arrogance, that even his ignominious dismissal from office was something that could be brushed aside?

## III

The Prince's triumph was short-lived. A few weeks later, owing to Palmerston's influence, the Government was defeated in the House, and Lord John resigned. Then, after a short interval, a coalition between the Whigs and the followers of Peel came into power, under the premiership of Lord Aberdeen. Once more, Palmerston was in the Cabinet. It was true that he did not return to the Foreign Office; that was something to the good; in the Home Department it might be hoped that his activities would be less dangerous and disagreeable. But the Foreign Secretary was no longer the complacent Granville; and in Lord Clarendon the Prince knew that he had a Minister to deal with, who, discreet and courteous as he was, had a mind of his own.

These changes, however, were merely the preliminaries of a far more serious development. Events, on every side, were moving towards a catastrophe. Suddenly the nation found itself under the awful shadow of imminent war. For several months, amid the shifting mysteries of diplomacy and the perplexed agitations of politics, the issue grew more doubtful and more dark, while the national temper was strained to the breaking-point. At the very crisis of the long and ominous negotiations, it was announced that Lord Palmerston had resigned. Then the pent-up fury of the people burst forth. They had felt that in the terrible complexity of events they were being guided by weak and embarrassed counsels; but they had been reassured by the knowledge that at the centre of power there was one man with strength, with courage, with determination, in whom they could put their trust. They now learnt that that man was no longer among their leaders. Why? In their rage, anxiety, and nervous exhaustion, they looked round desperately for some hidden and horrible explanation of what had occurred. They suspected plots, they smelt treachery in the air. It was easy to guess the object upon which their frenzy would vent itself. Was there not a foreigner in the highest of places, a foreigner whose hostility to their own adored champion was unrelenting and unconcealed? The moment that Palmerston's resignation was known, there was a universal outcry; and an extraordinary tempest of anger and hatred burst, with unparalleled violence, upon the head of the Prince.

It was everywhere asserted and believed that the Queen's husband was a traitor to the country, that he was a tool of the Russian Court, that in obedience to Russian influences he had forced Palmerston out of the Government, and that he was directing the foreign policy of England in the interests of England's enemies. For many weeks these accusations filled the whole of the press; repeated at public meetings, elaborated in private talk, they flew over the country, growing every moment more extreme and more improbable. While respectable newspapers thundered out their grave invectives, halfpenny broadsides, hawked through the streets of London, re-echoed in doggerel vulgarity the same sentiments and the same suspicions. At last the wildest rumours began to spread.

*Prince Albert skating on thin ice.*

In January 1854, it was whispered that the Prince had been seized, that he had been found guilty of high treason, that he was to be committed to the Tower. The Queen herself, some declared, had been arrested, and large crowds actually collected round the Tower to watch the incarceration of the royal miscreants. *

These fantastic hallucinations were the result of the fevered atmosphere of approaching war. The cause of Palmerston's resignation, indeed, remains wrapped in obscurity, and it is possible that it was brought about by the continued hostility of the Court. But the supposition that Albert's influence had been used to favour the interests of Russia was devoid of any basis in actual fact. As often happens in such cases, the Government had been swinging backwards and forwards between two incompatible policies—that of non-interference and that of threats supported by force—either of which, if consistently followed, might well have had a successful and peaceful issue, but which, mingled together, could only lead to war. Albert, with characteristic scrupulosity, attempted to thread his way through the complicated labyrinth of European diplomacy, and eventually was lost in the maze. But so was the whole of the Cabinet; and, when war came, his anti-Russian feelings were quite as vehement as those of the most bellicose of Englishmen.

Nevertheless, though the gravest of the charges levelled against the Prince were certainly without foundation, there were underlying elements in the situation which explained, if they did not justify, the popular state of mind. It was true that the Queen's husband was a foreigner, who had been brought up in a foreign Court, was impregnated with foreign ideas, and was closely related to a multitude of foreign princes. Clearly this, though perhaps an unavoidable, was an undesirable, state of affairs; nor were the objections to it merely theoretical; it had in fact produced unpleasant consequences of a serious kind. The Prince's German proclivities were perpetually lamented by English Ministers; Lord Palmerston, Lord Clarendon, Lord Aberdeen, all told the same tale; and it was constantly necessary, in the grave questions of national policy, to combat the prepossessions of a Court in which German views and German sentiments held a disproportionate place. As for Palmerston, his language on this topic was apt to be unbridled. At the height of his annoyance over his resignation, he roundly declared that he had been made a victim to foreign intrigue. He afterwards toned down this accusation; but the mere fact that such a suggestion from such a quarter was possible at all showed to what unfortunate consequences Albert's foreign birth and foreign upbringing might lead.

But this was not all. A constitutional question of the most profound importance was raised by the position of the Prince in England. His presence gave a new prominence to an old problem—the precise definition of the functions and the powers of the Crown. Those functions and powers had become, in effect, his; and what sort of use was he making of them? His views as to the place of the Crown in the Constitution are easily ascertainable; for they were Stockmar's; and it happens that we possess a detailed account of Stockmar's opinions upon the subject in a long letter addressed by him to the Prince at the time of this very crisis, just before the outbreak of the Crimean War. Constitutional Monarchy, according to the Baron, had suffered an eclipse since the passing of the Reform Bill. It was now 'constantly in danger of becoming a pure Ministerial Government.' The old race of Tories, who 'had a direct interest in upholding the prerogatives of the Crown,' had died out; and the Whigs were 'nothing but partly conscious, partly unconscious Republicans, who stand in the same relation to the Throne as the wolf does to the lamb.' There was a rule that it was unconstitutional to introduce 'the name and person of the irresponsible Sovereign' into parliamentary debates on constitutional matters; this was 'a constitutional fiction, which, although undoubtedly of old standing, was fraught with danger'; and the Baron warned the Prince that 'if the English Crown permit a Whig Ministry to follow this rule in practice, without exception, you must not wonder if in a little time you find the majority of the people impressed with the belief that the King, in the view of the law, is nothing but a mandarin figure, which has to nod its head in assent, or shake it in denial, as his Minister pleases.' To prevent this from happening, it was of extreme importance, said the Baron, 'that no opportunity should be let slip of vindicating the legitimate position of the Crown.' 'And this is not hard to do,' he added, 'and can never embarrass a Minister where such straightforward loyal personages as the Queen and the Prince are concerned.' In his opinion, the very lowest claim of the Royal Prerogative should include 'a right on the part of the King to be the permanent President of his Ministerial Council.' The Sovereign ought to be 'in the position of a permanent Premier, who takes rank above the temporary head of the Cabinet, and in matters of discipline exercises supreme authority.' The Sovereign 'may even take a part in the initiation and the maturing of the Government measures; for it would be unreasonable to expect that a King, himself as able, as accomplished, and as patriotic as the best of his Ministers, should be prevented from making use of these qualities at the deliberations of his Council.' 'The judicious exercise of this right,' concluded the Baron, 'which certainly requires a master mind, would not only be the best guarantee for Constitutional Monarchy, but would raise it to a height of power, stability, and symmetry, which has never been attained.'

Now it may be that this reading of the Constitution is a possible one, though indeed it is hard to see how it can be made compatible with the fundamental doctrine of ministerial responsibility. William III presided over his Council, and he was a constitutional monarch; and it seems that Stockmar had in his mind a conception of the Crown which would have given it a place in the Constitution analogous to that which it filled at the time of William III. But it is clear that such a theory, which would invest the

*The Charge of the Light Brigade at Balaclava on 25 October 1854 was the incident, above all, which typified the ineptitude of the management of the Crimean campaign. As a result of an ambiguously worded order, the brigade made a gallant, but senseless, attack on Russian gun emplacements which resulted in the loss of a third of the British cavalry. The Crimea was Britain's first major European engagement since the struggle against Napoleon; the troops, smart and orderly on the parade ground, fared badly on the hostile terrain. Badly led and inadequately supplied, they died in their thousands, mainly from disease and deprivation. 'What an awful time!' wrote the Queen. 'I never thought I should have lived to see and feel all this.'*

Crown with more power than it possessed even under George III, runs counter to the whole development of English public life since the Revolution; and the fact that it was held by Stockmar, and instilled by him into Albert, was of very serious importance. For there was good reason to believe not only that these doctrines were held by Albert in theory, but that he was making a deliberate and sustained attempt to give them practical validity. The history of the struggle between the Crown and Palmerston provided startling evidence that this was the case. That struggle reached its culmination when, in Stockmar's memorandum of 1850, the Queen asserted her 'constitutional right' to dismiss the Foreign Secretary if he altered a despatch which had received her sanction. The memorandum was, in fact, a plain declaration that the Crown intended to act independently of the Prime Minister. Lord John Russell, anxious at all costs to strengthen himself against Palmerston, accepted the memorandum, and thereby implicitly allowed the claim of the Crown. More than that; after the dismissal of Palmerston, among the grounds on which Lord John justified that dismissal in the House of Commons he gave a prominent place to the memorandum of 1850. It became apparent that the displeasure of the Sovereign might be a reason for the removal of a powerful and popular Minister. It seemed indeed as if, under the guidance of Stockmar and Albert, the 'Constitutional Monarchy' might in very truth be rising 'to a height of power, stability, and symmetry, which had never been attained.'

But this new development in the position of the Crown, grave as it was in itself, was rendered peculiarly disquieting by the unusual circumstances which surrounded it. For the functions of the Crown were now, in effect, being exercised by a person unknown to the Constitution, who wielded over the Sovereign an undefined and unbounded influence. The fact that this person was the Sovereign's husband, while it explained his influence and even made it inevitable, by no means diminished its strange and momentous import. An ambiguous, prepotent figure had come to disturb the ancient, subtle, and jealously guarded balance of the English Constitution. Such had been the unexpected outcome of the tentative and faint-hearted opening of Albert's political life. He himself made no attempt to minimise either the multiplicity or the significance of the functions he performed. He considered that it was his duty, he told the Duke of Wellington in 1850, to 'sink his *own individual* existence in that of his wife . . .—assume no separate responsibility before the public, but make this position entirely a part of hers—fill up every gap which, as a woman, she would naturally leave in the exercise of her regal functions—continually and anxiously watch every part of the public business, in order to be able to advise and assist her at any moment in any of the multifarious and difficult questions or duties brought before her, sometimes international, sometimes political, or social, or personal. As the natural head of her family, superintendent of her household, manager of her private affairs, sole *confidential* adviser in politics, and only assistant in her communications with the officers of the Government, he is, besides, the husband of the Queen, the tutor of the royal children, the private secretary of the Sovereign, and her permanent minister.' Stockmar's pupil had assuredly gone far and learnt well. Stockmar's pupil!—precisely; the public, painfully aware of Albert's predominance, had grown, too, uneasily conscious that Victoria's master had a master of his own. Deep in the darkness the Baron loomed. Another foreigner! Decidedly, there were elements in the situation which went far to justify the popular alarm. A foreign Baron controlled a foreign Prince, and the foreign Prince controlled the Crown of England. And the Crown itself was creeping forward ominously; and when, from under its shadow, the Baron and the Prince had frowned, a great Minister, beloved of the people, had fallen. Where was all this to end?

Within a few weeks Palmerston withdrew his resignation, and the public frenzy subsided as quickly as it had arisen. When Parliament met, the leaders of both the parties in both the Houses made speeches in favour of the Prince, asserting his unimpeachable loyalty to the country and vindicating his right to advise the Sovereign in all matters of State. Victoria was delighted. 'The position of my beloved lord and master,' she told the Baron, 'has been defined for *once and all* and his merits have been acknowledged on all sides most duly. There was an immense concourse of people assembled when we went to the House of Lords, and the people were very friendly.' Immediately afterwards, the country finally plunged into the Crimean War. In the struggle that followed, Albert's patriotism was put beyond a doubt, and the animosities of the past were forgotten. But the war had another consequence, less gratifying to the royal couple: it crowned the ambition of Lord Palmerston. In 1855, the man who five years before had been pronounced by Lord John Russell to be 'too old to do much in the future,' became Prime Minister of England, and, with one short interval, remained in that position for ten years.

*The Queen often sketched Prince Arthur, her seventh child. Here he parades in soldier's uniform, following the example of his famous godfather, the Duke of Wellington, on whose eighty-first birthday (1 May 1850) he was born. Victoria believed that Arthur inherited Prince Albert's upright moral character, and he was probably her favourite son. As Duke of Connaught, he made the army his career and rose to the rank of Field Marshal, but his mother's hopes of seeing him as Commander-in-Chief were disappointed when the position went to Lord Roberts. Prince Arthur lived to the great age of 92, dying in 1942.*

121

THE QUEEN AND PRINCE ALBERT TOURING IN THE HIGHLAND, SUMMER 1860,
ACCOMPANIED BY THE GILLIE JOHN BROWN.

# 6: LAST YEARS OF THE PRINCE CONSORT

THE weak-willed youth who took no interest in politics and never read a newspaper had grown into a man of unbending determination whose tireless energies were incessantly concentrated upon the laborious business of government and the highest questions of State. He was busy now from morning till night. In the winter, before the dawn, he was to be seen, seated at his writing-table, working by the light of the green reading-lamp which he had brought over with him from Germany, and the construction of which he had much improved by an ingenious device. Victoria was early too, but she was not so early as Albert; and when, in the chill darkness, she took her seat at her own writing-table, placed side by side with his, she invariably found upon it a neat pile of papers arranged for her inspection and her signature. The day, thus begun, continued in unremitting industry. At breakfast, the newspapers—the once hated newspapers—made their appearance, and the Prince, absorbed in their perusal, would answer no questions, or, if an article struck him, would read it aloud. After that there were ministers and secretaries to interview; there was a vast correspondence to be carried on; there were numerous memoranda to be made. Victoria, treasuring every word, preserving every letter, was all breathless attention and eager obedience. Sometimes Albert would actually ask her advice. He consulted her about his English: 'Lese recht aufmerksam, und sage wenn irgend ein Fehler ist,' he would say; or, as he handed her a draft for her signature, he would observe 'Ich hab' Dir hier ein Draft gemacht, lese es mal! Ich dächte es wäre recht so.'* Thus the diligent, scrupulous, absorbing hours passed by. Fewer and fewer grew the moments of recreation and of exercise. The demands of society were narrowed down to the smallest limits, and even then but grudgingly attended to. It was no longer a mere pleasure, it was a positive necessity, to go to bed as early as possible in order to be up and at

*Incognito on a Highland 'expedition', the Queen rides between the kilted figures of Prince Albert and her 'particular ghillie' John Brown, who strides along bearing Her Majesty's shawl. It was the Prince who first noticed 'the young J. Brown' as early as the 1840s; gradually the tall, blue-eyed Highlander was given charge of the Queen's safety when out riding or driving, 'combining the offices of groom, footman, page and maid, I might almost say, as he is so handy about cloaks and shawls,' as the Queen explained. It is true that the Queen came to rely more heavily on Brown after the Prince Consort's death, but he had already been a royal favourite for some years.*

*'Prince Albert the British farmer',
Punch, October 1843, refers to a
recent speech in his praise by the
Prime Minister Sir Robert Peel.
Although he is caricatured here in
top hat and regally emblazoned
smock, the Prince Consort took a
serious interest in agriculture. His
attitude to farming and stock-
breeding has been described as
'characteristically well-organized
and unfashionably hard-headed'.
Taking charge of the farms on the
Windsor estate, he employed
experts to design a dairy farm and
accommodation for his famous
herds of prize pigs. Soon he was
sending entries to agricultural shows
at home and abroad; his Devon
heifer, Bessy, took first prize at the
1855 Paris Show.*

work on the morrow betimes.

The important and exacting business of government, which became at last the dominating preoccupation in Albert's mind, still left unimpaired his old tastes and interests; he remained devoted to art, to science, to philosophy; and a multitude of subsidiary activities showed how his energies increased as the demands upon them grew. For whenever duty called, the Prince was all alertness. With indefatigable perseverance he opened museums, laid the foundation-stones of hospitals, made speeches to the Royal Agricultural Society, and attended meetings of the British Association. The National Gallery particularly interested him: he drew up careful regulations for the arrangement of the pictures according to schools; and he attempted—though in vain—to have the whole collection transported to South Kensington. Feodora, now the Princess Hohenlohe, after a visit to England, expressed in a letter to Victoria her admiration of Albert both as a private and a public character, Nor did she rely only on her own opinion. 'I must just copy out,' she said, 'what Mr. Klumpp wrote to me some little time ago, and which is quite true.—"Prince Albert is one of the few Royal personages who can sacrifice to any principle (as soon as it has become evident to them to be good and noble) all those notions (or sentiments) to which others, owing to their narrow-mindedness, or to the prejudices of their rank, are so thoroughly inclined strongly to cling."—There is something so truly religious in this,' the Princess added, 'as well as humane and just, most soothing to my feelings which are so often hurt and disturbed by what I hear and see.'

Victoria, from the depth of her heart, subscribed to all the eulogies of Feodora and Mr. Klumpp. She only found that they were insufficient. As she watched her beloved Albert, after toiling with state documents and public functions, devoting every spare moment of his time to domestic duties, to artistic appreciation, and to intellectual improvements; as she listened to him cracking his jokes at the luncheon-table, or playing Mendelssohn on the organ, or pointing out the merits of Sir Edwin Landseer's pictures; as she followed him round while he gave instructions about the breeding of cattle, or decided that the Gainsboroughs must be hung higher up so that the Winterhalters might be properly seen—she felt perfectly certain that no other wife had ever had such a husband. His mind was apparently capable of everything, and she was hardly surprised to learn that he had made an important discovery for the conversion of sewage into agricultural manure. Filtration from below upwards, he explained, through some appropriate medium, which retained the solids and set free the fluid sewage for irrigation, was the principle of the scheme. 'All previous plans,' he said, 'would have cost millions; mine costs next to nothing.' Unfortunately, owing to a slight miscalculation, the invention proved to be impracticable; but Albert's intelligence was unrebuffed, and he passed on, to plunge with all his accustomed ardour into a prolonged study of the rudiments of lithography.

But naturally it was upon his children that his private interests and those of Victoria were concentrated most vigorously. The royal nurseries showed no sign of emptying. The birth of the Prince Arthur in 1850 was followed, three years later, by that of the Prince Leopold; and in 1857 the Princess Beatrice was born. A family of nine must be, in any circumstances, a grave responsibility; and the Prince realised to the full how much the high destinies of his offspring intensified the need of parental care. It was inevitable that he should believe profoundly in the importance of education; he himself had been the product of education; Stockmar had made him what he was; it was for him, in his turn, to be a Stockmar—to be even more than a Stockmar— to the young creatures he had brought into the world. Victoria would assist him; a Stockmar, no doubt, she could hardly be; but she could be perpetually vigilant, she could mingle strictness with her affection, and she could always set a good example. These considerations, of course, applied pre-eminently to the education of the Prince of Wales. How tremendous was the significance of every particle of influence which went to the making of the future King of England! Albert set to work with a will. But, watching with Victoria the minutest details of the physical, intellectual, and moral training of his children, he soon perceived, to his distress, that there was something unsatisfactory in the development of his eldest son. The Princess Royal was an extremely intelligent child; but Bertie, though he was good-humoured and gentle, seemed to display a deep-seated repugnance to every form of mental exertion. This was most regrettable, but the remedy was obvious: the parental efforts must be redoubled; instruction must be multiplied; not for a single instant must the educational pressure be allowed to relax. Accordingly, more tutors were selected, the curriculum was revised, the time-table of studies was rearranged, elaborate memoranda dealing with every possible contingency were drawn up. It was above all essential that there should be no slackness: 'work,' said the Prince, 'must be work.' And work indeed it was. The boy grew up amid a ceaseless round of paradigms, syntactical exercises, dates, genealogical tables, and lists of capes. Constant notes flew backwards and forwards between the Prince, the Queen, and the tutors, with inquiries, with reports of progress, with detailed recommendations; and these notes were all carefully preserved for future reference. It was, besides, vital that the heir to the throne should be protected from the slightest possibility of contamination from the outside world. The Prince of Wales was not as other boys; he might, occasionally, be allowed to invite some sons of the nobility, boys of good character, to play with him in the garden of Buckingham Palace; but his father presided, with alarming precision, over their sports. In short, every possible precaution was taken, every conceivable effort was made. Yet, strange to say, the object of all this vigilance and solicitude continued to be unsatisfactory—appeared, in fact, to be positively growing worse. It was certainly very odd: the more lessons that Bertie had to do, the less he did them; and the more carefully he was guarded against excitements and frivolities, the more desirous of mere amusement he seemed to become. Albert was deeply grieved and Victoria was sometimes very angry; but grief and anger produced no more effect than supervision and time-tables. The Prince of Wales, in spite of everything, grew up into manhood without the faintest sign of 'adherence to and perserverance in the plan both of studies and life'—as one of the Royal memoranda put it—which had been laid down with such extraordinary forethought by his father.

'Bertie–The Boy', sketched by his mother just before his ninth birthday, boasts features already showing the Hanoverian inheritance which was to cause his parents such anxiety. Consulting a phrenologist they were told that 'in the Prince of Wales the organs of ostentativeness, destructiveness, self-esteem etc. are all large, intellectual organs only moderately developed. The result will be strong will, at times obstinacy.'

## II

*Tossing the caber at the Laggan Games, held by Cluny MacPherson to celebrate the Prince Consort's birthday on 26 August; the Queen and Prince were his guests. The caber was originally a rafter from a cottage, but this one was described as 'the trunk of a young fir, about 14 feet long, and nearly as thick as a man's thigh.'*

Against the insidious worries of politics, the boredom of society functions, and the pompous publicity of state ceremonies, Osborne had afforded a welcome refuge; but it soon appeared that even Osborne was too little removed from the world. After all, the Solent was a feeble barrier. Oh, for some distant, some almost inaccessible sanctuary, where, in true domestic privacy, one could make happy holiday, just as if—or at least very, very, nearly—one were anybody else! Victoria, ever since, together with Albert, she had visited Scotland in the early years of her marriage, had felt that her heart was in the Highlands. She had returned to them a few years later, and her passion had grown. How romantic they were! And how Albert enjoyed them too! His spirits rose quite wonderfully as soon as he found himself among the hills and the conifers. 'It is a happiness to see him,' she wrote. 'Oh! What can equal the beauties of nature!' she exclaimed in her journal, during one of these visits. 'What enjoyment there is in them! Albert enjoys it so much; he is in ecstasies here.' 'Albert said,' she noted next day, 'that the chief beauty of mountain scenery consists in its frequent changes. We came home at six o'clock.' Then she went on a longer expedition—up to the very top of a high hill. 'It was quite romantic. Here we were with only this Highlander behind us holding the ponies (for we got off twice and walked about). . . . We came home at half past eleven,—the most delightful, most romantic ride and walk I ever had. I had never been up such a mountain, and then the day was so fine.' The Highlanders, too, were such astonishing people. They 'never make difficulties,' she noted, 'but are cheerful, and happy, and merry, and ready to walk, and run, and do anything.' As for Albert he 'highly appreciated the good-breeding, simplicity, and intelligence, which make it so pleasant and even instructive to talk to them.' 'We were always in the habit,' wrote Her Majesty, 'of conversing with the Highlanders—with whom one comes so much in contact in the Highlands.' She loved everything about them—their customs, their dress, their dances, even their musical instruments. 'There were nine pipers at the castle,' she wrote, after staying with Lord Breadalbane; 'sometimes one and sometimes three played. They always played about breakfast-time, again during the morning, at luncheon, and also whenever we went in and out; again before dinner, and during most of dinner-time. We both have become quite fond of the bag-pipes.'

It was quite impossible not to wish to return to such pleasures again and again; and in 1848 the Queen took a lease of Balmoral House, a small residence near Braemar in the wilds of Aberdeenshire. Four years later she bought the place outright. Now she could be really happy every summer; now she could be simple and at her ease; now she could be romantic every evening, and dote upon Albert, without a single distraction, all day long. The diminutive scale of the house was in itself a charm. Nothing was more amusing than to find oneself living in two or three little sitting-rooms, with the children crammed away upstairs, and the Minister in attendance with only a tiny bedroom to do all his work in. And then to be able to run in and out of doors as one liked, and to sketch, and to walk, and to watch the red deer coming so surprisingly close, and to pay visits to the cottagers! And occasionally one could be more adventurous still—one could go and stay for a night or two at the Bothie at Alt-na-giuthasach—a mere couple of huts with 'a wooden addition'—and only eleven people in the whole party! And there were mountains to be climbed and cairns to be built in solemn pomp. 'At last, when the cairn, which is, I think, seven or eight feet high, was nearly completed, Albert climbed up to the top of it, and placed the last stone; after which three cheers were given. It was a gay, pretty, and touching sight; and I felt almost inclined to cry. The view was so beautiful over the dear hills; the day so fine; the whole so *gemüthlich*.' And in the evening there were sword-dances and reels.

But Albert had determined to pull down the little old house, and to build in its place a Castle of his own designing. With great ceremony, in accordance with a memorandum drawn up by the Prince for the occasion, the foundation-stone of the new edifice was laid, and by 1855 it was habitable. Spacious, built of granite in the Scotch baronial style, with a tower 100 feet high, and minor turrets and castellated gables, the Castle was skilfully arranged to command the finest views of the surrounding mountains and of the neighbouring River Dee. Upon the interior decorations Albert and Victoria lavished all their care. The walls and the floors were of pitch-pine, and covered with specially manufactured tartans. The Balmoral tartan, in red and grey, designed by the Prince, and the Victoria tartan, with a white stripe, designed by the Queen, were to be seen in every room: there were tartan curtains, and tartan chair-covers, and even tartan linoleums. Occasionally the Royal Stuart tartan appeared, for Her Majesty always maintained that she was an ardent Jacobite. Water-colour sketches by Victoria hung upon the walls, together with innumerable stags' antlers, and the head of a boar, which had been shot by Albert in Germany. In an alcove in the hall stood a life-sized statue of Albert in Highland dress.

Victoria declared that it was perfection. 'Every year,' she wrote, 'my heart becomes more fixed in this dear paradise, and so much more so now, that *all* has become my dear Albert's *own* creation, own work, own building, own laying-out; . . . and his great taste, and the impress of his dear hand, have been stamped everywhere.'

And here, in very truth, her happiest days were passed. In after years, when she looked back upon them, a kind of glory, a radiance as of an unearthly holiness, seemed to glow about these golden hours. Each hallowed moment stood out clear, beautiful, eternally significant. For, at the time, every experience there, sentimental, or grave, or trivial, had come upon her with a peculiar vividness, like a flashing of marvellous lights. Albert's stalkings—an evening walk when she lost her way—Vicky sitting down on a wasps' nest—a torchlight dance—with what intensity such things, and ten thousand like them, impressed themselves upon her eager consciousness! And how she flew to her journal to note them down! The news of the Duke's death! What a moment!—when, as she sat sketching after a picnic by a loch in the lonely hills, Lord Derby's letter had been brought to her, and she had learnt that '*England's*, or rather *Britain's* pride, her glory, her hero, the

*Leaping at the Laggan Games; the £5 prize went to Archibald Gunn, a bank clerk from Inverness; a reporter noted that 'whilst the others puffed, and strained, and sweated, and after all hit their legs against the wand they wished to clear, the winner took two or three quiet steps, and leapt as softly, as deftly, and as lightly as a cat.'*

A morning call at Balmoral: Queen Victoria took a personal interest in her tenants on the Balmoral estate and enjoyed her regular visits to them. The Scots bard William McGonagall, celebrated as one of the world's worst poets, wrote:
'Long may she be spared to roam
Among the bonnie Highland
   floral,
And spend many a happy day
In the palace of Balmoral.

Because she is very kind
To the old women there,
And allows them bread, tea,
   and sugar,
And each one gets a share.'

greatest man she had ever produced, was no more!' For such were her reflections upon the 'old rebel' of former days. But that past had been utterly obliterated—no faintest memory of it remained. For years she had looked up to the Duke as a figure almost superhuman. Had he not been a supporter of good Sir Robert? Had he not asked Albert to succeed him as Commander-in-Chief? And what a proud moment it had been when he stood as sponsor to her son Arthur, who was born on his eighty-first birthday! So now she filled a whole page of her diary with panegyrical regrets. 'His position was the highest a subject ever had—above party,—looked up to by all,—revered by the whole nation,—the friend of the Sovereign . . . The Crown never possessed,—and I fear never *will*—so *devoted*, loyal, and faithful a subject, so staunch a supporter! To *us* his loss is *irreparable* . . . To Albert he showed the greatest kindness and the utmost confidence . . . Not an eye will be dry in the whole country.' These were serious thoughts; but they were soon succeeded by others hardly less moving—by events as impossible to forget—by Mr. MacLeod's sermon on Nicodemus,—by the gift of a red flannel petticoat to Mrs. P. Farquharson, and another to old Kitty Kear.

But, without doubt, most memorable, most delightful of all were the expeditions—the rare, exciting expeditions up distant mountains, across broad rivers, through strange country, and lasting several days. With only two gillies—Grant and Brown—for servants, and with assumed names . . . it was more like something in a story than real life. 'We had decided to call ourselves *Lord and Lady Churchill and party*—Lady Churchill passing as *Miss*

*Spencer* and General Grey as *Dr. Grey!* Brown once forgot this and called me "Your Majesty" as I was getting into the carriage, and Grant on the box once called Albert "Your Royal Highness," which set us off laughing, but no one observed it.' Strong, vigorous, enthusiastic, bringing, so it seemed, good fortune with her—the Highlanders declared she had 'a lucky foot'—she relished everything—the scrambles and the views and the contretemps and the rough inns with their coarse fare and Brown and Grant waiting at table. She could have gone on for ever and ever, absolutely happy with Albert beside her and Brown at her pony's head. But the time came for turning homewards; alas! the time came for going back to England. She could hardly bear it; she sat disconsolate in her room and watched the snow falling. The last day! Oh! If only she could be snowed up!

# III

The Crimean War brought new experiences, and most of them were pleasant ones. It was pleasant to be patriotic and pugnacious, to look out appropriate prayers to be read in the churches, to have news of glorious victories, and to know oneself, more proudly than ever, the representative of England. With that spontaneity of feeling which was so peculiarly her own, Victoria poured out her emotion, her admiration, her pity, her love, upon her 'dear soldiers.' When she gave them their medals her exultation knew no bounds. 'Noble fellows!' she wrote to the King of the Belgians. 'I own I feel as if these were *my own children*; my heart beats for *them* as for my *nearest and dearest*. They were so touched, so pleased; many, I hear, cried—and they won't hear of giving up their medals to have their names engraved upon them for fear they should *not* receive the *identical one* put into *their hands by me*, which is quite touching. Several came by in a sadly mutilated state.' She and they were at one. They felt that she had done them a splendid honour, and she, with perfect genuineness, shared their feeling. Albert's attitude towards such things was different; there was an austerity in him which quite prohibited the expansions of emotion. When General Williams returned from the heroic defence of Kars and was presented at Court, the quick, stiff, distant bow with which the Prince received him struck like ice upon the beholders. He was a stranger still.

But he had other things to occupy him, more important, surely, than the personal impressions of military officers and people who went to Court. He was at work—ceaselessly at work—on the tremendous task of carrying through the war to a successful conclusion. State papers, despatches, memoranda, poured from him in an overwhelming stream. Between 1853 and 1857 fifty folio volumes were filled with the comments of his pen upon the Eastern question. Nothing would induce him to stop. Weary ministers staggered under the load of his advice; but his advice continued, piling itself up over their writing-tables, and flowing out upon them from red box after red box. Nor was it advice to be ignored. The talent for administration which had reorganised the royal palaces and planned the Great Exhibition asserted

*The Queen's admiration for the heroism of private soldiers in the Crimea led to the institution of the Victoria Cross in 1856, for which all ranks in the Army and Navy were eligible. Inscribed 'For Valour', it was awarded only to men who had served in the presence of the enemy and performed an act of outstanding bravery or devotion. A pension of £10 a year was given with the medal.*

itself no less in the confused complexities of war. Again and again the Prince's suggestions, rejected or unheeded at first, were adopted under the stress of circumstances and found to be full of value. The enrolment of a foreign legion, the establishment of a depôt for troops at Malta, the institution of periodical reports and tabulated returns as to the condition of the army at Sebastopol—such were the contrivances and the achievements of his indefatigable brain. He went further: in a lengthy minute he laid down the lines for a radical reform in the entire administration of the army. This was premature, but his proposal that 'a camp of evolution' should be created, in which troops should be concentrated and drilled, proved to be the germ of Aldershot.

Meanwhile Victoria had made a new friend: she had suddenly been captivated by Napoleon III. Her dislike of him had been strong at first. She considered that he was a disreputable adventurer who had usurped the throne of poor old Louis Philippe; and besides he was hand-in-glove with Lord Palmerston. For a long time, although he was her ally, she was unwilling to meet him; but at last a visit of the Emperor and Empress to England was arranged. Directly he appeared at Windsor her heart began to soften. She found that she was charmed by his quiet manners, his low, soft voice, and by the soothing simplicity of his conversation. The good-will of England was essential to the Emperor's position in Europe, and he had determined to fascinate the Queen. He succeeded. There was something deep within her which responded immediately and vehemently to natures that offered a romantic contrast with her own. Her adoration of Lord Melbourne was intimately interwoven with her half-unconscious appreciation of the exciting unlikeness between herself and that sophisticated, subtle, aristocratical old man. Very different was the quality of her unlikeness to Napoleon; but its quantity was at least as great. From behind the vast solidity of her respectability, her conventionality, her established happiness, she peered out with a strange delicious pleasure at that unfamiliar, darkly-glittering foreign object, moving so meteorically before her, an ambiguous creature of wilfulness and Destiny. And, to her surprise, where she had dreaded antagonisms, she discovered only sympathies. He was, she said, 'so quiet, so simple, *naïf* even, so pleased to be informed about things he does not know, so gentle, so full of tact, dignity, and modesty, so full of kind attention towards us, never saying a word, or doing a thing, which could put me out . . . There is something fascinating, melancholy, and engaging, which draws you to him, in spite of any *prévention* you may have against him, and certainly without the assistance of any outward appearance, though I like his face.' She observed that he rode 'extremely well, and looks well on horseback, as he sits high.' And he danced 'with great dignity and spirit.' Above all, he listened to Albert; listened with the most respectful attention; showed, in fact, how pleased he was 'to be informed about things he did not know'; and afterwards was heard to declare that he had never met the Prince's equal. On one occasion, indeed—but only on one—he had seemed to grow slightly restive. In a diplomatic conversation, 'I expatiated a little on the Holstein question,' wrote the Prince in a memorandum, 'which appeared to bore the Emperor as "*très-compliquée.*"'

Victoria, too, became much attached to the Empress, whose looks and graces she admired without a touch of jealousy. Eugénie, indeed, in the plenitude of her beauty, exquisitely dressed in wonderful Parisian crinolines which set off to perfection her tall and willowy figure, might well have caused some heartburning in the breast of her hostess, who, very short, rather stout, quite plain, in garish middle-class garments, could hardly be expected to feel at her best in such company. But Victoria had no misgivings. To her it mattered nothing that her face turned red in the heat and that her purple pork-pie hat was of last year's fashion, while Eugénie, cool and modish, floated in an infinitude of flounces by her side. She was Queen of England, and was not that enough? It certainly seemed to be; true majesty was hers, and she knew it. More than once, when the two were together in public, it was the woman to whom, as it seemed, nature and art had given so little, who, by the sheer force of an inherent grandeur, completely threw her adorned and beautiful companion into the shade.

There were tears when the moment came for parting, and Victoria felt 'quite wehmüthig,' as her guests went away from Windsor. But before long she and Albert paid a return visit to France, where everything was very delightful, and she drove incognito through the streets of Paris in 'a common bonnet,' and saw a play in the theatre at St. Cloud, and, one evening, at a great party given by the Emperor in her honour at the Château of Versailles, talked a little to a distinguished-looking Prussian gentleman, whose name was Bismarck. Her rooms were furnished so much to her taste that she declared they gave her quite a home feeling—that, if her little dog were there, she should really imagine herself at home. Nothing was said, but three days later her little dog barked a welcome to her as she entered the apartments. The Emperor himself, sparing neither trouble nor expense, had personally arranged the charming surprise. Such were his attentions. She returned to England more enchanted than ever. 'Strange indeed,' she exclaimed, 'are the dispensations and ways of Providence!'

The alliance prospered, and the war drew towards a conclusion. Both the Queen and the Prince, it is true, were most anxious that there should not be a premature peace. When Lord Aberdeen wished to open negotiations Albert attacked him in a '*geharnischten*' letter, while Victoria rode about on horseback reviewing the troops. At last, however, Sebastopol was captured. The news reached Balmoral late at night, and 'in a few minutes Albert and all the gentlemen in every species of attire sallied forth, followed by all the servants, and gradually by all the population of the village—keepers, gillies, workmen—up to the top of the cairn.' A bonfire was lighted, the pipes were played, and guns were shot off. 'About three-quarters of an hour after Albert came down and said the scene had been wild and exciting beyond everything. The people had been drinking healths in whisky and were in great ecstasy.' The 'great ecstasy,' perhaps, would be replaced by other feelings next morning; but at any rate the war was over—though, to be sure, its end seemed as difficult to account for as its beginning. The dispensations and ways of Providence continued to be strange.

*Eugénie de Montijo, wife of Napoleon III, Emperor of the French. Victoria analysed her appeal: 'It is not such great beauty, but such grace, elegance, sweetness, and nature. Her manners are charming; the profile and figure beautiful and particularly distingués.' After Napoleon's downfall in 1870, Victoria remained a staunch friend to Eugénie, who sought refuge in England.*

# IV

An unexpected consequence of the war was a complete change in the relations between the royal pair and Palmerston. The Prince and the Minister drew together over their hostility to Russia, and thus it came about that when Victoria found it necessary to summon her old enemy to form an administration she did so without reluctance. The premiership, too, had a sobering effect upon Palmerston; he grew less impatient and dictatorial; considered with attention the suggestions of the Crown, and was, besides, genuinely impressed by the Prince's ability and knowledge. Friction, no doubt, there still occasionally was, for, while the Queen and the Prince devoted themselves to foreign politics as much as ever, their views, when the war was over, became once more antagonistic to those of the Prime Minister. This was especially the case with regard to Italy. Albert, theoretically the friend of constitutional government, distrusted Cavour, was horrified by Garibaldi, and dreaded the danger of England being drawn into war with Austria. Palmerston, on the other hand, was eager for Italian independence; but he was no longer at the Foreign Office, and the brunt of the royal displeasure had now to be borne by Lord John Russell. In a few years the situation had curiously altered. It was Lord John who now filled the subordinate and the ungrateful rôle; but the Foreign Secretary, in his struggle with the Crown, was supported, instead of opposed, by the Prime Minister. Nevertheless the struggle was fierce, and the policy, by which the vigorous sympathy of England became one of the decisive factors in the final achievement of Italian unity, was only carried through in face of the violent opposition of the Court.

Towards the other European storm-centre, also, the Prince's attitude continued to be very different from that of Palmerston. Albert's great wish was for a united Germany under the leadership of a constitutional and virtuous Prussia; Palmerston did not think that there was much to be said for the scheme, but he took no particular interest in German politics, and was ready enough to agree to a proposal which was warmly supported by both the Prince and the Queen—that the royal Houses of England and Prussia should be united by the marriage of the Princess Royal with the Prussian Crown Prince. Accordingly, when the Princess was not yet fifteen, the Prince, a young man of twenty-four, came over on a visit to Balmoral, and the betrothal took place. Two years later, in 1858, the marriage was celebrated. At the last moment, however, it seemed that there might be a hitch. It was pointed out in Prussia that it was customary for Princes of the blood-royal to be married in Berlin, and it was suggested that there was no reason why the present case should be treated as an exception. When this reached the ears of Victoria, she was speechless with indignation. In a note, emphatic even for Her Majesty, she instructed the Foreign Secretary to tell the Prussian Ambassador 'not to *entertain* the *possibility* of such a question. . . . The Queen *never* could consent to it, both for public and for private reasons, and the assumption of its being *too much* for a Prince Royal of Prussia to *come* over to marry *the Princess Royal of Great Britain in* England is too *absurd* to say the least. . . . Whatever may be the usual practice of Prussian princes, it is not *every* day that one marries the eldest daughter of the Queen of England. The question must therefore be considered as settled and closed.' It was, and the wedding took place in St. James's Chapel. There were great festivities—illuminations, state concerts, immense crowds, and general rejoicings. At Windsor a magnificent banquet was given to the bride and bridegroom in the Waterloo room, at which, Victoria noted in her diary, 'everybody was most friendly and kind about Vicky and full of the universal enthusiasm, of which the Duke of Buccleuch gave us most pleasing instances, he having been in the very thick of the crowd and among the lowest of the low.' Her feelings during several days had been growing more and more emotional, and when the time came for the young couple to depart she very nearly broke down—but not quite. 'Poor dear child!' she wrote afterwards. 'I clasped her in my arms and blessed her, and knew not what to say. I kissed good Fritz and pressed his hand again and again. He was unable to speak and the tears were in his eyes. I embraced them both again at the carriage door, and Albert got into the carriage, an open one, with them and Bertie. . . . The band struck up. I wished good-bye to the good Perponchers. General Schreckenstein was much affected. I pressed his hand, and the good Dean's, and then went quickly upstairs.'

Albert, as well as General Schreckenstein, was much affected. He was losing his favourite child, whose opening intelligence had already begun to display a marked resemblance to his own—an adoring pupil, who, in a few years, might have become an almost adequate companion. An ironic fate had determined that the daughter who was taken from him should be sympathetic, clever, interested in the arts and sciences, and endowed with a strong taste for memoranda, while not a single one of these qualities could be discovered in the son who remained. For certainly the Prince of Wales did not take after his father. Victoria's prayer had been unanswered, and with each succeeding year it became more obvious that Bertie was a true scion of the House of Brunswick. But these evidences of innate characteristics served only to redouble the efforts of his parents; it still might not be too late to incline the young branch, by ceaseless pressure and careful fastenings, to grow in the proper direction. Everything was tried. The boy was sent on a continental tour with a picked body of tutors, but the results were unsatisfactory. At his father's request he kept a diary which, on his return, was inspected by the Prince. It was found to be distressingly meagre: what a multitude of highly interesting reflections might have been arranged under the heading: 'The First Prince of Wales visiting the Pope!' But there was not a single one. 'Le jeune prince plaisait à tout le monde,' old Metternich reported to Guizot, 'mais avait l'air embarrassé et très triste.' On his seventeenth birthday a memorandum was drawn up over the names of the Queen and the Prince informing their eldest son that he was now entering upon the period of manhood, and directing him henceforward to perform the duties of a Christian gentleman. 'Life is composed of duties,' said the memorandum, 'and in the due, punctual and cheerful performance of them the true Christian, true soldier, and true gentleman is recognised. . . . A new sphere of life will open for you in which you will have to be taught what to do and what not to do, a subject requiring study more important than any

*Victoria, the Princess Royal, on the day of her wedding to the Crown Prince of Prussia, 25 January 1858. The Queen wrote, 'it is terrible to give up one's poor child'; but she was pleased that the Princess's popularity with the English public showed, 'in spite of a few newspaper follies and absurdities, how really sound and monarchical everything is in this country'. The eldest son of their marriage, the future Kaiser Wilhelm II of Germany, was Victoria's favourite grandchild.*

in which you have hitherto been engaged.' On receipt of the memorandum Bertie burst into tears. At the same time another memorandum was drawn up, headed 'Confidential: for the guidance of the gentlemen appointed to attend on the Prince of Wales.' This long and elaborate document laid down 'certain principles' by which the 'conduct and demeanour' of the gentlemen were to be regulated 'and which it is thought may conduce to the benefit of the Prince of Wales.' 'The qualities which distinguish a gentleman in society,' continued this remarkable paper, 'are:—

(1) His appearance, his deportment and dress.

(2) The character of his relations with, and treatment of, others.

(3) His desire and power to acquit himself creditably in conversation or whatever is the occupation of the society with which he mixes.'

A minute and detailed analysis of these sub-headings followed, filling several pages, and the memorandum ended with a final exhortation to the gentlemen: 'If they will duly appreciate the responsibility of their position, and taking the points above laid down as the outline, will exercise their own good sense in acting *upon all occasions* upon these principles, thinking no point of detail too minute to be important, but maintaining one steady consistent line of conduct, they may render essential service to the young Prince and justify the flattering selection made by the royal parents.' A year later the young Prince was sent to Oxford, where the greatest care was taken that he should not mix with the undergraduates. Yes, everything had been tried—everything . . . with one single exception. The experiment had never been made of letting Bertie enjoy himself. But why should it have been? 'Life is composed of duties.' What possible place could there be for enjoyment in the existence of a Prince of Wales?

The same year which deprived Albert of the Princess Royal brought him another and a still more serious loss. The Baron had paid his last visit to England. For twenty years, as he himself said in a letter to the King of the Belgians, he had performed 'the laborious and exhausting office of a paternal friend and trusted adviser' to the Prince and the Queen. He was seventy; he was tired, physically and mentally; it was time to go. He returned to his home in Coburg, exchanging, once for all, the momentous secrecies of European statecraft for the tittle-tattle of a provincial capital and the gossip of family life. In his stiff chair by the fire he nodded now over old stories—not of emperors and generals, but of neighbours and relatives and the domestic adventures of long ago—the burning of his father's library—and the goat that ran upstairs to his sister's room and ran twice round the table and then ran down again. Dyspepsia and depression still attacked him; but, looking back over his life, he was not dissatisfied. His conscience was clear. 'I have worked as long as I had strength to work,' he said, 'and for a purpose no one can impugn. The consciousness of this is my reward—the only one which I desired to earn.'

Apparently, indeed, his 'purpose' had been accomplished. By his wisdom, his patience, and his example he had brought about, in the fullness of time, the miraculous metamorphosis of which he had dreamed. The Prince was his creation. An indefatigable toiler, presiding, for the highest ends, over a great nation—that was his achievement; and he looked upon his work and it was

*Princess Helena, known as 'Lenchen', was the Queen's fifth child. Born in 1846, she disgraced herself at her christening by sucking her thumb and crying; much later the Queen found her an invaluable help and companion, and persuaded her to settle at Frogmore instead of living abroad after her marriage to the penniless, cigar-smoking Prince Christian of Schleswig-Holstein. The couple had two daughters (about whom Queen Victoria once sent the bulletin, 'Children very well but poor little Louise very ugly') and two sons—the elder, Christian Victor, known as Prince 'Christle', was to die of enteric fever on active service in the Boer War. Princess Helena lived until 1923.*

good. But had the Baron no misgivings? Did he never wonder whether, perhaps, he might have accomplished not too little but too much? How subtle and how dangerous are the snares which fate lays for the wariest of men! Albert, certainly, seemed to be everything that Stockmar could have wished—virtuous, industrious, persevering, intelligent. And yet—why was it?—all was not well with him. He was sick at heart.

For in spite of everything he had never reached to happiness. His work, for which at last he came to crave with an almost morbid appetite, was a solace and not a cure; the dragon of his dissatisfaction devoured with dark relish that ever-growing tribute of laborious days and nights; but it was hungry still. The causes of his melancholy were hidden, mysterious, unanalysable perhaps— too deeply rooted in the innermost recesses of his temperament for the eye of reason to apprehend. There were contradictions in his nature, which, to some of those who knew him best, made him seem an inexplicable enigma: he was severe and gentle; he was modest and scornful; he longed for affection and he was cold. He was lonely, not merely with the loneliness of exile but with the loneliness of conscious and unrecognised superiority. He had the pride, at once resigned and overweening, of a doctrinaire. And yet to say that he was simply a doctrinaire would be a false description; for the pure doctrinaire rejoices always in an internal contentment, and Albert was very far from doing that. There was something that he wanted that he could never get. What was it? Some absolute, some ineffable sympathy? Some extraordinary, some sublime success? Possibly, it was a mixture of both. To dominate and to be understood! To conquer, by the same triumphant influence, the submission and the appreciation of men—that would be worth while indeed! But, to such imaginations, he saw too clearly how faint were the responses of his actual environment. Who was there who appreciated him, really and truly? Who *could* appreciate him in England? And, if the gentle virtue of an inward excellence availed so little, could he expect more from the hard ways of skill and force? The terrible land of his exile loomed before him a frigid, an impregnable mass. Doubtless he had made some slight impression: it was true that he had gained the respect of his fellow workers, that his probity, his industry, his exactitude, had been recognised, that he was a highly influential, an extremely important man. But how far, how very far, was all this from the goal of his ambitions! How feeble and futile his efforts seemed against the enormous coagulation of dullness, of folly, of slackness, of ignorance, of confusion that confronted him! He might have the strength or the ingenuity to make some small change for the better here or there—to rearrange some detail, to abolish some anomaly, to insist upon some obvious reform; but the heart of the appalling organism remained untouched. England lumbered on, impervious and self-satisfied, in her old intolerable course. He threw himself across the path of the monster with rigid purpose and set teeth, but he was brushed aside. Yes! even Palmerston was still unconquered—was still there to afflict him with his jauntiness, his muddle-headedness, his utter lack of principle. It was too much. Neither nature nor the Baron had given him a sanguine spirit; the seeds of pessimism, once lodged within him, flourished in a propitious soil. He:

*Princess Louise was the Queen's sixth child, born in March 1848 and named after Prince Albert's mother. A slow developer at first, she grew up to be a talented sculptor. On her twentieth birthday the Queen felt able to describe her as 'a clever, dear girl (and who would some years ago have thought it?)' Two years later Princess Louise fell in love with Lord Lorne, son of the Duke of Argyll. Although the Princess Royal disapproved of a match between her sister and 'a subject' the Queen supported the young couple in the hope of bringing 'new blood' into the royal family. Unfortunately, the marriage turned out badly; Louise and her husband lived apart and there were no children.*

135

'questioned things, and did not find
One that would answer to his mind;
And all the world appeared unkind.'

He believed that he was a failure and he began to despair.

Yet Stockmar had told him that he must 'never relax,' and he never would. He would go on, working to the utmost and striving for the highest, to the bitter end. His industry grew almost maniacal. Earlier and earlier was the green lamp lighted; more vast grew the correspondence; more searching the examination of the newspapers; the interminable memoranda more punctilious, analytical, and precise. His very recreations became duties. He enjoyed himself by time-table, went deer-stalking with meticulous gusto, and made puns at lunch—it was the right thing to do. The mechanism worked with astonishing efficiency, but it never rested and it was never oiled. In dry exactitude the innumerable cog-wheels perpetually revolved. No, whatever happened, the Prince would not relax; he had absorbed the doctrines of Stockmar too thoroughly. He knew what was right, and, at all costs, he would pursue it. That was certain. But alas! in this our life what are the certainties? 'In nothing be over-zealous!' says an old Greek. 'The due measure in all the works of man is best. For often one who zealously pushes towards some excellence, though he be pursuing a gain, is really being led utterly astray by the will of some Power, which makes those things that are evil seem to him good, and those things seem to him evil that are for his advantage.' Surely, both the Prince and the Baron might have learnt something from the frigid wisdom of Theognis.

Victoria noticed that her husband sometimes seemed to be depressed and overworked. She tried to cheer him up. Realising uneasily that he was still regarded as a foreigner, she hoped that by conferring upon him the title of Prince Consort (1857) she would improve his position in the country. 'The Queen has a right to claim that her husband should be an Englishman,' she wrote. But unfortunately, in spite of the Royal Letters Patent, Albert remained as foreign as before; and as the years passed his dejection deepened. She worked with him, she watched over him, she walked with him through the woods at Osborne, while he whistled to the nightingales, as he had whistled once at Rosenau so long ago. When his birthday came round, she took the greatest pains to choose him presents that he would really like. In 1858, when he was thirty-nine, she gave him 'a picture of Beatrice, life-size, in oil, by Horsley, a complete collection of photographic views of Gotha and the country round, which I had taken by Bedford, and a paper-weight of Balmoral granite and deers' teeth, designed by Vicky.' Albert was of course delighted, and his merriment at the family gathering was more pronounced than ever: and yet . . . what was there that was wrong?

No doubt it was his health. He was wearing himself out in the service of the country; and certainly his constitution, as Stockmar had perceived from the first, was ill-adapted to meet a serious strain. He was easily upset; he constantly suffered from minor ailments. His appearance in itself was enough to indicate the infirmity of his physical powers. The handsome youth of twenty years since with the flashing eyes and the soft complexion had grown

*The Queen, the devoted wife, admires a portrait of 'that most perfect of human beings, my adored Husband!' The royal couple often commissioned pictures and statuettes of themselves, their children and their pets; these mementoes would then be exchanged as Christmas or birthday presents. In her widowhood Queen Victoria viewed representations of Albert almost as holy relics, and made a practice of giving these memorial images as christening gifts to her increasing numbers of grandchildren.*

136

into a sallow, tired-looking man, whose body, in its stoop and its loose fleshiness, betrayed the sedentary labourer, and whose head was quite bald on the top. Unkind critics, who had once compared Albert to an operatic tenor, might have remarked that there was something of the butler about him now. Beside Victoria, he presented a painful contrast. She, too, was stout, but it was with the plumpness of a vigorous matron; and an eager vitality was everywhere visible—in her energetic bearing, her protruding, enquiring glances, her small, fat, capable, and commanding hands. If only, by some sympathetic magic, she could have conveyed into that portly, flabby figure, that dessicated and discouraged brain, a measure of the stamina and the self-assurance which were so pre-eminently hers!

But suddenly she was reminded that there were other perils besides those of ill-health. During a visit to Coburg in 1860, the Prince was very nearly killed in a carriage accident. He escaped with a few cuts and bruises; but Victoria's alarm was extreme, though she concealed it. 'It is when the Queen feels most deeply,' she wrote afterwards, 'that she always appears calmest, and she could not and dared not allow herself to speak of what might have been, or even to admit to herself (and she cannot and dare not now) the entire danger, for her head would turn!' Her agitation, in fact, was only surpassed by her thankfulness to God. She felt, she said, that she could not rest 'without doing something to mark permanently her feelings,' and she decided that she would endow a charity in Coburg. '£1,000, or even £2,000, given either at once, or in instalments yearly, would not, in the Queen's opinion, be too much.' Eventually, the smaller sum having been fixed upon, it was invested in a trust, called the 'Victoria-Stift,' in the names of the Burgomaster and chief clergyman of Coburg, who were directed to distribute the interest yearly among a certain number of young men and women of exemplary character belonging to the humbler ranks of life.

Shortly afterwards the Queen underwent, for the first time in her life, the actual experience of close personal loss. Early in 1861 the Duchess of Kent was taken seriously ill, and in March she died. The event overwhelmed Victoria. With a morbid intensity, she filled her diary for pages with minute descriptions of her mother's last hours, her dissolution, and her corpse, interspersed with vehement apostrophes, and the agitated outpourings of emotional reflection. In the grief of the present the disagreements of the past were totally forgotten. It was the horror and the mystery of Death—Death present and actual—that seized upon the imagination of the Queen. Her whole being, so instinct with vitality, recoiled in agony from the grim spectacle of the triumph of that awful power. Her own mother, with whom she had lived so closely and so long that she had become a part almost of her existence, had fallen into nothingness before her very eyes! She tried to forget it, but she could not. Her lamentations continued with a strange abundance, a strange persistency. It was almost as if, by some mysterious and unconscious precognition, she realised that for her, in an especial manner, that grisly Majesty had a dreadful dart in store.

For indeed, before the year was out, a far more terrible blow was to fall upon her. Albert, who had for long been suffering from sleeplessness, went, on a cold and drenching day towards the end of November, to inspect the

*The Prince Consort in middle age, robbed by overwork and anxiety of his youthful good looks. As he approached forty he began to suffer from a variety of ailments which the robust Queen did not always take seriously. 'Papa never allows he is any better or will try to get over it,' she complained to Vicky when the Prince felt wretched with stomach trouble and inflamed gums. 'He makes such a miserable face that people always think he's very ill. It is quite the contrary with me always; I never show it, so people believe I am never ill or ever suffer. His nervous system is easily excited and irritated, and he's so completely overpowered by everything'.*

buildings for the new Military Academy at Sandhurst. On his return, it was clear that the fatigue and exposure to which he had been subjected had seriously affected his health. He was attacked by rheumatism, his sleeplessness continued, and he complained that he felt thoroughly unwell. Three days later a painful duty obliged him to visit Cambridge. The Prince of Wales, who had been placed at that University in the previous year, was behaving in such a manner that a parental visit and a parental admonition had become necessary. The disappointed father, suffering in mind and body, carried through his task; but, on his return journey to Windsor, he caught a fatal chill. During the next week he gradually grew weaker and more miserable. Yet, depressed and enfeebled as he was, he continued to work. It so happened that at that very moment a grave diplomatic crisis had arisen. Civil war had broken out in America, and it seemed as if England, owing to a violent quarrel with the Northern States, was upon the point of being drawn into the conflict. A severe despatch by Lord John Russell was submitted to the Queen; and the Prince perceived that, if it were sent off unaltered, war would be the almost inevitable consequence. At seven o'clock on the morning of December 1, he rose from his bed, and with a quavering hand wrote a series of suggestions for the alteration of the draft, by which its language might be softened, and a way left open for a peaceful solution of the question. These changes were accepted by the Government, and war was averted. It was the Prince's last memorandum.

He had always declared that he viewed the prospect of death with equanimity. 'I do not cling to life,' he had once said to Victoria. 'You do; but I set no store by it.' And then he added: 'I am sure, if I had a severe illness, I should give up at once, I should not struggle for life. I have no tenacity of life.' He had judged correctly. Before he had been ill many days, he told a friend that he was convinced he would not recover. He sank and sank. Nevertheless, if his case had been properly understood and skilfully treated from the first, he might conceivably have been saved; but the doctors failed to diagnose his symptoms; and it is noteworthy that his principal physician was Sir James Clark. When it was suggested that other advice should be taken, Sir James pooh-poohed the idea: 'there was no cause for alarm,' he said. But the strange illness grew worse. At last, after a letter of fierce remonstrance from Palmerston, Dr. Watson was sent for; and Dr. Watson saw at once that he had come too late. The Prince was in the grip of typhoid fever. 'I think that everything so far is satisfactory,' said Sir James Clark. •

The restlessness and the acute suffering of the earlier days gave place to a settled torpor and an ever-deepening gloom. Once the failing patient asked for music—'a fine chorale at a distance'; and a piano having been placed in the adjoining room, Princess Alice played on it some of Luther's hymns, after which the Prince repeated 'The Rock of Ages.' Sometimes his mind wandered; sometimes the distant past came rushing upon him; he heard the birds in the early morning, and was at Rosenau again, a boy. Or Victoria would come and read to him 'Peveril of the Peak,' and he showed that he could follow the story, and then she would bend over him, and he would murmur 'liebes Frauchen' and 'gutes Weibchen,' stroking her cheek. Her distress and her agitation were great, but she was not seriously frightened.

*The eighteen-year-old Princess Alice reads to her father during his last illness; she proved a great help both in nursing the invalid and calming the anxious Queen. At times the dying Prince asked for music, which Alice would play on the piano in an adjoining room. She and her mother took turns in reading to him, often from Sir Walter Scott's novel,* Peveril of the Peak. *The year before, Victoria had acknowledged, in a letter to Stockmar, that all was not well with Albert: 'I wish I could think', she wrote, 'I had made one as happy as he has made me. But this is not for want of love and devotion.'*

Buoyed up by her own abundant energies, she would not believe that Albert's might prove unequal to the strain. She refused to face such a hideous possibility. She declined to see Dr. Watson. Why should she? Had not Sir James Clark assured her that all would be well? Only two days before the end, which was seen now to be almost inevitable by everyone about her, she wrote, full of apparent confidence, to the King of the Belgians: 'I do not sit up with him at night,' she said, 'as I could be of no use; and there is nothing to cause alarm.' The Princess Alice tried to tell her the truth, but her hopefulness would not be daunted. On the morning of December 14, Albert, just as she had expected, seemed to be better; perhaps the crisis was over. But in the course of the day there was a serious relapse. Then at last she allowed herself to see that she was standing on the edge of an appalling gulf. The whole family was summoned, and, one after another, the children took a silent farewell of their father. 'It was a terrible moment,' Victoria wrote in her diary, 'but, thank God! I was able to command myself, and to be perfectly calm, and remained sitting by his side.' He murmured something, but she could not hear what it was; she thought he was speaking in French. Then all at once he began to arrange his hair, 'just as he used to do when well and he was dressing.' 'Es ist kleines Frauchen,' she whispered to him; and he seemed to understand. For a moment, towards the evening, she went into another room, but was immediately called back: she saw at a glance that a ghastly change had taken place. As she knelt by the bed, he breathed deeply, breathed gently, breathed at last no more. His features became perfectly rigid. She shrieked—one long wild shriek that rang through the terror-stricken Castle—and understood that she had lost him for ever.

# 7: WIDOWHOOD

THE death of the Prince Consort was the central turning-point in the history of Queen Victoria. She herself felt that her true life had ceased with her husband's, and that the remainder of her days upon earth was of a twilight nature—an epilogue to a drama that was done. Nor is it possible that her biographer should escape a similar impression. For him, too, there is a darkness over the latter half of that long career. The first forty-two years of the Queen's life are illuminated by a great and varied quantity of authentic information. With Albert's death a veil descends. Only occasionally, at fitful and disconnected intervals, does it lift for a moment or two; a few main outlines, a few remarkable details may be discerned; the rest is all conjecture and ambiguity. Thus, though the Queen survived her great bereavement for almost as many years as she had lived before it, the chronicle of those years can bear no proportion to the tale of her earlier life. We must be content in our ignorance with a brief and summary relation.

The sudden removal of the Prince was not merely a matter of overwhelming personal concern to Victoria; it was an event of national, of European importance. He was only forty-two, and in the ordinary course of nature he might have been expected to live at least thirty years longer. Had he done so it can hardly be doubted that the whole development of the English polity would have been changed. Already at the time of his death he filled a unique place in English public life; already among the inner circle of politicians he was accepted as a necessary and useful part of the mechanism of the State. Lord Clarendon, for instance, spoke of his death as 'a national calamity of far greater importance than the public dream of,' and lamented the loss of his 'sagacity and foresight,' which, he declared, would have been 'more than ever valuable' in the event of an American war. And, as time

*The Queen joins in Hallowe'en celebrations at Balmoral in 1867: 'We had been driving,' she wrote, 'but turned back in time for the celebration. Close to Donald Stewart's house we were met by two ghillies, bearing torches. Louise got out and took one, walking by the side of the carriage like one of the witches in Macbeth. As we approached Balmoral, the keepers, with their wives and children, the ghillies, and other people met us, all with torches, Brown also carrying one. We got out at the house, where Leopold joined us, and a torch was also given to him. We walked round the house with Ross playing the pipes, going down the steps of the terrace. . . . After this, a bonfire was made of all the torches, close to the house, and they danced reels while Ross played the pipes.' After her bereavement the Queen spent much of her time in Scotland, where she had been so happy with Albert; she continued to take a keen interest in Scottish pastimes and customs.*

went on, the Prince's influence must have enormously increased. For, in addition to his intellectual and moral qualities, he enjoyed, by virtue of his position, one supreme advantage which every other holder of high office in the country was without: he was permanent. Politicians came and went, but the Prince was perpetually installed at the centre of affairs. Who can doubt that, towards the end of the century, such a man, grown grey in the service of the nation, virtuous, intelligent, and with the unexampled experience of a whole lifetime of government, would have acquired an extraordinary prestige? If, in his youth, he had been able to pit the Crown against the mighty Palmerston and to come off with equal honours from the contest, of what might he not have been capable in his old age? What Minister, however able, however popular, could have withstood the wisdom, the irreproachability, the vast prescriptive authority, of the venerable Prince? It is easy to imagine how, under such a ruler, an attempt might have been made to convert England into a State as exactly organised, as elaborately trained, as efficiently equipped, and as autocratically controlled, as Prussia herself. Then perhaps, eventually, under some powerful leader—a Gladstone or a Bright— the democratic forces in the country might have rallied together, and a struggle might have followed in which the Monarchy would have been shaken to its foundations. Or, on the other hand, Disraeli's hypothetical prophecy might have come true. 'With Prince Albert,' he said, 'we have buried our sovereign. This German Prince has governed England for twenty-one years with a wisdom and energy such as none of our kings have ever shown. . . . If he had outlived some of our "old stagers" he would have given us the blessings of absolute government.'

The English Constitution—that indescribable entity—is a living thing, growing with the growth of men, and assuming ever-varying forms in accordance with the subtle and complex laws of human character. It is the child of wisdom and chance. The wise men of 1688 moulded it into the shape we know; but the chance that George I could not speak English gave it one of its essential peculiarities—the system of a Cabinet independent of the Crown and subordinate to the Prime Minister. The wisdom of Lord Grey saved it from petrifaction and destruction, and set it upon the path of Democracy. Then chance intervened once more; a female sovereign happened to marry an able and pertinacious man; and it seemed likely that an element which had been quiescent within it for years—the element of irresponsible administrative power—was about to become its predominant characteristic and to change completely the direction of its growth. But what chance gave, chance took away. The Consort perished in his prime; and the English Constitution, dropping the dead limb with hardly a tremor, continued its mysterious life as if he had never been.

One human being, and one alone, felt the full force of what had happened. The Baron, by his fireside at Coburg, suddenly saw the tremendous fabric of his creation crash down into sheer and irremediable ruin. Albert was gone, and he had lived in vain. Even his blackest hypochondria had never envisioned quite so miserable a catastrophe. Victoria wrote to him, visited him, tried to console him by declaring with passionate conviction that she would carry on her husband's work. He smiled a sad smile and looked into the

*For Queen and subjects alike, 'going into mourning' was an important aspect of bereavement, though not everyone kept up official mourning for as long as the Queen's ten years. Mourning clothes and accessories were often needed quickly, and so were amongst the first garments to be supplied ready-made by a developing retail trade. Mantles, caps, bonnets, jackets, cloaks, collars, cuffs and similar articles could be selected at establishments like Jay's Mourning Warehouse in Regent Street, where they might be packed into boxes lined with special paper appropriately patterned with hearses, tombstones and angels.*

fire. Then he murmured that he was going where Albert was—that he would not be long. He shrank into himself. His children clustered round him and did their best to comfort him, but it was useless: the Baron's heart was broken. He lingered for eighteen months, and then, with his pupil, explored the shadow and the dust.

## II

With appalling suddenness Victoria had exchanged the serene radiance of happiness for the utter darkness of woe. In the first dreadful moments those about her had feared that she might lose her reason, but the iron strain within her held firm, and in the intervals between the intense paroxysms of grief it was observed that the Queen was calm. She remembered, too, that Albert had always disapproved of exaggerated manifestations of feeling, and her one remaining desire was to do nothing but what he would have wished. Yet there were moments when her royal anguish would brook no restraints. One day she sent for the Duchess of Sutherland, and, leading her to the Prince's room, fell prostrate before his clothes in a flood of weeping, while she adjured the Duchess to tell her whether the beauty of Albert's character had ever been surpassed. At other times a feeling akin to indignation swept over her. 'The poor fatherless baby of eight months,' she wrote to the King of the Belgians, 'is now the utterly heart-broken and crushed widow of forty-two! My *life* as a *happy* one is *ended!* The world is gone for *me!* . . . Oh! to be cut off in the prime of life—to see our pure, happy, quiet, domestic life, which *alone* enabled me to bear my *much* disliked position, CUT OFF at forty-two—when I *had* hoped with such instinctive certainty that God never *would* part us, and would let us grow old together (though *he* always talked of the shortness of life)—is *too awful,* too cruel!' The tone of outraged Majesty seems to be discernible. Did she wonder in her heart of hearts how the Deity could have dared?

But all other emotions gave way before her over-mastering determination to continue, absolutely unchanged, and for the rest of her life on earth, her reverence, her obedience, her idolatry. 'I am anxious to repeat *one* thing,' she told her uncle, 'and *that one* is *my firm* resolve, my *irrevocable decision,* viz. that *his* wishes—*his* plans—about everything, *his* views about *every* thing are to be *my law!* And *no human power* will make me swerve from *what he* decided and wished.' She grew fierce, she grew furious, at the thought of any possible intrusion between her and her desire. Her uncle was coming to visit her, and it flashed upon her that *he* might try to interfere with her and seek to 'rule the roast' as of old. She would give him a hint. 'I am *also determined,*' she wrote, 'that *no one* person—may *he* be ever so good, ever so devoted among my servants—is to lead or guide or dictate *to me.* I know *how he* would disapprove it . . . Though miserably weak and utterly shattered, my spirit rises when I think *any* wish or plan of his is to be touched or changed, or I am to be *made to do* anything.' She ended her letter in grief and affection. She was, she said, his 'ever wretched but devoted child, Victoria R.' And then she looked at the date: it was the 24th of December. An agonising pang assailed her, and she dashed down a postscript—'What a Xmas! I won't think of it.'

*The Glasallt Shiel, Queen Victoria's Highland retreat, was built at the end of Loch Muick in 1868. It was not associated with memories of Albert, and her Private Secretary Ponsonby noted that a stay there always improved her spirits. She enjoyed the relatively small scale of its fifteen rooms: 'Felt quite lost in my big sitting-room after the snug little one at the Glasallt,' she commented once on her return to Balmoral.*

At first, in the tumult of her distresses, she declared that she could not see her Ministers, and the Princess Alice, assisted by Sir Charles Phipps, the keeper of the Privy Purse, performed, to the best of her ability, the functions of an intermediary. After a few weeks, however, the Cabinet, through Lord John Russell, ventured to warn the Queen that this could not continue. She realised that they were right: Albert would have agreed with them; and so she sent for the Prime Minister. But when Lord Palmerston arrived at Osborne, in the pink of health, brisk, with his whiskers freshly dyed, and dressed in a brown overcoat, light grey trousers, green gloves, and blue studs, he did not create a very good impression.

Nevertheless, she had grown attached to her old enemy, and the thought of a political change filled her with agitated apprehensions. The Government, she knew, might fall at any moment; she felt she could not face such an eventuality; and therefore, six months after the death of the Prince, she took the unprecedented step of sending a private message to Lord Derby, the leader of the Opposition, to tell him that she was not in a fit state of mind or body to undergo the anxiety of a change of Government, and that if he turned the present Ministers out of office it would be at the risk of sacrificing her life—or her reason. When this message reached Lord Derby he was considerably surprised. 'Dear me!' was his cynical comment. 'I didn't think she was so fond of them as *that*.'

Though the violence of her perturbations gradually subsided, her cheerfulness did not return. For months, for years, she continued in settled gloom. Her life became one of almost complete seclusion. Arrayed in thickest *crêpe*, she passed dolefully from Windsor to Osborne, from Osborne to Balmoral. Rarely visiting the capital, refusing to take any part in the ceremonies of state, shutting herself off from the slightest intercourse with society, she became almost as unknown to her subjects as some potentate of the East. They might murmur, but they did not understand. What had she to do with empty shows and vain enjoyments? No! She was absorbed by very different preoccupations. She was the devoted guardian of a sacred trust. Her place was in the inmost shrine of the house of mourning—where she alone had the right to enter, where she could feel the effluence of a mysterious presence, and interpret, however faintly and feebly, the promptings of a still living soul. That, and that only, was her glorious, her terrible duty. For terrible indeed it was. As the years passed her depression seemed to deepen and her loneliness to grow more intense. 'I am on a dreary sad pinnacle of solitary grandeur,' she said. Again and again she felt that she could bear her situation no longer—that she would sink under the strain. And then, instantly, that Voice spoke: and she braced herself once more to perform, with minute conscientiousness, her grim and holy task.

Above all else, what she had to do was to make her own the master-impulse of Albert's life—she must work, as he had worked, in the service of the country. That vast burden of toil which he had taken upon his shoulders it was now for her to bear. She assumed the gigantic load; and naturally she staggered under it. While he had lived, she had worked, indeed, with regularity and application; but it was work made easy, made delicious, by his care, his forethought, his advice, and his infallibility. The mere sound of his voice, asking her to sign a paper, had thrilled her; in such a presence she could have laboured gladly for ever. But now there was a hideous change. Now there were no neat piles and docketings under the green lamp; now there were no simple explanations of difficult matters; now there was nobody to tell her what was right and what was wrong. She had her secretaries, no doubt: there were Sir Charles Phipps, and General Grey, and Sir Thomas Biddulph; and they did their best. But they were mere subordinates: the whole weight of initiative and responsibility rested upon her alone. For so it had to be. 'I am *determined*'—had she not declared it?—'that *no one* person is to lead or guide or dictate *to me*'; anything else would be a betrayal of her trust. She would follow the Prince in all things. He had refused to delegate authority; he had examined into every detail with his own eyes; he had made it a rule never to sign a paper without having first, not merely read it, but made notes on it too. She would do the same. She sat from morning till night surrounded by huge heaps of despatch-boxes, reading and writing at her desk—at her desk, alas! which stood alone now in the room.

Within two years of Albert's death a violent disturbance in foreign politics put Victoria's faithfulness to a crucial test. The fearful Schleswig-Holstein dispute, which had been smouldering for more than a decade, showed signs of bursting out into conflagration. The complexity of the questions at issue was indescribable. 'Only three people,' said Palmerston, 'have ever really understood the Schleswig-Holstein business—the Prince Consort, who is dead—a German professor, who has gone mad—and I, who have forgotten

*This copy of William Theed's statue of Prince Albert in Highland dress was unveiled at Balmoral in 1867. Other Scottish memorials included a cairn on the top of Craig Lowrigan, inscribed 'To the Memory of Albert, the Great and Good, Prince Consort.'*

145

*The Prince of Wales married the eighteen-year-old Danish Princess Alexandra in St. George's Chapel, Windsor, on 10 May 1863. Dressed in deep mourning, the Queen watched from the 'royal closet' as Jenny Lind sang a chorale composed by the late Prince Consort, and little Prince Wilhelm of Prussia bit the bare knees of his kilted royal uncles. Queen Victoria hoped that a wife like 'Alix' might be the 'SALVATION' of the pleasure-loving Bertie, but expressed doubts as to their suitability as parents. 'Are you aware', she asked her daughter Vicky, 'that Alix has the smallest head ever seen? I dread that—with his small empty brain—very much for future children.'*

all about it.' But, though the Prince might be dead, had he not left a vicegerent behind him? Victoria threw herself into the seething embroilment with the vigour of inspiration. She devoted hours daily to the study of the affair in all its windings; but she had a clue through the labyrinth: whenever the question had been discussed, Albert, she recollected it perfectly, had always taken the side of Prussia. Her course was clear. She became an ardent champion of the Prussian point of view. It was a legacy of the Prince, she said. She did not realise that the Prussia of the Prince's days was dead, and that a new Prussia, the Prussia of Bismarck, was born. Perhaps Palmerston, with his queer prescience, instinctively apprehended the new danger; at any rate, he and Lord John were agreed upon the necessity of supporting

Denmark against Prussia's claims. But opinion was sharply divided, not only in the country but in the Cabinet. For eighteen months the controversy raged; while the Queen, with persistent vehemence, opposed the Prime Minister and the Foreign Secretary. When at last the final crisis arose—when it seemed possible that England would join forces with Denmark in a war against Prussia—Victoria's agitation grew febrile in its intensity. Towards her German relatives she preserved a discreet appearance of impartiality; but she poured out upon her Ministers a flood of appeals, protests, and expostulations. She invoked the sacred cause of Peace. 'The only chance of preserving peace for Europe,' she wrote, 'is by not assisting Denmark, who has brought this entirely upon herself. . . . The Queen suffers much, and her nerves are more and more totally shattered. . . . But though all this anxiety is wearing her out, it will not shake her firm purpose of resisting any attempt to involve this country in a mad and useless combat.' She was, she declared, 'prepared to make a stand,' even if the resignation of the Foreign Secretary should follow. 'The Queen,' she told Lord Granville, 'is completely exhausted by the anxiety and suspense, and misses her beloved husband's help, advice, support, and love in an overwhelming manner.' She was so worn out by her efforts for peace that she could 'hardly hold up her head or hold her pen.' England did not go to war, and Denmark was left to her fate; but how far the attitude of the Queen contributed to this result it is impossible, with our present knowledge, to say. On the whole, however, it seems probable that the determining factor in the situation was the powerful peace party in the Cabinet rather than the imperious and pathetic pressure of Victoria.

It is, at any rate, certain that the Queen's enthusiasm for the sacred cause of peace was short-lived. Within a few months her mind had completely altered. Her eyes were opened to the true nature of Prussia, whose designs upon Austria were about to culminate in the Seven Weeks' War. Veering precipitately from one extreme to the other, she now urged her Ministers to interfere by force of arms in support of Austria. But she urged in vain.

Her political activity, no more than her social seclusion, was approved by the public. As the years passed, and the royal mourning remained as unrelieved as ever, the animadversions grew more general and more severe. It was observed that the Queen's protracted privacy not only cast a gloom over high society, not only deprived the populace of its pageantry, but also exercised a highly deleterious effect upon the dress-making, millinery, and hosiery trades. This latter consideration carried great weight. At last, early in 1864, the rumour spread that Her Majesty was about to go out of mourning, and there was much rejoicing in the newspapers; but unfortunately it turned out that the rumour was quite without foundation. Victoria, with her own hand, wrote a letter to *The Times* to say so. 'This idea,' she declared, 'cannot be too explicitly contradicted.' 'The Queen,' the letter continued, 'heartily appreciates the desire of her subjects to see her, and whatever she *can* do to gratify them in this loyal and affectionate wish, she *will* do. . . . But there are other and higher duties than those of mere representation which are now thrown upon the Queen, alone and unassisted—duties which she cannot neglect without injury to the public service, which weigh unceasingly upon her, overwhelming her with work and anxiety.' The justification might have been considered more cogent had it not been known that those 'other and higher duties' emphasised by the Queen consisted for the most part of an attempt to counteract the foreign policy of Lord Palmerston and Lord John Russell. A large section—perhaps a majority—of the nation were violent partisans of Denmark in the Schleswig-Holstein quarrel; and Victoria's support of Prussia was widely denounced. A wave of unpopularity, which reminded old observers of the period preceding the Queen's marriage more than twenty-five years before, was beginning to rise. The press was rude; Lord Ellenborough attacked the Queen in the House of Lords; there were curious whispers in high quarters that she had had thoughts of abdicating—whispers followed by regrets that she had not done so. Victoria, outraged and injured, felt that she was misunderstood. She was profoundly unhappy. After Lord Ellenborough's speech, General Grey declared that he 'had never seen the Queen so completely upset.' 'Oh, how fearful it is,' she herself wrote to Lord Granville, 'to be suspected—uncheered—unguided and unadvised—and how alone the poor Queen feels!' Nevertheless, suffer as she might, she was as resolute as ever; she would not move by a hair's-breadth from the course that a supreme obligation marked out for her; she would be faithful to the end.

And so, when Schleswig-Holstein was forgotten, and even the image of the Prince had begun to grow dim in the fickle memories of men, the solitary watcher remained immutably concentrated at her peculiar task. The world's hostility, steadily increasing, was confronted and outfaced by the impenetrable weeds of Victoria. Would the world never understand? It was not mere sorrow that kept her so strangely sequestered; it was devotion, it was self-immolation; it was the laborious legacy of love. Unceasingly the pen moved over the black-edged paper. The flesh might be weak, but that vast burden must be borne. And fortunately, if the world would not understand, there were faithful friends who did. There was Lord Granville, and there was kind Mr. Theodore Martin. Perhaps Mr. Martin, who was so clever, would find means to make people realise the facts. She would send him a letter, pointing out her arduous labours and the difficulties under which she struggled, and then he might write an article for one of the magazines. It is not, she told him in 1863, 'the Queen's *sorrow* that keeps her secluded. . . . It is her *overwhelming work* and her health, which is greatly shaken by her sorrow, and the totally overwhelming amount of work and responsibility— work which she feels really wears her out. Alice Helps was wonderstruck at the Queen's room; and if Mrs. Martin will look at it, she can tell Mr. Martin what surrounds her. From the hour she gets out of bed till she gets into it again there is work, work, work,—letter-boxes, questions, &c., which are dreadfully exhausting—and if she had not comparative rest and quiet in the evening she would most likely not be *alive*. Her brain is constantly overtaxed.' It was too true.

## III

To carry on Albert's work—that was her first duty; but there was another, second only to that, and yet nearer, if possible, to her heart—to impress the true nature of his genius and character upon the minds of her subjects. She realised that during his life he had not been properly appreciated; the full extent of his powers, the supreme quality of his goodness, had been necessarily concealed; but death had removed the need of barriers, and now her husband, in his magnificent entirety, should stand revealed to all. She set to work methodically. She directed Sir Arthur Helps to bring out a collection of the Prince's speeches and addresses, and the weighty tome appeared in 1862. Then she commanded General Grey to write an account of the Prince's early years—from his birth to his marriage; she herself laid down the design of the book, contributed a number of confidential documents, and added numerous notes; General Grey obeyed, and the work was completed in 1866. But the principal part of the story was still untold, and Mr. Martin was forthwith instructed to write a complete biography of the Prince Consort. Mr. Martin laboured for fourteen years. The mass of material with which he had to deal was almost incredible, but he was extremely industrious, and he enjoyed throughout the gracious assistance of Her Majesty. The first bulky volume was published in 1874; four others slowly followed; so that it was not until 1880 that the monumental work was finished.

Mr. Martin was rewarded by a knighthood; and yet it was sadly evident that neither Sir Theodore nor his predecessors had achieved the purpose which the Queen had in view. Perhaps she was unfortunate in her coadjutors, but, in reality, the responsibility for the failure must lie with Victoria herself. Sir Theodore and the others faithfully carried out the task which she had set them—faithfully put before the public the very image of Albert that filled her own mind. The fatal drawback was that the public did not find that image attractive. Victoria's emotional nature, far more remarkable for vigour than for subtlety, rejecting utterly the qualifications which perspicacity, or humour, might suggest, could be satisfied with nothing but the absolute and the categorical. When she disliked she did so with an unequivocal emphasis which swept the object of her repugnance at once and finally outside the pale of consideration; and her feelings of affection were equally unmitigated. In the case of Albert her passion for superlatives reached its height. To have conceived of him as anything short of perfect—perfect in virtue, in wisdom, in beauty, in all the glories and graces of man—would have been an unthinkable blasphemy: perfect he was, and perfect he must be shown to have been. And so Sir Arthur, Sir Theodore, and the General painted him. In the circumstances, and under such supervision, to have done anything else would have required talents considerably more distinguished than any that those gentlemen possessed. But that was not all. By a curious mischance Victoria was also able to press into her service another writer, the distinction of whose talents was this time beyond a doubt. The Poet Laureate, adopting, either from complaisance or conviction, the tone of his sovereign, joined in the chorus, and endowed the royal formula with the magical resonance of verse. This settled the matter. Henceforward it was impossible to forget that Albert had worn the white flower of a blameless life.

The result was doubly unfortunate. Victoria, disappointed and chagrined, bore a grudge against her people for their refusal, in spite of all her efforts, to rate her husband at his true worth. She did not understand that the picture of an embodied perfection is distasteful to the majority of mankind. The cause of this is not so much an envy of the perfect being as a suspicion that he must be inhuman; and thus it happened that the public, when it saw displayed for its admiration a figure resembling the sugary hero of a moral story-book rather than a fellow man of flesh and blood, turned away with a shrug, a smile, and a flippant ejaculation. But in this the public was the loser as well as Victoria. For in truth Albert was a far more interesting personage than the public dreamed. By a curious irony an impeccable waxwork had been fixed by the Queen's love in the popular imagination, while the creature whom it represented—the real creature, so full of energy and stress and torment, so mysterious and so unhappy, and so fallible, and so very human—had altogether disappeared.

# IV

Words and books may be ambiguous memorials; but who can misinterpret the visible solidity of bronze and stone? At Frogmore, near Windsor, where her mother was buried, Victoria constructed, at the cost of £200,000, a vast and elaborate mausoleum for herself and her husband. But that was a private and domestic monument, and the Queen desired that wherever her subjects might be gathered together they should be reminded of the Prince. Her desire was gratified; all over the country—at Aberdeen, at Perth, and at Wolverhampton—statues of the Prince were erected; and the Queen, making an exception to her rule of retirement, unveiled them herself. Nor did the capital lag behind. A month after the Prince's death a meeting was called together at the Mansion House to discuss schemes for honouring his memory. Opinions, however, were divided upon the subject. Was a statue or an institution to be preferred? Meanwhile a subscription was opened; an influential committee was appointed, and the Queen was consulted as to her wishes in the matter. Her Majesty replied that she would prefer a granite obelisk, with sculptures at the base, to an institution. But the committee hesitated: an obelisk, to be worthy of the name, must clearly be a monolith; and where was the quarry in England capable of furnishng a granite block of the required size? It was true that there was granite in Russian Finland; but the committee were advised that it was not adapted to resist exposure to the open air. On the whole, therefore, they suggested that a Memorial Hall should be erected, together with a statue of the Prince. Her Majesty assented; but then another difficulty arose. It was found that not more than £60,000 had been subscribed—a sum insufficient to defray the double expense. The Hall, therefore, was abandoned; a statue alone was to be erected; and certain eminent architects were asked to prepare designs. Eventually the committee had at their disposal a total sum of £120,000, since the public subscribed another £10,000, while £50,000 was voted by Parliament. Some years later a joint-stock company was formed and built, as a private speculation, the Albert Hall.

The architect whose design was selected, both by the committee and by the Queen, was Mr. Gilbert Scott, whose industry, conscientiousness, and

Prince Albert had requested that, if he died first, the Queen should not 'raise even a single marble image' to his memory, but his widow ignored that and commissioned numerous models, paintings and statues. Much of the memorial sculpture was executed by William Theed, an artist favoured by the Prince Consort in life. In this photograph taken in 1862 by Prince Alfred, the Queen and Princess Alice gaze disconsolately at a bust begun by Theed only two weeks after the Prince's death, and pronounced by the Queen to be 'life itself'.

genuine piety had brought him to the head of his profession. His lifelong zeal for the Gothic style having given him a special prominence, his handiwork was strikingly visible, not only in a multitude of original buildings, but in most of the cathedrals of England. Protests, indeed, were occasionally raised against his renovations; but Mr. Scott replied with such vigour and unction in articles and pamphlets that not a Dean was unconvinced, and he was permitted to continue his labours without interruption. On one occasion, however, his devotion to Gothic had placed him in an unpleasant situation. The Government offices in Whitehall were to be rebuilt; Mr. Scott competed, and his designs were successful. Naturally, they were in the Gothic style, combining 'a certain squareness and horizontality of outline' with pillar-mullions, gables, high-pitched roofs, and dormers; and the drawings, as Mr. Scott himself observed, 'were, perhaps, the best ever sent in to a competition, or nearly so.' After the usual difficulties and delays the work was at last to be put in hand, when there was a change of Government and Lord Palmerston became Prime Minister. Lord Palmerston at once sent for Mr. Scott. 'Well, Mr. Scott,' he said, in his jaunty way, 'I can't have anything to do with this Gothic style. I must insist on your making a design in the Italian manner, which I am sure you can do very cleverly.' Mr. Scott was appalled; the style of the Italian renaissance was not only unsightly, it was positively immoral, and he sternly refused to have anything to do with it. Thereupon Lord Palmerston assumed a fatherly tone. 'Quite true; a Gothic architect can't be expected to put up a Classical building; I must find someone else.' This was intolerable, and Mr. Scott, on his return home, addressed to the Prime Minister a strongly-worded letter, in which he dwelt upon his position as an architect, upon his having won two European competitons, his being an A.R.A., a gold medallist of the Institute, and a lecturer on architecture at the Royal Academy; but it was useless—Lord Palmerston did not even reply. It then occurred to Mr. Scott that, by a judicious mixture, he might, while preserving the essential character of the Gothic, produce a design which would give a superficial impression of the Classical style. He did so, but no effect was produced upon Lord Palmerston. The new design, he said, was 'neither one thing nor t'other—a regular mongrel affair—and he would have nothing to do with it either.' After that Mr. Scott found it necessary to recruit for two months at Scarborough, 'with a course of quinine.' He recovered his tone at last, but only at the cost of his convictions. For the sake of his family he felt that it was his unfortunate duty to obey the Prime Minister; and, shuddering with horror, he constructed the Government offices in a strictly Renaissance style.

Shortly afterwards Mr. Scott found some consolation in building the St. Pancras Hotel in a style of his own.

And now another and yet more satisfactory task was his. 'My idea in designing the Memorial,' he wrote, 'was to erect a kind of ciborium to protect a statue of the Prince; and its special characteristic was that the ciborium was designed in some degree on the principles of the ancient shrines. These shrines were models of imaginary buildings, such as had never in reality been erected; and my idea was to realise one of these imaginary structures with its precious materials, its inlaying, its enamels, &c. &c.' His idea was particularly appropriate since it chanced that a similar conception, though in the reverse order of magnitude, had occurred to the Prince himself, who had designed and executed several silver cruet-stands upon the same model. At the Queen's request a site was chosen in Kensington Gardens as near as possible to that of the Great Exhibition; and in May 1864 the first sod was turned. The work was long, complicated, and difficult; a great number of workmen were employed, besides several subsidiary sculptors and metal-workers under Mr. Scott's direction, while at every stage sketches and models were submitted to Her Majesty, who criticised all the details with minute care, and constantly suggested improvements. The frieze, which encircles the base of the monument, was in itself a very serious piece of work. 'This,' said Mr. Scott, 'taken as a whole, is perhaps one of the most laborious works of sculpture ever undertaken, consisting, as it does, of a continuous range of figure-sculpture of the most elaborate description, in the highest *alto-relievo* of

*Previous page: Queen Victoria after the opera, from a painting by Edmund Thomas Parris. 'I am a terribly modern person, and I must say I prefer Bellini, Rossini, Donizetti, etc., to anything else,' she wrote. Her preferences were no doubt in part the result of the influence of her singing teacher, Luigi Lablache, the greatest bass of the age. He had sung at Beethoven's funeral, and became one of the finest interpreters of the new Italian opera.*

*Above: Queen Victoria receiving the news of her accession to the throne, 20 June 1837, by H.T. Wells. She recorded in her journal: 'I was awoke at 6 o'clock by Mamma, who told me that the Archbishop of Canterbury and Lord Conyngham were here, and wished to see me. I got out of bed and went into my sitting-room (only in my dressing-gown) and alone, and saw them. Lord Conyngham (the Lord Chamberlain) then acquainted me that my poor Uncle, the King, was no more, and had expired at 12 minutes past 2 this morning, and consequently that I am Queen.'*

Above: the Queen and Prince
Albert, accompanied by the
Princess Royal, the Prince of Wales
and Princess Alice, enjoy the
opulent furnishings of the Great
Western Railway Company's
special state carriage on the first leg
of their journey to Scotland in the
early 1840s. Following the
widowed Queen Adelaide's
adventurous example, the royal
couple had made their first train
journey, from Slough, for Windsor,
to Paddington, in 1842; the Queen
was 'quite charmed' by the trip, and
henceforth used trains all over the
British Isles.

Following pages: the royal
entourage arrives at Cherbourg in
August 1858, from a painting by
Jules Achille Noel. France and
Great Britain had been victorious
allies in the Crimean War, and on
a previous state visit the Queen had
been fascinated by the dapper
Emperor, and 'came back with
feelings of real affection for and
interest in France.' This time,
despite dazzling festivities, both
political and personal relationships
were strained: British observers
were alarmed by Louis Napoleon's
show of naval strength, and Queen
Victoria refused to greet his mistress
with a kiss.

RECEPTION de S.M. LA REINE D'ANGLETERRE
PAR S.M. L'EMPEREUR NAPOLÉON III, A BORD
DU VAISSEAU LA BRETAGNE, RADE de CHERBOURG.

Previous pages: Tuxen's group portrait of the royal family shows them gathered to celebrate the 1887 Golden Jubilee. On the far right stands the resplendent figure of Crown Prince Frederick of Prussia, Victoria's son-in-law, already mortally ill with throat cancer. He became Emperor the following year, but died three months later.

Above: this magnificent Durbar was held in Delhi in 1876 to celebrate the Queen's new title of Empress of India; presiding over it was the Viceroy of India, Lord Lytton (a great friend of Lady Strachey, who named her fourth son after him). Since the days of the East India Company, British control had been spreading over the whole sub-continent, while at home Britons were fascinated by tales of the rich and startling contrasts of Indian life. Her Majesty's troops apparently paraded with faultless precision; native princes dwelt in sophisticated splendour; English ladies held tea-parties at the hill-stations and, it was said, in remote areas propitiatory goats were sacrificed before images of Queen Victoria.

life-size, of more than 200 feet in length, containing about 170 figures, and executed in the hardest marble which could be procured.' After three years of toil the memorial was still far from completion, and Mr. Scott thought it advisable to give a dinner to the workmen, 'as a substantial recognition of his appreciation of their skill and energy.' 'Two long tables,' we are told, 'constructed of scaffold planks, were arranged in the workshops, and covered with newspapers, for want of table-cloths. Upwards of eighty men sat down. Beef and mutton, plum-pudding and cheese, were supplied in abundance, and each man who desired it had three pints of beer, gingerbeer and lemonade being provided for the teetotalers, who formed a very considerable proportion. . . . Several toasts were given and many of the workmen spoke, almost all of them commencing by "Thanking God that they enjoyed good health"; some alluded to the temperance that prevailed amongst them, others observed how little swearing was ever heard, whilst all said how pleased and proud they were to be engaged on so great a work.'

Gradually the edifice approached completion. The one hundred and seventieth life-size figure in the frieze was chiselled, the granite pillars arose, the mosaics were inserted in the allegorical pediments, the four colossal statues representing the greater Christian virtues, the four other colossal statues representing the greater moral virtues, were hoisted into their positions, the eight bronzes representing the greater sciences—Astronomy, Chemistry, Geology, Geometry, Rhetoric, Medicine, Philosophy, and Physiology—were fixed on their glittering pinnacles, high in air. The statue of Physiology was particularly admired. 'On her left arm,' the official description informs us, 'she bears a new-born infant, as a representation of the development of the highest and most perfect of physiological forms; her hand points towards a microscope, the instrument which lends its assistance for the investigation of the minuter forms of animal and vegetable organisms.' At last the gilded cross crowned the dwindling galaxies of superimposed angels, the four continents in white marble stood at the four corners of the base, and, seven years after its inception, in July 1872, the monument was thrown open to the public.

But four more years were to elapse before the central figure was ready to be placed under its starry canopy. It was designed by Mr. Foley, though in one particular the sculptor's freedom was restricted by Mr. Scott. 'I have chosen the sitting posture,' Mr. Scott said, 'as best conveying the idea of dignity befitting a royal personage.' Mr. Foley ably carried out the conception of his principal. 'In the attitude and expression,' he said, 'the aim has been, with the individuality of portraiture, to embody rank, character, and enlightenment, and to convey a sense of that responsive intelligence indicating an active, rather than a passive, interest in those pursuits of civilisation illustrated in the surrounding figures, groups, and relievos. . . . To identify the figure with one of the most memorable undertakings of the public life of the Prince—the International Exhibition of 1851—a catalogue of the works collected in that first gathering of the industry of all nations, is placed in the right hand.' The statue was of bronze gilt and weighed nearly ten tons. It was rightly supposed that the simple word 'Albert,' cast on the base, would be a sufficient means of identification.

*George Gilbert Scott's National Albert Memorial in Kensington Gardens was the most lavish and impressive of the many civic tributes to the late consort.*

# OUT!

(BUT IT WAS THE UNDERHAND BOWLING THAT DID IT.)

# 8: MR. GLADSTONE
# AND LORD BEACONSFIELD

ORD PALMERSTON'S laugh—a queer metallic 'Ha! ha! ha!' with reverberations in it from the days of Pitt and the Congress of Vienna—was heard no more in Piccadilly; Lord John Russell dwindled into senility; Lord Derby tottered from the stage. A new scene opened; and new protagonists—Mr. Gladstone and Mr. Disraeli—struggled together in the limelight. Victoria, from her post of vantage, watched these developments with that passionate and personal interest which she invariably imported into politics. Her prepossessions were of an unexpected kind. Mr. Gladstone had been the disciple of her revered Peel, and had won the approval of Albert; Mr. Disraeli had hounded Sir Robert to his fall with hideous virulence, and the Prince had pronounced that he 'had not one single element of a gentleman in his composition.' Yet she regarded Mr. Gladstone with a distrust and dislike which steadily deepened, while upon his rival she lavished an abundance of confidence, esteem, and affection such as Lord Melbourne himself had hardly known.

Her attitude towards the Tory Minister had suddenly changed when she found that he alone among public men had divined her feelings at Albert's death. Of the others she might have said 'they pity me and not my grief'; but Mr. Disraeli had understood; and all his condolences had taken the form of reverential eulogies of the departed. The Queen declared that he was 'the only person who appreciated the Prince.' She began to show him special favour; gave him and his wife two of the coveted seats in St. George's Chapel at the Prince of Wales's wedding, and invited him to stay a night at Windsor. When the grant for the Albert Memorial came before the House of Commons, Disraeli, as leader of the Opposition, eloquently supported the project. He was rewarded by a copy of the Prince's speeches, bound in white morocco, with an inscription in the royal hand. In his letter of thanks he

*'Out! (But it was the underhand bowling that did it.)': a game of political cricket for William Ewart Gladstone and his rival Benjamin Disraeli. This cartoon appeared in* Fun *in 1866, before either statesman had held office as Prime Minister, although both were party leaders and both had served as Chancellor of the Exchequer. The 'underhand bowling' was the Conservative opposition's proposed amendment to the Parliamentary reform bill, which would manipulate property valuation to affect voting qualifications, while 'rating', represented by the cricket ball, was the specific issue over which Lord John Russell's Liberal administration was forced to resign. Disraeli was soon to climb to 'the top of the greasy pole' by becoming Prime Minister for a brief term in 1868, followed by a longer period from 1874 to 1880. Gladstone headed four governments: 1868 to 1874; 1880 to 1885; February— August 1886, and 1892 to 1894.*

'ventured to touch upon a sacred theme,' and, in a strain which re-echoed with masterly fidelity the sentiments of his correspondent, dwelt at length upon the absolute perfection of Albert. 'The Prince,' he said, 'is the only person whom Mr. Disraeli has ever known who realised the Ideal. None with whom he is acquainted have ever approached it. There was in him an union of the manly grace and sublime simplicity, of chivalry with the intellectual splendour of the Attic Academe. The only character in English history that would, in some respects, draw near to him is Sir Philip Sidney: the same high tone, the same universal accomplishment, the same blended tenderness and vigour, the same rare combination of romantic energy and classic repose.' As for his own acquaintance with the Prince, it had been, he said, 'one of the most satisfactory incidents of his life: full of refined and beautiful memories, and exercising, as he hopes, over his remaining existence, a soothing and exalting influence.' Victoria was much affected by 'the depth and delicacy of these touches,' and henceforward Disraeli's place in her affections was assured. When, in 1866, the Conservatives came into office, Disraeli's position as Chancellor of the Exchequer and leader of the House necessarily brought him into a closer relation with the Sovereign. Two years later Lord Derby resigned, and Victoria, with intense delight and peculiar graciousness, welcomed Disraeli as her First Minister.

But only for nine agitated months did he remain in power. The Ministry, in a minority in the Commons, was swept out of existence by a general election. Yet by the end of that short period the ties which bound together the Queen and her Premier had grown far stronger than ever before; the relationship between them was now no longer merely that between a grateful mistress and a devoted servant: they were friends. His official letters, in which the personal element had always been perceptible, developed into racy records of political news and social gossip, written, as Lord Clarendon said, 'in his best novel style.' Victoria was delighted; she had never, she declared, had such letters in her life, and had never before known *everything*. In return, she sent him, when the spring came, several bunches of flowers, picked by her own hands. He despatched to her a set of his novels, for which, she said, she was 'most grateful, and which she values much.' She herself had lately published her 'Leaves from the Journal of our Life in the Highlands,' and it was observed that the Prime Minister, in conversing with Her Majesty at this period, constantly used the words 'we authors, ma'am.' Upon political questions, she was his staunch supporter. 'Really there never was such conduct as that of the Opposition,' she wrote. And when the Government was defeated in the House she was 'really shocked at the way in which the House of Commons go on; they really bring discredit on Constitutional Government.' She dreaded the prospect of a change; she feared that if the Liberals insisted upon disestablishing the Irish Church, her Coronation Oath might stand in the way. But a change there had to be, and Victoria vainly tried to console herself for the loss of her favourite Minister by bestowing a peerage upon Mrs. Disraeli.

Mr. Gladstone was in his shirt-sleeves at Hawarden, cutting down a tree, when the royal message was brought to him. 'Very significant,' he remarked, when he had read the letter, and went on cutting down his tree. His secret thoughts on the occasion were more explicit, and were committed to his diary. 'The Almighty,' he wrote, 'seems to sustain and spare me for some purpose of His own, deeply unworthy as I know myself to be. Glory be to His name.'

The Queen, however, did not share her new Minister's view of the Almighty's intentions. She could not believe that there was any divine purpose to be detected in the programme of sweeping changes which Mr. Gladstone was determined to carry out. But what could she do? Mr. Gladstone, with his daemonic energy and his powerful majority in the House of Commons, was irresistible; and for five years (1869–74) Victoria found herself condemned to live in an agitating atmosphere of interminable reform—reform in the Irish Church and the Irish land system, reform in education, reform in parliamentary elections, reform in the organisation of the Army and the Navy, reform in the administration of justice. She disapproved, she struggled, she grew very angry; she felt that if Albert had been living things would never have happened so; but her protests and her complaints were alike unavailing. The mere effort of grappling with the mass of documents which poured in upon her in an ever-growing flood was terribly exhausting. When the draft of the lengthy and intricate Irish Church Bill came before her, accompanied by an explanatory letter from Mr. Gladstone covering a dozen closely-written quarto pages, she almost despaired. She turned from the Bill to the explanation, and from the explanation back again to the Bill, and she could not decide which was the most confusing. But she had to do her duty: she had not only to read, but to make notes. At last she handed the whole heap of papers to Mr. Martin, who happened to be staying at Osborne, and requested him to make a précis of them. When he had done so, her disapproval of the measure became more marked than ever; but, such was the strength of the Government, she actually found herself obliged to urge moderation upon the Opposition, lest worse should ensue.

In the midst of this crisis, when the future of the Irish Church was hanging in the balance, Victoria's attention was drawn to another proposed reform. It was suggested that the sailors in the Navy should henceforward be allowed to wear beards. 'Has Mr. Childers ascertained anything on the subject of the beards?' the Queen wrote anxiously to the First Lord of the Admiralty. On the whole, Her Majesty was in favour of the change. 'Her own personal feeling,' she wrote, 'would be for the beards without the moustaches, as the latter have rather a soldierlike appearance; but then the object in view would not be obtained, viz. to prevent the necessity of shaving. Therefore it had better be as proposed, the entire beard, only it should be kept short and very clean.' After thinking over the question for another week, the Queen wrote a final letter. She wished, she said, 'to make one additional observation respecting the beards, viz. that on no account should moustaches be allowed without beards. That must be clearly understood.'

Changes in the Navy might be tolerated; to lay hands upon the Army was a more serious matter. From time immemorial there had been a particularly close connection between the Army and the Crown; and Albert had devoted even more time and attention to the details of military business than to the processes of fresco-painting or the planning of sanitary cottages for the

*'An ample supply of excellent boys is always available' for recruitment to the Royal Navy, noted an article written in 1897. This group have not yet grown the nautical beards in which the Queen took such an interest, although the officer at the end of the line provides them with a splendid example. During the last decades of the Queen's reign the Navy was transformed by new technology as part of the arms race against imperial Germany. By the end of their training period, these 'excellent boys' would probably be able to handle the big cordite propellant guns of the latest 'Magnificent' class battleships.*

deserving poor. But now there was to be a great alteration: Mr. Gladstone's fiat had gone forth, and the Commander-in-Chief was to be removed from his direct dependence upon the Sovereign, and made subordinate to Parliament and the Secretary of State for War. Of all the liberal reforms this was the one which aroused the bitterest resentment in Victoria. She considered that the change was an attack upon her personal position—almost an attack upon the personal position of Albert. But she was helpless, and the Prime Minister had his way. When she heard that the dreadful man had yet another reform in contemplation—that he was about to abolish the purchase of military commissions—she could only feel that it was just what might have been expected. For a moment she hoped that the House of Lords would come to the rescue; the Peers opposed the change with unexpected vigour; but Mr. Gladstone, more conscious than ever of the support of the Almighty, was ready with an ingenious device. The purchase of commissions had been originally allowed by Royal Warrant; it should now be disallowed by the same agency. Victoria was faced by a curious dilemma: she abominated the abolition of purchase; but she was asked to abolish it by an exercise of sovereign power which was very much to her taste. She did not hesitate for long; and when the Cabinet, in a formal minute, advised her to sign the Warrant, she did so with a good grace.

Unacceptable as Mr. Gladstone's policy was, there was something else about him which was even more displeasing to Victoria. She disliked his personal demeanour towards herself. It was not that Mr. Gladstone, in his intercourse with her, was in any degree lacking in courtesy or respect. On the contrary, an extraordinary reverence permeated his manner, both in his conversation and his correspondence with the Sovereign. Indeed, with that deep and passionate conservatism which, to the very end of his incredible career, gave such an unexpected colouring to his inexplicable character, Mr. Gladstone viewed Victoria through a haze of awe which was almost religious—as a sacrosanct embodiment of venerable traditions—a vital element in the British Constitution—a Queen by Act of Parliament. But unfortunately the lady did not appreciate the compliment. The well-known complaint—'He speaks to me as if I were a public meeting'—whether authentic or no—and the turn of the sentence is surely a little too epigrammatic to be genuinely Victorian—undoubtedly expresses the essential element of her antipathy. She had no objection to being considered as an institution; she was one, and she knew it. But she was a woman too, and to be considered *only* as an institution—that was unbearable. And thus all Mr. Gladstone's zeal and devotion, his ceremonious phrases, his low bows, his punctilious correctitudes, were utterly wasted; and when, in the excess of his loyalty, he went further, and imputed to the object of his veneration, with obsequious blindness, the subtlety of intellect, the wide reading, the grave enthusiasm, which he himself possessed, the misunderstanding became complete. The discordance between the actual Victoria and this strange Divinity made in Mr. Gladstone's image produced disastrous results. Her discomfort and dislike turned at last into positive animosity, and, though her manners continued to be perfect, she never for a moment unbent; while he on his side was overcome with disappointment, perplexity, and mortification.

Yet his fidelity remained unshaken. When the Cabinet met, the Prime Minister, filled with his beatific vision, would open the proceedings by reading aloud the letters which he had received from the Queen upon the questions of the hour. The assembly sat in absolute silence while, one after another, the royal missives, with their emphases, their ejaculations, and their grammatical peculiarities, boomed forth in all the deep solemnity of Mr. Gladstone's utterance. Not a single comment, of any kind, was ever hazarded; and, after a fitting pause, the Cabinet proceeded with the business of the day.

## II

Little as Victoria appreciated her Prime Minister's attitude towards her, she found that it had its uses. The popular discontent at her uninterrupted seclusion had been gathering force for many years, and now burst out in a new and alarming shape. Republicanism was in the air. Radical opinion in England, stimulated by the fall of Napoleon III and the establishment of a republican government in France, suddenly grew more extreme than it had ever been since 1848. It also became for the first time almost respectable. Chartism had been entirely an affair of the lower classes; but now Members of Parliament, learned professors, and ladies of title openly avowed the most subversive views. The monarchy was attacked both in theory and in practice. And it was attacked at a vital point: it was declared to be too expensive. What benefits, it was asked, did the nation reap to counterbalance the enormous sums which were expended upon the Sovereign? Victoria's retirement gave an unpleasant handle to the argument. It was pointed out

*William Ewart Gladstone (1809–98) retained his immense mental and physical vigour into advanced old age. The 'Grand Old Man' was still chopping down trees on his Hawarden estate in his seventies, and he became Prime Minister for the fourth and last time at the age of eighty-two.*

that the ceremonial functions of the Crown had virtually lapsed; and the awkward question remained whether any of the other functions which it did continue to perform were really worth £385,000 per annum. The royal balance-sheet was curiously examined. An anonymous pamphlet entitled 'What does she do with it?' appeared, setting forth the financial position with malicious clarity. The Queen, it stated, was granted by the Civil List £60,000 a year for her private use; but the rest of her vast annuity was given, as the Act declared, to enable her 'to defray the expenses of her royal household and to support the honour and dignity of the Crown.' Now it was obvious that, since the death of the Prince, the expenditure for both these purposes must have been very considerably diminished, and it was difficult to resist the conclusion that a large sum of money was diverted annually from the uses for which it had been designed by Parliament, to swell the private fortune of Victoria. The precise amount of that private fortune it was impossible to discover; but there was reason to suppose that it was gigantic; perhaps it reached a total of five million pounds. The pamphlet protested against such a state of affairs, and its protests were repeated vigorously in newspapers and at public meetings. Though it is certain that the estimate of Victoria's riches was much exaggerated, it is equally certain that she was an exceedingly wealthy woman. She probably saved £20,000 a year from the Civil List, the revenues of the Duchy of Lancaster were steadily increasing, she had inherited a considerable property from the Prince Consort, and she had been left, in 1852, an estate of half a million by Mr. John Neild, an eccentric miser. In these circumstances it was not surprising that when, in 1871, Parliament was asked to vote a dowry of £30,000 to the Princess Louise on her marriage with the eldest son of the Duke of Argyll, together with an annuity of £6,000, there should have been a serious outcry. *

In order to conciliate public opinion, the Queen opened Parliament in person, and the vote was passed almost unanimously. But a few months later another demand was made: the Prince Arthur had come of age, and the nation was asked to grant him an annuity of £15,000. The outcry was redoubled. The newspapers were filled with angry articles; Bradlaugh thundered against 'princely paupers' to one of the largest crowds that had ever been seen in Trafalgar Square; and Sir Charles Dilke expounded the case for a republic in a speech to his constituents at Newcastle. The Prince's annuity was ultimately sanctioned in the House of Commons by a large majority; but a minority of fifty members voted in favour of reducing the sum to £10,000.

Towards every aspect of this distasteful question, Mr. Gladstone presented an iron front. He absolutely discountenanced the extreme section of his followers. He declared that the whole of the Queen's income was justly at her personal disposal, argued that to complain of royal savings was merely to encourage royal extravagance, and successfully convoyed through Parliament the unpopular annuities, which, he pointed out, were strictly in accordance with precedent. When, in 1872, Sir Charles Dilke once more returned to the charge in the House of Commons, introducing a motion for a full enquiry into the Queen's expenditure with a view to a root-and-branch reform of the Civil List, the Prime Minister brought all the resources of his powerful and ingenious eloquence to the support of the Crown. He was completely successful; and amid a scene of great disorder the motion was ignominiously dismissed. Victoria was relieved; but she grew no fonder of Mr. Gladstone.

It was perhaps the most miserable moment of her life. The Ministers, the press, the public, all conspired to vex her, to blame her, to misinterpret her actions, to be unsympathetic and disrespectful in every way. She was 'a cruelly misunderstood woman,' she told Mr. Martin, complaining to him bitterly of the unjust attacks which were made upon her, and declaring that 'the great worry and anxiety and hard work for ten years, alone, unaided, with increasing age and never very strong health,' were breaking her down, and 'almost drove her to despair.' The situation was indeed deplorable. It seemed as if her whole existence had gone awry; as if an irremediable antagonism had grown up between the Queen and the nation. If Victoria had died in the early seventies, there can be little doubt that the voice of the world would have pronounced her a failure.

## III

But she was reserved for a very different fate. The outburst of republicanism had been in fact the last flicker of an expiring cause. The liberal tide, which had been flowing steadily ever since the Reform Bill, reached its height with Mr. Gladstone's first administration; and towards the end of that administration the inevitable ebb began. The reaction, when it came, was sudden and complete. The General Election of 1874 changed the whole face of politics. Mr. Gladstone and the Liberals were routed; and the Tory party, for the first time for over forty years, attained an unquestioned supremacy in England. It was obvious that their surprising triumph was pre-eminently due to the skill and vigour of Disraeli. He returned to office no longer the dubious commander of an insufficient host, but with drums beating and flags flying, a conquering hero. And as a conquering hero Victoria welcomed her new Prime Minister.

Then there followed six years of excitement, of enchantment, of felicity, of glory, of romance. The amazing being, who now at last, at the age of seventy, after a lifetime of extraordinary struggles, had turned into reality the absurdest of his boyhood's dreams, knew well enough how to make his own, with absolute completeness, the heart of the Sovereign Lady whose servant, and whose master, he had so miraculously become. In women's hearts he had always read as in an open book. His whole career had turned upon those curious entities; and the more curious they were, the more intimately at home with them he seemed to be. But Lady Beaconsfield, with her cracked idolatry, and Mrs. Brydges-Williams, with her clogs, her corpulence, and her legacy, were gone: an even more remarkable phenomenon stood in their place. He surveyed what was before him with the eye of a past-master; and he was not for a moment at a loss. He realised everything—the interacting complexities of circumstance and character, the pride of place mingled so inextricably with personal arrogance, the superabundant emotionalism, the ingenuousness of outlook, the solid, the laborious respectability, shot through so incongruously by temperamental cravings for the coloured and the strange, the singular intellectual limitations, and the mysteriously essential

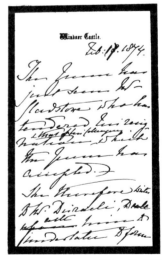

*The Queen's letter to Disraeli of 17 February 1874, informing him of Gladstone's resignation and asking him to form a government. She was delighted, writing in her journal, 'What an important turn the elections have taken! It shows that the country is not Radical.' The letter is edged as always with mourning black.*

169

*In the winter of 1877 the Queen demonstrated her support for Disraeli's handling of the tricky Eastern Question by paying him the great compliment of lunching with him at his home. After meeting the Queen and Princess Beatrice at High Wycombe railway station, the elderly statesman escorted them to Hughenden Manor, passing under a triumphal arch constructed of chairs 'representing the staple manufacture of the town'. Later the Queen was distressed to learn that the day of her visit had coincided with the anniversary of the recent death of Disraeli's wife, Mary Anne.*

female element impregnating every particle of the whole. A smile hovered over his impassive features, and he dubbed Victoria 'the Faery.' The name delighted him, for, with that epigrammatic ambiguity so dear to his heart, it precisely expressed his vision of the Queen. The Spenserian allusion was very pleasant—the elegant evocation of Gloriana; but there was more in it than that: there was the suggestion of a diminutive creature, endowed with magical—and mythical—properties, and a portentousness almost ridiculously out of keeping with the rest of her make-up. The Faery, he determined, should henceforward wave her wand for him alone. Detachment is always a rare quality, and rarest of all, perhaps, among politicians; but that veteran egotist possessed it in a supreme degree. Not only did he know what he had to do, not only did he do it; he was in the audience as well as on the stage; and he took in with the rich relish of a connoisseur every feature of the entertaining situation, every phase of the delicate drama, and every detail of his own consummate performance.

The smile hovered and vanished, and, bowing low with Oriental gravity and Oriental submissiveness, he set himself to his task. He had understood from the first that in dealing with the Faery the appropriate method of approach was the very antithesis of the Gladstonian; and such a method was naturally his. It was not his habit to harangue and exhort and expatiate in official conscientiousness; he liked to scatter flowers along the path of business, to compress a weighty argument into a happy phrase, to insinuate what was in his mind with an air of friendship and confidential courtesy. He was nothing if not personal; and he had perceived that personality was the key that opened the Faery's heart. Accordingly, he never for a moment allowed his intercourse with her to lose the personal tone; he invested all the transactions of State with the charms of familiar conversation; she was always the royal lady, the adored and revered mistress, he the devoted and respectful friend. When once the personal relation was firmly established, every difficulty disappeared. But to maintain that relation uninterruptedly in a smooth and even course, a particular care was necessary: the bearings had to be most assiduously oiled. Nor was Disraeli in any doubt as to the nature of the lubricant. 'You have heard me called a flatterer,' he said to Matthew Arnold, 'and it is true. Everyone likes flattery; and when you come to royalty you should lay it on with a trowel.' He practised what he preached. His adulation was incessant, and he applied it in the very thickest slabs. 'There is no honour and no reward,' he declared, 'that with him can ever equal the possession of your Majesty's kind thoughts. All his own thoughts and feelings and duties and affections are now concentrated in your Majesty, and he desires nothing more for his remaining years than to serve your Majesty, or, if that service ceases, to live still on its memory as a period of his existence most interesting and fascinating.' 'In life,' he told her, 'one must have for one's thoughts a sacred depository, and Lord Beaconsfield ever presumes to see that in his Sovereign Mistress.' She was not only his own solitary support; she was the one prop of the State. 'If your Majesty is ill,' he wrote during a grave political crisis, 'he is sure he will himself break down. All, really, depends upon your Majesty.' 'He lives only for Her,' he asseverated, 'and works only for Her, and without Her all is lost.' When her birthday came he produced an elaborate confection of hyperbolic compliment. 'To-day Lord Beaconsfield ought fitly, perhaps, to congratulate a powerful Sovereign on her imperial sway, the vastness of her Empire, and the success and strength of her fleets and armies. But he cannot, his mind is in another mood. He can only think of the strangeness of his destiny that it has come to pass that he should be the servant of one so great, and whose infinite kindness, the brightness of whose intelligence and the firmness of whose will, have enabled him to undertake labours to which he otherwise would be quite unequal, and supported him in all things by a condescending sympathy, which in the hour of difficulty alike charms and inspires. Upon the Sovereign of many lands and many hearts may an omnipotent Providence shed every blessing that the wise can desire and the virtuous deserve!' In those expert hands the trowel seemed to assume the qualities of some lofty masonic symbol—to be the ornate and glittering vehicle of verities unrealised by the profane.

Such tributes were delightful, but they remained in the nebulous region of words, and Disraeli had determined to give his blandishments a more significant solidity. He deliberately encouraged those high views of her own position which had always been native to Victoria's mind and had been reinforced by the principles of Albert and the doctrines of Stockmar. He professed to a belief in a theory of the Constitution which gave the Sovereign a leading place in the councils of government; but his pronouncements upon the subject were indistinct; and when he emphatically declared that there ought to be 'a real Throne,' it was probably with the mental addition that that throne would be a very unreal one indeed whose occupant was unamenable to his cajoleries. But the vagueness of his language was in itself an added stimulant to Victoria. Skilfully confusing the woman and the Queen, he threw, with a grandiose gesture, the government of England at her feet, as if in doing so he were performing an act of personal homage. In his first audience after returning to power, he assured her that 'whatever she wished should be done.' When the intricate Public Worship Regulation Bill was being discussed by the Cabinet, he told the Faery that his 'only object' was 'to further your Majesty's wishes in this matter.' When he brought off his great *coup* over the Suez Canal, he used expressions which implied that the only gainer by the transaction was Victoria. 'It is just settled,' he wrote in triumph; 'you have it, Madam . . . Four millions sterling! and almost immediately. There was only one firm that could do it—Rochschilds. They behaved admirably; advanced the money at a low rate, and the entire interest of the Khedive is now yours, Madam.' Nor did he limit himself to highly-spiced insinuations. Writing with all the authority of his office, he advised the Queen that she had the constitutional right to dismiss a Ministry which was supported by a large majority in the House of Commons; he even urged her to do so, if, in her opinion, 'your Majesty's Government have from wilfulness, or even from weakness, deceived your Majesty.' To the horror of Mr. Gladstone, he not only kept the Queen informed as to the general course of business in the Cabinet, but revealed to her the part taken in its discussions by individual members of it. Lord Derby, the son of the late Prime Minister and Disraeli's Foreign Secretary, viewed these developments with grave mistrust. 'Is there not,' he ventured to write to his Chief, 'just a risk of encouraging her in too large ideas of her personal power, and too great indifference to what the public expects? I only ask; it is for you to judge.'

As for Victoria, she accepted everything—compliments, flatteries, Elizabethan prerogatives—without a single qualm. After the long gloom of her bereavement, after the chill of the Gladstonian discipline, she expanded to the rays of Disraeli's devotion like a flower in the sun. The change in her situation was indeed miraculous. No longer was she obliged to puzzle for hours over the complicated details of business, for now she had only to ask Mr. Disraeli for an explanation, and he would give it her in the most concise, in the most amusing, way. No longer was she worried by alarming novelties; no longer was she put out at finding herself treated, by a reverential gentleman in high collars, as if she were some embodied precedent, with a recondite knowledge of Greek. And her deliverer was surely the most fascinating of men. The strain of charlatanism, which had unconsciously captivated her in Napoleon III, exercised the same enchanting effect in the case of Disraeli. Like a dram-drinker, whose ordinary life is passed in dull sobriety, her unsophisticated intelligence gulped down his rococo allurements with peculiar zest. She became intoxicated, entranced. Believing all that he told her of herself, she completely regained the self-confidence which had been slipping away from her throughout the dark period that followed Albert's death. She swelled with a new elation, while he, conjuring up before her wonderful Oriental visions, dazzled her eyes with an imperial grandeur of which she had only dimly dreamed. Under the compelling influence, her very demeanour altered. Her short, stout figure, with its folds of black velvet, its muslin streamers, its heavy pearls at the heavy neck, assumed an almost menacing air. In her countenance, from which the charm of youth had long since vanished, and which had not yet been softened by age, the traces of grief, of disappointment, and of displeasure were still visible, but they were overlaid by looks of arrogance and sharp lines of peremptory hauteur. Only, when Mr. Disraeli appeared, the expression changed in an instant, and the forbidding visage became charged with smiles. For him she would do anything. Yielding to his encouragements, she began to emerge from her seclusion; she appeared in London in semi-state, at hospitals and concerts; she opened Parliament; she reviewed troops and distributed medals at Aldershot. But such public signs of favour were trivial in comparison with her private attentions. During his hours of audience, she could hardly restrain her excitement and delight. 'I can only describe my reception,' he wrote to a friend on one occasion, 'by telling you that I really thought she was going to embrace me. She was wreathed with smiles, and, as she tattled, glided about the room like a bird.' In his absence, she talked of him perpetually, and there was a note of unusual vehemence in her solicitude for his health. 'John Manners,' Disraeli told Lady Bradford, 'who has just come from Osborne, says that the Faery only talked of one subject, and that was her Primo. According to him, it was her gracious opinion that the Government should make my health a Cabinet question. Dear John seemed quite surprised at what she said; but you are more used to these ebullitions.' She often sent him presents; an illustrated album arrived for him regularly from Windsor on Christmas Day. But her most valued gifts were the bunches of spring flowers which, gathered by herself and her ladies in the woods at Osborne, marked in an especial manner the warmth and tenderness of her sentiments. Among these it was, he declared, the primroses that he loved the best. They were, he said, 'the ambassadors of Spring,' 'the gems and jewels of Nature.' He liked them, he assured her, 'so much better for their being wild; they seem an offering from the Fauns and Dryads of Osborne.' 'They show,' he told her, 'that your Majesty's sceptre has touched the enchanted Isle.' He sat at dinner with heaped-up bowls of them on every side, and told his guests that 'they were all sent to me this morning by the Queen from Osborne, as she knows it is my favourite flower.'

As time went on, and as it became clearer and clearer that the Faery's thraldom was complete, his protestations grew steadily more highly coloured and more unabashed. At last he ventured to import into his blandishments a strain of adoration that was almost avowedly romantic. In phrases of baroque

convolution, he delivered the message of his heart. The pressure of business, he wrote, had 'so absorbed and exhausted him, that towards the hour of post he has not had clearness of mind, and vigour of pen, adequate to convey his thoughts and facts to the most loved and illustrious being, who deigns to consider them.' She sent him some primroses, and he replied that he could 'truly say they are "more precious than rubies," coming, as they do, and at such a moment, from a Sovereign whom he adores.' She sent him snowdrops, and his sentiment overflowed into poetry. 'Yesterday eve,' he wrote, 'there appeared, in Whitehall Gardens, a delicate looking case, with a royal superscription, which, when he opened, he thought, at first, that your Majesty had graciously bestowed upon him the stars of your Majesty's principal orders. And, indeed, he was so impressed with this graceful illusion, that, having a banquet, where there were many stars and ribbons, he could not resist the temptation, by placing some snowdrops on his heart, of showing that he, too, was decorated by a gracious Sovereign.

'Then, in the middle of the night, it occurred to him, that it might all be an enchantment, and that, perhaps, it was a Faery gift and came from another monarch: Queen Titania, gathering flowers, with her Court, in a soft and sea-girt isle, and sending magic blossoms, which, they say, turn the heads of those who receive them.'

A Faery gift! Did he smile as he wrote the words? Perhaps; and yet it would be rash to conclude that his perfervid declarations were altogether without sincerity. Actor and spectator both, the two characters were so intimately blended together in that odd composition that they formed an inseparable unity, and it was impossible to say that one of them was less genuine than the other. With one element, he could coldly appraise the Faery's intellectual capacity, note with some surprise that she could be on occasion 'most interesting and amusing,' and then continue his use of the trowel with an ironical solemnity; while, with the other, he could be overwhelmed by the immemorial panoply of royalty, and, thrilling with the sense of his own strange elevation, dream himself into a gorgeous phantasy of crowns and powers and chivalric love. When he told Victoria that 'during a somewhat romantic and imaginative life, nothing has ever occurred to him so interesting as this confidential correspondence with one so exalted and so inspiring,' was he not in earnest after all? When he wrote to a lady about the Court, 'I love the Queen—perhaps the only person in this world left to me that I do love,' was he not creating for himself an enchanted palace out of the Arabian Nights, full of melancholy and spangles, in which he actually believed? Victoria's state of mind was far more simple; untroubled by imaginative yearnings, she never lost herself in that nebulous region of the spirit where feeling and fancy grow confused. Her emotions, with all their intensity and all their exaggeration, retained the plain prosaic texture of everyday life. And it was fitting that her expression of them should be equally commonplace. She was, she told her Prime Minister, at the end of an official letter, 'yours aff'ly V.R. and I.' In such a phrase the deep reality of her feeling is instantly manifest. The Faery's feet were on the solid earth; it was the rusé cynic who was in the air.

He had taught her, however, a lesson, which she had learnt with alarming

The Queen's ambition to become Empress of India—and Disraeli's eagerness to fulfil it—was ideal material for the cartoonist. Here Prime Minister Disraeli, proprietress of 'Dizzy's Crown and Coronet Establishment', urges her to try her new imperial headgear for size. Trained in the satirical traditions of Rowlandson and Gillray, Victorian artists could be merciless in their portrayal of racial or personal traits, and Disraeli's Jewish origins and distinctive appearance made him an easy and frequent target. But the banter of 'saucy Ben the Jew, the leader of the Tory crew' was edged with respect. Lytton Strachey alludes in his text to the tribute paid to Disraeli by the German Chancellor Bismarck after the Congress of Berlin in 1878, held to settle the Eastern Question: 'Der alte Jude, das ist der Mann!' It was a judgement echoed by both friends and rivals at home, when Disraeli returned, announcing 'peace with honour'.

175

rapidity. A second Gloriana, did he call her? Very well, then, she would show that she deserved the compliment. Disquieting symptoms followed fast. In May 1874, the Tsar, whose daughter had just been married to Victoria's second son, the Duke of Edinburgh, was in London, and, by an unfortunate error, it had been arranged that his departure should not take place until two days after the date on which his royal hostess had previously decided to go to Balmoral. Her Majesty refused to modify her plans. It was pointed out to her that the Tsar would certainly be offended, that the most serious consequences might follow; Lord Derby protested; Lord Salisbury, the Secretary of State for India, was much perturbed. But the Faery was unconcerned; she had settled to go to Balmoral on the 18th, and on the 18th she would go. At last Disraeli, exercising all his influence, induced her to agree to stay in London for two days more. 'My head is still on my shoulders,' he told Lady Bradford. 'The great lady has absolutely postponed her departure! Everybody had failed, even the Prince of Wales; . . . and I have no doubt I am not in favour. I can't help it. Salisbury says I have saved an Afghan War, and Derby compliments me on my unrivalled triumph.' But before very long, on another issue, the triumph was the Faery's. Disraeli, who had suddenly veered towards a new Imperialism, had thrown out the suggestion that the Queen of England ought to become the Empress of India. Victoria seized upon the idea with avidity, and, in season and out of season, pressed upon her Prime Minister the desirability of putting his proposal into practice. He demurred; but she was not to be baulked; and in 1876, in spite of his own unwillingness and that of his entire Cabinet, he found himself obliged to add to the troubles of a stormy session by introducing a bill for the alteration of the Royal Title. His compliance, however, finally conquered the Faery's heart. The measure was angrily attacked in both Houses, and Victoria was deeply touched by the untiring energy with which Disraeli defended it. She was, she said, much grieved by 'the worry and annoyance' to which he was subjected; she feared she was the cause of it; and she would never forget what she owed to 'her kind, good, and considerate friend.' At the same time, her wrath fell on the Opposition. Their conduct, she declared, was 'extraordinary, incomprehensible, and mistaken,' and, in an emphatic sentence which seemed to contradict both itself and all her former proceedings, she protested that she 'would be glad if it were more generally known that it was *her* wish, as people *will* have it, that it has been *forced upon her!*' When the affair was successfully over, the imperial triumph was celebrated in a suitable manner. On the day of the Delhi Proclamation, the new Earl of Beaconsfield went to Windsor to dine with the new Empress of India. That night the Faery, usually so homely in her attire, appeared in a glittering panoply of enormous uncut jewels, which had been presented to her by the reigning Prince of her *Raj*. At the end of the meal the Prime Minister, breaking through the rules of etiquette, arose, and in a flowery oration proposed the health of the Queen-Empress. His audacity was well received, and his speech was rewarded by a smiling curtsey.

These were significant episodes; but a still more serious manifestation of Victoria's temper occurred in the following year, during the crowning crisis of Beaconsfield's life. His growing imperialism, his desire to magnify the power and prestige of England, his insistence upon a 'spirited foreign policy,' had brought him into collision with Russia; the terrible Eastern Question loomed up; and, when war broke out between Russia and Turkey, the gravity of the situation became extreme. The Prime Minister's policy was fraught with difficulty and danger. Realising perfectly the appalling implications of an Anglo-Russian war, he was yet prepared to face even that eventuality if he could obtain his ends by no other method; but he believed that Russia in reality was still less desirous of a rupture, and that, if he played his game with sufficient boldness and adroitness, she would yield, when it came to the point, all that he required without a blow. It was clear that the course he had marked out for himself was full of hazard, and demanded an extraordinary nerve; a single false step, and either himself, or England, might be plunged in disaster. But nerve he had never lacked; he began his diplomatic egg-dance with high assurance; and then he discovered that, besides the Russian Government, besides the Liberals and Mr. Gladstone, there were two additional sources of perilous embarrassment with which he would have to reckon. In the first place there was a strong party in the Cabinet, headed by Lord Derby, the Foreign Secretary, which was unwilling to take the risk of war; but his culminating anxiety was the Faery.

From the first, her attitude was uncompromising. The old hatred of Russia, which had been engendered by the Crimean War, surged up again within her; she remembered Albert's prolonged animosity; she felt the prickings of her own greatness; and she flung herself into the turmoil with passionate heat. Her indignation with the Opposition—with anyone who ventured to sympathise with the Russians in their quarrel with the Turks—was unbounded. When anti-Turkish meetings were held in London, presided over by the Duke of Westminster and Lord Shaftesbury, and attended by Mr. Gladstone and other prominent Radicals, she considered that 'the Attorney-General ought to be set at these men'; 'it can't,' she exclaimed, 'be constitutional.' Never in her life, not even in the crisis over the Ladies of the Bedchamber, did she show herself a more furious partisan. But her displeasure was not reserved for the Radicals; the backsliding Conservatives equally felt its force. She was even discontented with Lord Beaconsfield himself. Failing entirely to appreciate the delicate complexity of his policy, she constantly assailed him with demands for vigorous action, interpreted each finesse as a sign of weakness, and was ready at every juncture to let slip the dogs of war. As the situation developed, her anxiety grew feverish. 'The Queen,' she wrote, 'is feeling terribly anxious lest delay should cause us to be too late and lose our prestige for ever! It worries her night and day.' 'The Faery,' Beaconsfield told Lady Bradford, 'writes every day and telegraphs every hour; this is almost literally the case.' She raged loudly against the Russians. 'And the language,' she cried, 'the insulting language—used by the Russians against us! It makes the Queen's blood boil!' 'Oh,' she wrote a little later, 'if the Queen were a man, she would like to go and give those Russians, whose word one cannot believe, such a beating! We shall never be friends again till we have it out. This the Queen feels sure of.'

The unfortunate Prime Minister, urged on to violence by Victoria on one side, had to deal, on the other, with a Foreign Secretary who was fundamentally opposed to any policy of active interference at all. Between the Queen and Lord Derby he held a harassed course. He gained, indeed, some slight satisfaction in playing off the one against the other—in stimulating Lord Derby with the Queen's missives, and in appeasing the Queen by repudiating Lord Derby's opinions; on one occasion he actually went so far as to compose, at Victoria's request, a letter bitterly attacking his colleague, which her Majesty forthwith signed, and sent, without alteration, to the Foreign Secretary. But such devices gave only a temporary relief; and it soon became evident that Victoria's martial ardour was not to be side-tracked by hostilities against Lord Derby; hostilities against Russia were what she wanted, what she would, what she must, have. For now, casting aside the last relics of moderation, she began to attack her friend with a series of extraordinary threats. Not once, not twice, but many times she held over his head the formidable menace of her imminent abdication. 'If England,' she wrote to Beaconsfield, 'is to kiss Russia's feet, she will not be a party to the humiliation of England and would lay down her crown,' and she added that the Prime Minister might, if he thought fit, repeat her words to the Cabinet. 'This delay,' she ejaculated, 'this uncertainty by which, abroad, we are losing our prestige and our position, while Russia is advancing and will be before Constantinople in no time! Then the Government will be fearfully blamed and the Queen so humiliated that she thinks she would abdicate at once. Be bold!' 'She feels,' she reiterated, 'she cannot, as she before said, remain the Sovereign of a country that is letting itself down to kiss the feet of the great barbarians, the retarders of all liberty and civilisation that exists.' When the Russians advanced to the outskirts of Constantinople she fired off three letters in a day demanding war; and when she learnt that the Cabinet had only decided to send the Fleet to Gallipoli she declared that 'her first impulse' was 'to lay down the thorny crown, which she feels little satisfaction in retaining if the position of this country is to remain as it is now.' It is easy to imagine the agitating effect of such a correspondence upon Beaconsfield. This was no longer the Faery; it was a genie whom he had rashly called out of her bottle, and who was now intent upon showing her supernal power. More than once, perplexed, dispirited, shattered by illness, he had thoughts of withdrawing altogether from the game. One thing alone, he told Lady Bradford, with a wry smile, prevented him. 'If I could only,' he wrote, 'face the scene which would occur at headquarters if I resigned, I would do so at once.'

He held on, however, to emerge victorious at last. The Queen was pacified; Lord Derby was replaced by Lord Salisbury; and at the Congress of Berlin *der alte Jude* carried all before him. He returned to England in triumph, and assured the delighted Victoria that she would very soon be, if she was not already, the 'Dictatress of Europe.'

But soon there was an unexpected reverse. At the General Election of 1880 the country, mistrustful of the forward policy of the Conservatives, and carried away by Mr. Gladstone's oratory, returned the Liberals to power. Victoria was horrified, but within a year she was to be yet more nearly hit. The grand romance had come to its conclusion. Lord Beaconsfield, worn out with age and maladies, but moving still, an assiduous mummy, from dinner-

*In Harry Furniss's poignant drawing, the ageing Disraeli, Byronic love-lock firmly in place on his balding brow, looks down from the Peers' Gallery for the last time on the scene of his triumphs in the House of Commons. Failing health had influenced his decision to exchange the demanding Commons for the more sedate Upper Chamber. Asked how he felt on taking his seat as Lord Beaconsfield he answered, 'I am dead; dead but in the Elysian fields.' He died in 1881, aged seventy-seven.*

party to dinner-party, suddenly moved no longer. When she knew that the end was inevitable, she seemed, by a pathetic instinct, to divest herself of her royalty, and to shrink, with hushed gentleness, beside him, a woman and nothing more. 'I send some Osborne primroses,' she wrote to him with touching simplicity, 'and I meant to pay you a little visit this week but I thought it better you should be quite quiet and not speak. And I beg you will be very good and obey the doctors.' She would see him, she said, 'when we come back from Osborne, which won't be long.' 'Everyone is so distressed at your not being well,' she added; and she was, 'Ever yours very aff'ly, V.R.I.' When the royal letter was given him, the strange old comedian, stretched on his bed of death, poised it in his hand, appeared to consider deeply, and then whispered to those about him: 'This ought to be read to me by a Privy Councillor.'

# 9: OLD AGE

EANWHILE in Victoria's private life many changes and developments had taken place. With the marriages of her elder children her family circle widened; grandchildren appeared; and a multitude of new domestic interests sprang up. The death of King Leopold in 1865 had removed the predominant figure of the older generation, and the functions he had performed as the centre and adviser of a large group of relatives in Germany and in England devolved upon Victoria. These functions she discharged with unremitting industry, carrying on an enormous correspondence, and following with absorbed interest every detail in the lives of the ever-ramifying cousinhood. And she tasted to the full both the joys and the pains of family affection. She took a particular delight in her grandchildren, to whom she showed an indulgence which their parents had not always enjoyed, though, even to her grandchildren, she could be, when the occasion demanded it, severe. The eldest of them, the little Prince Wilhelm of Prussia, was a remarkably headstrong child; he dared to be impertinent even to his grandmother; and once, when she told him to bow to a visitor at Osborne, he disobeyed her outright. This would not do: the order was sternly repeated, and the naughty boy, noticing that his kind grandmama had suddenly turned into a most terrifying lady, submitted his will to hers, and bowed very low indeed.

It would have been well if all the Queen's domestic troubles could have been got over as easily. Among her more serious distresses was the conduct of the Prince of Wales. The young man was now independent and married; he had shaken the parental yoke from his shoulders; he was positively beginning to do as he liked. Victoria was much perturbed, and her worst fears seemed to be justified when in 1870 he appeared as a witness in a society divorce case. It was clear that the heir to the throne had been mixing with people of whom

'Today is the day on which I have reigned longer, by a day, than any English sovereign,' wrote the Queen shortly before celebrating her Diamond Jubilee in 1897. Wearing a dress of black moiré with panels of pigeon grey, embroidered with silver roses, thistles and shamrocks, she pressed an electric button to transmit a telegraph message to the farthest corners of her mighty Empire: 'From my heart I thank my beloved people. May God bless them.' Despite lameness, failing eyesight and a tendency to doze off during long carriage drives, the seventy-eight-year-old sovereign retained much of her zest for life. Her appetite remained healthy in spite of occasional stomach upsets. When prescribed Bengers Food (a patent food substitute), she added it to her already substantial diet. 'Of course when she devours a huge chocolate ice followed by a couple of apricots washed down with ice water, the Queen ought to expect a dig from the indigestion fiend,' wrote a lady-in-waiting when the Queen was over eighty.

she did not at all approve. What was to be done? She saw that it was not only her son that was to blame—that it was the whole system of society; and so she despatched a letter to Mr. Delane, the editor of *The Times*, asking him if he would 'frequently *write* articles pointing out the *immense* danger and evil of the wretched frivolity and levity of the views and lives of the Higher Classes.' And five years later Mr. Delane did write an article upon that very subject. Yet it seemed to have very little effect.

Ah! if only the Higher Classes would learn to live as she lived in the domestic sobriety of her sanctuary at Balmoral! For more and more did she find solace and refreshment in her Highland domain; and twice yearly, in the spring and in the autumn, with a sigh of relief, she set her face northwards, in spite of the humble protests of Ministers, who murmured vainly in the royal ears that to transact the affairs of State over an interval of six hundred miles added considerably to the cares of government. Her ladies, too, felt occasionally a slight reluctance to set out, for, especially in the early days, the long pilgrimage was not without its drawbacks. For many years the Queen's conservatism forbade the continuation of the railway up Deeside, so that the last stages of the journey had to be accomplished in carriages. But, after all, carriages had their good points; they were easy, for instance, to get in and out of, which was an important consideration, for the royal train remained for long immune from modern conveniences, and when it drew up, on some border moorland, far from any platform, the high-bred dames were obliged to descend to earth by the perilous foot-board, the only pair of folding steps being reserved for Her Majesty's saloon. In the days of crinolines such moments were sometimes awkward; and it was occasionally necessary to summon Mr. Johnstone, the short and sturdy Manager of the Caledonian Railway, who, more than once, in a high gale and drenching rain with great difficulty 'pushed up'—as he himself described it—some unlucky Lady Blanche or Lady Agatha into her compartment. But Victoria cared for none of these things. She was only intent upon regaining, with the utmost swiftness, her enchanted Castle, where every spot was charged with memories, where every memory was sacred, and where life was passed in an incessant and delightful round of absolutely trivial events.

And it was not only the place that she loved; she was equally attached to 'the simple mountaineers,' from whom, she said, 'she learnt many a lesson of resignation and faith.' Smith and Grant and Ross and Thompson—she was devoted to them all; but, beyond the rest, she was devoted to John Brown. The Prince's gillie had now become the Queen's personal attendant—a body servant from whom she was never parted, who accompanied her on her drives, waited on her during the day, and slept in a neighbouring chamber at night. She liked his strength, his solidity, the sense he gave her of physical security; she even liked his rugged manners and his rough unaccommodating speech. She allowed him to take liberties with her which would have been unthinkable from anybody else. To bully the Queen, to order her about, to reprimand her—who could dream of venturing upon such audacities? And yet, when she received such treatment from John Brown, she positively seemed to enjoy it. The eccentricity appeared to be extraordinary; but, after all, it is no uncommon thing for an autocratic dowager to allow some trusted

*John Brown, the former ghillie, was by December 1865 the 'permanent personal attendant' of the Queen, who valued his 'strong arm and wise advice, warm heart and cheery original way of saying things, and sympathy in any large or small circumstances.' The Queen's children sometimes resented her growing dependence on Brown's 'strong arm' and straight talking ('You've said enough,' he once admonished the prolix Gladstone), and he quarrelled with both Prince Alfred and the Prince of Wales. Sir Henry Ponsonby, the Queen's Private Secretary, summed him up as 'the only person who could fight and make the Queen do what she did not wish.' The warmth of the Queen's feelings for her 'poor faithful Brown' was clear when, grief-stricken at his death at the age of fifty-seven in 1883, she told her grandson Prince George of York, 'I have lost my dearest, best friend who no-one in this world can ever replace . . . never forget your poor sorrowing old Grandmama's best and truest friend . . .'*

indispensable servant to adopt towards her an attitude of authority which is jealously forbidden to relatives or friends: the power of a dependant still remains, by a psychological sleight-of-hand, one's own power, even when it is exercised over oneself. When Victoria meekly obeyed the abrupt commands of her henchman to get off her pony or put on her shawl, was she not displaying, and in the highest degree, the force of her volition? People might wonder; she could not help that; this was the manner in which it pleased her to act, and there was an end of it. To have submitted her judgment to a son or a Minister might have seemed wiser or more natural; but if she had done so, she instinctively felt, she would indeed have lost her independence. And yet upon somebody she longed to depend. Her days were heavy with the long process of domination. As she drove in silence over the moors she leaned back in the carriage, oppressed and weary; but what a relief!—John Brown was behind on the rumble, and his strong arm would be there for her to lean upon when she got out.

He had, too, in her mind, a special connection with Albert. In their expeditions the Prince had always trusted him more than anyone; the gruff, kind, hairy Scotsman was, she felt, in some mysterious way, a legacy from the dead. She came to believe at last—or so it appeared—that the spirit of Albert was nearer when Brown was near. Often, when seeking inspiration over some complicated question of political or domestic import, she would gaze with deep concentration at her late husband's bust. But it was also noticed that sometimes in such moments of doubt and hesitation Her Majesty's looks would fix themselves upon John Brown.

Eventually, the 'simple mountaineer' became almost a state personage. The influence which he wielded was not to be overlooked. Lord Beaconsfield was careful, from time to time, to send courteous messages to 'Mr. Brown' in his letters to the Queen, and the French Government took particular pains to provide for his comfort during the visits of the English Sovereign to France. It was only natural that among the elder members of the royal family he should not have been popular, and that his failings—for failings he had, though Victoria would never notice his too acute appreciation of Scotch whisky—should have been the subject of acrimonious comment at Court. But he served his mistress faithfully, and to ignore him would be a sign of disrespect in her biographer. For the Queen, far from making a secret of her affectionate friendship, took care to publish it to the world. By her orders two gold medals were struck in his honour; on his death, in 1883, a long and eulogistic obituary notice of him appeared in the *Court Circular*; and a Brown memorial brooch—of gold, with the late gillie's head on one side and the royal monogram on the other—was designed by Her Majesty for presentation to her Highland servants and cottagers, to be worn by them on the anniversary of his death, with a mourning scarf and pins. In the second series of extracts from the Queen's Highland Journal, published in 1884, her 'devoted personal attendant and faithful friend' appears upon almost every page, and is in effect the hero of the book. With an absence of reticence remarkable in royal persons, Victoria seemed to demand, in this private and delicate matter, the sympathy of the whole nation; and yet—such is the world!—there were those who actually treated the relations between their Sovereign and her

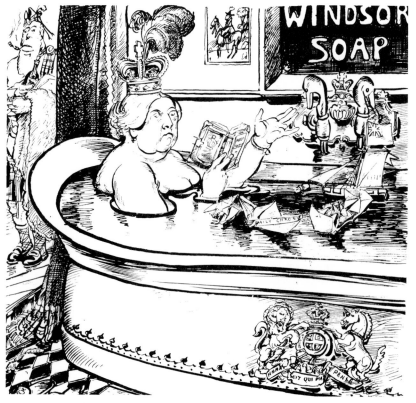

*The respect which the aged Queen commanded at home did not protect her from scurrilous comment abroad. This cartoon, published in Le Rire in 1899, has the temerity to show the Queen in her bath, evidently using the appropriately named Windsor Soap. Her reading matter pokes fun at her piety, the fleet of paper boats mocks the Royal Navy, while a Highland attendant lurks, whisky in hand, in the doorway. The Garter arms, emblazoned on the side of the bath, warn ironically: 'Shamed be he who thinks evil of it.'*

servant as a theme for ribald jests.

## II

The busy years hastened away; the traces of Time's unimaginable touch grew manifest; and old age, approaching, laid a gentle hold upon Victoria. The grey hair whitened; the mature features mellowed; the short firm figure amplified and moved more slowly, supported by a stick. And, simultaneously, in the whole tenour of the Queen's existence an extraordinary transformation came to pass. The nation's attitude towards her, critical and even hostile as it had been for so many years, altogether changed; while there was a corresponding alteration in the temper of Victoria's own mind.

Many causes led to this result. Among them were the repeated strokes of personal misfortune which befell the Queen during a cruelly short space of years. In 1878 the Princess Alice, who had married in 1862 the Prince Louis of Hesse-Darmstadt, died in tragic circumstances. In the following year the Prince Imperial, the only son of the Empress Eugénie, to whom Victoria, since the catastrophe of 1870, had become devotedly attached, was killed in the Zulu War. Two years later, in 1881, the Queen lost Lord Beaconsfield, and, in 1883, John Brown. In 1884 the Prince Leopold, Duke of Albany, who had been an invalid from birth, died prematurely, shortly after his marriage. Victoria's cup of sorrows was indeed overflowing; and the public, as it watched the widowed mother weeping for her children and her friends, displayed a constantly increasing sympathy.

An event which occurred in 1882 revealed and accentuated the feelings of the nation. As the Queen, at Windsor, was walking from the train to her carriage, a youth named Roderick Maclean fired a pistol at her from a distance of a few yards. An Eton boy struck up Maclean's arm with an umbrella before the pistol went off; no damage was done, and the culprit was at once arrested. This was the last of a series of seven attempts upon the Queen—attempts which, taking place at sporadic intervals over a period of forty years, resembled one another in a curious manner. All, with a single exception, were perpetrated by adolescents, whose motives were apparently not murderous, since, save in the case of Maclean, none of their pistols was loaded. These unhappy youths, who, after buying their cheap weapons, stuffed them with gunpowder and paper, and then went off, with the certainty of immediate detection, to click them in the face of royalty, present a strange problem to the psychologist. But, though in each case their actions and their purposes seemed to be so similar, their fates were remarkably varied. The first of them, Edward Oxford, who fired at Victoria within a few months of her marriage, was tried for high treason, declared to be insane, and sent to an asylum for life. It appears, however, that this sentence did not commend itself to Albert, for when, two years later, John Francis committed the same offence, and was tried upon the same charge, the Prince pronounced that there was no insanity in the matter. 'The wretched creature,' he told his father, was 'not out of his mind, but a thorough scamp.' 'I hope,' he added 'his trial will be conducted with the greatest strictness.' Apparently it was; at any rate, the jury shared the view of the Prince, the plea of insanity was set aside, and Francis was found guilty of high treason and condemned to death; but, as there was no proof of an intent to kill or even to wound, this sentence, after a lengthened deliberation between the Home Secretary and the Judges, was commuted for one of transportation for life. As the law stood, these assaults, futile as they were, could be treated only as high treason; the discrepancy between the actual deed and the tremendous penalties involved was obviously grotesque; and it was, besides, clear that a jury, knowing that a verdict of guilty implied a sentence of death, would tend to the alternative course, and find the prisoner not guilty but insane—a conclusion which, on the face of it, would have appeared to be the more reasonable. In 1842, therefore, an Act was passed making any attempt to hurt the Queen a misdemeanour, punishable by transportation for seven years, or imprisonment, with or without hard labour, for a term not exceeding three years—the misdemeanant, at the discretion of the Court, 'to be publicly or privately whipped, as often, and in such manner and form, as the Court shall direct, not exceeding thrice.' The four subsequent attempts were all dealt with under this new law; William Bean, in 1842, was sentenced to eighteen months' imprisonment; William Hamilton, in 1849, was transported for seven years; and, in 1850, the same sentence was passed upon Lieutenant Robert Pate, who struck the Queen on the head with his cane in Piccadilly. Pate, alone among these delinquents, was of mature years; he had held a commission in the Army, dressed himself as a dandy, and was, the Prince declared, 'manifestly deranged.' In 1872 Arthur O'Connor, a youth of seventeen, fired an unloaded pistol at the Queen outside Buckingham Palace; he was immediately seized by John Brown, and sentenced to one year's imprisonment and twenty strokes of the birch rod. It was for his bravery upon this occasion that Brown was presented with one of his gold medals. In all these cases the jury had refused to allow the plea of insanity; but Roderick Maclean's attempt in 1882 had a different issue. On this occasion the pistol was found to have been loaded, and the public indignation, emphasised as it was by Victoria's growing popularity, was particularly great. Either for this or for some other reason the procedure of the last forty years was abandoned, and Maclean was tried for high treason. The result was what might have been expected: the jury brought in a verdict of 'not guilty, but insane'; and the prisoner was sent to an asylum during Her Majesty's pleasure. Their verdict, however, produced a remarkable consequence. Victoria, who doubtless carried in her mind some memory of Albert's disapproval of a similar verdict in the case of Oxford, was very much annoyed. What did the jury mean, she asked, by saying that Maclean was not guilty? It was perfectly clear that he was guilty—she had seen him fire off the pistol herself. It was in vain that Her Majesty's constitutional advisers reminded her of the principle of English law which lays down that no man can be found guilty of a crime unless he be proved to have had a criminal intention. Victoria was quite unconvinced. 'If that is the law,' she said, 'the law must be altered': and altered it was. In 1883 an Act was passed changing the form of the verdict in cases of insanity, and the confusing anomaly remains upon the Statute Book to this day.

But it was not only through the feelings—commiserating or indignant—of personal sympathy that the Queen and her people were being drawn more nearly together; they were beginning, at last, to come to a close and permanent agreement upon the conduct of public affairs. Mr. Gladstone's second administration (1880–85) was a succession of failures, ending in disaster and disgrace; liberalism fell into discredit with the country, and Victoria perceived with joy that her distrust of her Ministers was shared by an ever-increasing number of her subjects. During the crisis in the Sudan, the popular temper was her own. She had been among the first to urge the necessity of an expedition to Khartoum, and, when the news came of the catastrophic death of General Gordon, her voice led the chorus of denunciation which raved against the Government. In her rage, she despatched a fulminating telegram to Mr. Gladstone, not in the usual cypher, but open; and her letter of condolence to Miss Gordon, in which she attacked her Ministers for breach of faith, was widely published. It was rumoured that she had sent for Lord Hartington, the Secretary of State for War, and vehemently upbraided him. 'She rated me,' he was reported to have told a friend, 'as if I'd been a footman.' 'Why didn't she send for the butler?' asked his friend. 'Oh,' was the reply, 'the butler generally manages to keep out of the way on such occasions.'

But the day came when it was impossible to keep out of the way any longer. Mr. Gladstone was defeated, and resigned. Victoria, at a final interview, received him with her usual amenity, but, besides the formalities demanded by the occasion, the only remark which she made to him of a personal nature

'I was trembling vy. much and a sort of shiver ran through me,' recorded a shaken Queen Victoria after the assassination attempt depicted here in 1872. The pistol with which the young Irishman Arthur O'Connor menaced the Queen in fact proved to be unloaded, but John Brown's bravery in seizing the 'weak-minded' assailant was rewarded with public thanks, a gold medal and a yearly annuity of £25. The last of the seven attacks made on her life came in 1882 when the deranged Roderick Maclean fired at her outside Windsor station. William McGonagall, as always, produced a verse for the occasion:
'Maclean must be a madman,
Which is obvious to be seen,
Or else he wouldn't have tried to shoot
Our most beloved Queen.'

was to the effect that she supposed Mr. Gladstone would now require some rest. He remembered with regret how, at a similar audience in 1874, she had expressed her trust in him as a supporter of the throne; but he noted the change without surprise. 'Her mind and opinions,' he wrote in his diary afterwards, 'have since that day been seriously warped.'

Such was Mr. Gladstone's view; but the majority of the nation by no means agreed with him; and, in the General Election of 1886, they showed decisively that Victoria's politics were identical with theirs by casting forth the contrivers of Home Rule—that abomination of desolation—into outer darkness, and placing Lord Salisbury in power. Victoria's satisfaction was profound. A flood of new unwonted hopefulness swept over her, stimulating her vital spirits with a surprising force. Her habit of life was suddenly altered; abandoning the long seclusion which Disraeli's persuasions had only momentarily interrupted, she threw herself vigorously into a multitude of public activities. She appeared at drawing-rooms, at concerts, at reviews; she laid foundation-stones; she went to Liverpool to open an international exhibition, driving through the streets in her open carriage in heavy rain amid vast applauding crowds. Delighted by the welcome which met her everywhere, she warmed to her work. She visited Edinburgh, where the ovation of Liverpool was repeated and surpassed. In London, she opened in high state the Colonial and Indian Exhibition at South Kensington. On this occasion the ceremonial was particularly magnificent; a blare of trumpets announced the approach of Her Majesty; the 'National Anthem' followed; and the Queen, seated on a gorgeous throne of hammered gold, replied with her own lips to the address that was presented to her. Then she rose, and, advancing upon the platform with regal port, acknowledged the acclamations of the great assembly by a succession of curtseys, of elaborate and commanding grace.

Next year was the fiftieth of her reign, and in June the splendid anniversary was celebrated in solemn pomp. Victoria, surrounded by the highest dignitaries of her realm, escorted by a glittering galaxy of kings and princes, drove through the crowded enthusiasm of the capital to render thanks to God in Westminster Abbey. In that triumphant hour the last remaining traces of past antipathies and past disagreements were altogether swept away. The Queen was hailed at once as the mother of her people and as the embodied symbol of their imperial greatness; and she responded to the double sentiment with all the ardour of her spirit. England and the people of England, she knew it, she felt it, were, in some wonderful and yet quite simple manner, *hers*. Exultation, affection, gratitude, a profound sense of obligation, an unbounded pride—such were her emotions; and, colouring and intensifying the rest, there was something else. At last, after so long, happiness—fragmentary, perhaps, and charged with gravity, but true and unmistakable none the less—had returned to her. The unaccustomed feeling filled and warmed her consciousness. When, at Buckingham Palace again, the long ceremony over, she was asked how she was, 'I am very tired, but very happy,' she said.

*This advertisement, using the Queen's image for a typically excruciating nineteenth-century pun, exemplifies the strong undercurrent of popular irreverence beneath the bland conformity of Victorian society.*

# III

And so, after the toils and tempests of the day, a long evening followed—mild, serene, and lighted with a golden glory. For an unexampled atmosphere of success and adoration invested the last period of Victoria's life. Her triumph was the summary, the crown, of a greater triumph—the culminating prosperity of a nation. The solid splendour of the decade between Victoria's two jubilees can hardly be paralleled in the annals of England. The sage counsels of Lord Salisbury seemed to bring with them not only wealth and power, but security; and the country settled down, with calm assurance, to the enjoyment of an established grandeur. And—it was only natural—Victoria settled down too. For she was a part of the establishment—an essential part as it seemed—a fixture—a magnificent, immovable sideboard in the huge saloon of state. Without her the heaped-up banquet of 1890 would have lost its distinctive quality—the comfortable order of the substantial unambiguous dishes, with their background of weighty glamour, half out of sight.

Her own existence came to harmonise more and more with what was around her. Gradually, imperceptibly, Albert receded. It was not that he was forgotten—that would have been impossible—but that the void created by his absence grew less agonising, and even, at last, less obvious. Eventually Victoria found it possible to regret the bad weather without immediately reflecting that her 'dear Albert always said we could not alter it, but must leave it as it was'; she could even enjoy a good breakfast without considering how 'dear Albert' would have liked the buttered eggs. And, as that figure slowly faded, its place was taken, inevitably, by Victoria's own. Her being, revolving for so many years round an external object, now changed its motion and found its centre in itself. It had to be so: her domestic position, the pressure of her public work, her indomitable sense of duty, made anything else impossible. Her egotism proclaimed its rights. Her age increased still further the surrounding deference; and her force of character, emerging at length in all its plenitude, imposed itself absolutely upon its environment by the conscious effort of an imperious will.

Little by little it was noticed that the outward vestiges of Albert's posthumous domination grew less complete. At Court the stringency of mourning was relaxed. As the Queen drove through the Park in her open carriage with her Highlanders behind her, nursery-maids canvassed eagerly the growing patch of violet velvet in the bonnet with its jet appurtenances on the small bowing head.

It was in her family that Victoria's ascendancy reached its highest point. All her offspring were married; the number of her descendants rapidly increased; there were many marriages in the third generation; and no fewer than thirty-seven of her great-grandchildren were living at the time of her death. A picture of the period displays the royal family collected together in one of the great rooms at Windsor—a crowded company of more than fifty persons, with the imperial matriarch in their midst. Over them all she ruled with a most potent sway. The small concerns of the youngest aroused her

*On holiday in the Highlands, a middle-aged Prince of Wales poses for a family portrait with his youthful-looking wife, Alix, his children and pet. His eldest son Prince Eddy was to predecease him in 1892, leaving George, Duke of York, next in line to the throne. Of the three rather plain daughters, Louise married the Duke of Fife, Victoria (favourite sister of the future King George V) remained single and Maud became Queen of Norway. Bertie had done his duty in marrying and raising a family, but it seems unlikely that he heeded the warnings of the popular ballad which urged him 'not to go astray' by 'going out with the girls and staying till morning'.*

passionate interest; and the oldest she treated as if they were children still. The Prince of Wales, in particular, stood in tremendous awe of his mother. She had steadily refused to allow him the slightest participation in the business of government; and he had occupied himself in other ways. Nor could it be denied that he enjoyed himself—out of her sight; but, in that redoubtable presence, his abounding manhood suffered a miserable eclipse. Once, at Osborne, when, owing to no fault of his, he was too late for a dinner party, he was observed standing behind a pillar and, wiping the sweat from his forehead, trying to nerve himself to go up to the Queen. When at last he did so, she gave him a stiff nod, whereupon he vanished immediately behind another pillar, and remained there until the party broke up. At the time of this incident the Prince of Wales was over fifty years of age.

It was inevitable that the Queen's domestic activities should occasionally trench upon the domain of high diplomacy; and this was especially the case when the interests of her eldest daughter, the Crown Princess of Prussia, were at stake. The Crown Prince held liberal opinions; he was much influenced by his wife; and both were detested by Bismarck, who declared with scurrilous emphasis that the Englishwoman and her mother were a menace to the

Prussian State. The feud was still further intensified when, on the death of the old Emperor (1888), the Crown Prince succeeded to the throne. A family entanglement brought on a violent crisis. One of the daughters of the new Empress had become betrothed to Prince Alexander of Battenberg, who had lately been ejected from the throne of Bulgaria owing to the hostility of the Tsar. Victoria, as well as the Empress, highly approved of the match. Of the two brothers of Prince Alexander, the elder had married another of her grand-daughters, and the younger was the husband of her daughter, the Princess Beatrice; she was devoted to the handsome young men; and she was delighted by the prospect of the third brother—on the whole the handsomest, she thought, of the three—also becoming a member of her family. Unfortunately, however, Bismarck was opposed to the scheme. He perceived that the marriage would endanger the friendship between Germany and Russia, which was vital to his foreign policy, and he announced that it must not take place. A fierce struggle between the Empress and the Chancellor followed. Victoria, whose hatred of her daughter's enemy was unbounded, came over to Charlottenburg to join in the fray. Bismarck, over his pipe and his lager, snorted out his alarm. The Queen of England's object, he said, was clearly political—she wished to estrange Germany and Russia— and very likely she would have her way. 'In family matters,' he added, 'she is not used to contradiction'; she would 'bring the parson with her in her travelling-bag and the bridegroom in her trunk, and the marriage would come off on the spot.' But the man of blood and iron was not to be thwarted so easily, and he asked for a private interview with the Queen. The details of their conversation are unknown; but it is certain that in the course of it Victoria was forced to realise the meaning of resistance to that formidable personage, and that she promised to use all her influence to prevent the marriage. The engagement was broken off; and in the following year Prince Alexander of Battenberg united himself to Fräulein Loisinger, an actress at the court theatre of Darmstadt.

But such painful incidents were rare. Victoria was growing very old; with no Albert to guide her, with no Beaconsfield to enflame her, she was willing enough to abandon the dangerous questions of diplomacy to the wisdom of Lord Salisbury, and to concentrate her energies upon objects which touched her more nearly and over which she could exercise an undisputed control. Her home—her court—the monuments at Balmoral—the livestock at Windsor—the organisation of her engagements—the supervision of the multitudinous details of her daily routine—such matters played now an even greater part in her existence than before. Her life passed in an extraordinary exactitude. Every moment of her day was mapped out beforehand; the succession of her engagements was immutably fixed; the dates of her journeys—to Osborne, to Balmoral, to the South of France, to Windsor, to London—were hardly altered from year to year. She demanded from those who surrounded her a rigid precision in details, and she was preternaturally quick in detecting the slightest deviation from the rules which she had laid down. Such was the irresistible potency of her personality, that anything but the most implicit obedience to her wishes was felt to be impossible; but sometimes somebody was unpunctual; and unpunctuality was one of the most heinous of sins. Then her displeasure—her dreadful displeasure—became all too visible. At such moments there seemed nothing surprising in her having been the daughter of a martinet.

But these storms, unnerving as they were while they lasted, were quickly over, and they grew more and more exceptional. With the return of happiness a gentle benignity flowed from the aged Queen. Her smile, once so rare a visitant to those saddened features, flitted over them with an easy alacrity; the blue eyes beamed; the whole face, starting suddenly from its pendulous expressionlessness, brightened and softened and cast over those who watched it an unforgettable charm. For in her last years there was a fascination in Victoria's amiability which had been lacking even from the vivid impulse of her youth. Over all who approached her—or very nearly all—she threw a peculiar spell. Her grandchildren adored her; her ladies waited upon her with a reverential love. The honour of serving her obliterated a thousand inconveniences—the monotony of a court existence, the fatigue of standing, the necessity for a superhuman attentiveness to the minutiæ of time and space. As one did one's wonderful duty one could forget that one's legs were aching from the infinitude of the passages at Windsor, or that one's bare arms were turning blue in the Balmoral cold.

What, above all, seemed to make such service delightful was the detailed interest which the Queen took in the circumstances of those around her. Her absorbing passion for the comfortable commonplaces, the small crises, the recurrent sentimentalities, of domestic life constantly demanded wider fields for its activity; the sphere of her own family, vast as it was, was not enough; she became the eager confidante of the household affairs of her ladies; her sympathies reached out to the palace domestics; even the housemaids and scullions—so it appeared—were the objects of her searching inquiries, and of her heartfelt solicitude when their lovers were ordered to a foreign station, or their aunts suffered from an attack of rheumatism which was more than usually acute.

Nevertheless the due distinctions of rank were immaculately preserved. The Queen's mere presence was enough to ensure that; but, in addition, the dominion of court etiquette was paramount. For that elaborate code, which had kept Lord Melbourne stiff upon the sofa and ranged the other guests in silence about the round table according to the order of precedence, was as punctiliously enforced as ever. Every evening after dinner, the hearth-rug, sacred to royalty, loomed before the profane in inaccessible glory, or, on one or two terrific occasions, actually lured them magnetically forward to the very edge of the abyss. The Queen, at the fitting moment, moved towards her guests; one after the other they were led up to her; and, while duologue followed duologue in constraint and embarrassment, the rest of the assembly stood still, without a word. Only in one particular was the severity of the etiquette allowed to lapse. Throughout the greater part of the reign the rule that ministers must stand during their audiences with the Queen had been absolute. When Lord Derby, the Prime Minister, had an audience of Her Majesty after a serious illness, he mentioned it afterwards, as a proof of the royal favour, that the Queen had remarked 'How sorry she was she could not ask him to be seated.' Subsequently, Disraeli, after an attack of gout and in a

*Victoria's loyalty to her servants, and theirs to her, was striking. Ann Birkin, pictured here in 1898, embroidered the Queen's stockings for over sixty years.*

moment of extreme expansion on the part of Victoria, had been offered a chair; but he had thought it wise humbly to decline the privilege. In her later years, however, the Queen invariably asked Mr. Gladstone and Lord Salisbury to sit down.

Sometimes the solemnity of the evening was diversified by a concert, an opera, or even a play. One of the most marked indications of Victoria's enfranchisement from the thraldom of widowhood had been her resumption—after an interval of thirty years—of the custom of commanding dramatic companies from London to perform before the Court at Windsor. On such occasions her spirits rose high. She loved acting; she loved a good plot; above all, she loved a farce. Engrossed by everything that passed upon the stage, she would follow, with childlike innocence, the unwinding of the story; or she would assume an air of knowing superiority and exclaim in triumph, 'There! You didn't expect *that*, did you?' when the *dénouement* came. Her sense of humour was of a vigorous though primitive kind. She had been one of the very few persons who had always been able to appreciate the Prince Consort's jokes; and, when those were cracked no more, she could still roar with laughter, in the privacy of her household, over some small piece of fun—some oddity of an ambassador, or some ignorant Minister's *faux pas*. When the jest grew subtle she was less pleased; but, if it approached the confines of the indecorous, the danger was serious. To take a liberty called down at once Her Majesty's most crushing disapprobation; and to say something improper was to take the greatest liberty of all. Then the royal lips sank down at the corners, the royal eyes stared in astonished protrusion, and in fact the royal countenance became inauspicious in the highest degree. The transgressor shuddered into silence, while the awful 'We are not amused' annihilated the dinner table. Afterwards, in her private entourage, the Queen would observe that the person in question was, she very much feared, 'not discreet'; it was a verdict from which there was no appeal.

In general, her æsthetic tastes had remained unchanged since the days of Mendelssohn, Landseer, and Lablache. She still delighted in the roulades of Italian opera; she still demanded a high standard in the execution of a pianoforte duet. Her views on painting were decided; Sir Edwin, she declared, was perfect; she was much impressed by Lord Leighton's manners; and she profoundly distrusted Mr. Watts. From time to time she ordered engraved portraits to be taken of members of the royal family; on these occasions she would have the first proofs submitted to her, and, having inspected them with minute particularity, she would point out their mistakes to the artists, indicating at the same time how they might be corrected. The artists invariably discovered that Her Majesty's suggestions were of the highest value. In literature her interests were more restricted. She was devoted to Lord Tennyson; and, as the Prince Consort had admired George Eliot, she perused 'Middlemarch': she was disappointed. There is reason to believe, however, that the romances of another female writer, whose popularity among the humbler classes of Her Majesty's subjects was at one time enormous, secured, no less, the approval of Her Majesty. Otherwise she did not read very much.

Once, however, the Queen's attention was drawn to a publication which it

The Queen's smile, usually eclipsed by the technical demands of Victorian photography, beams out in this family portrait of 1886 which she described as 'very successful'. In the background Princess Beatrice stands behind one of the Queen's favourite grand-daughters, Princess Victoria, whose mother, Princess Alice, had died in 1878. The round-eyed baby, Princess Victoria's eldest child, grew up to marry Prince Andrew of Greece, and became the mother of Prince Philip, Duke of Edinburgh.

was impossible for her to ignore. 'The Greville Memoirs,' filled with a mass of historical information of extraordinary importance, but filled also with descriptions, which were by no means flattering, of George IV, William IV, and other royal persons, was brought out by Mr. Reeve. Victoria read the book, and was appalled. It was, she declared, a 'dreadful and really scandalous book,' and she could not say 'how *horrified* and *indignant*' she was at Greville's 'indiscretion, indelicacy, ingratitude towards friends, betrayal of confidence and shameful disloyalty towards his Sovereign.' She wrote to Disraeli to tell him that in her opinion it was '*very important* that the book should be severely censured and discredited.' 'The tone in which he speaks of royalty,' she added, 'is unlike anything one sees in history even, and is most reprehensible.' Her anger was directed with almost equal vehemence against Mr. Reeve for his having published 'such an abominable book,' and she charged Sir Arthur Helps to convey to him her deep displeasure. Mr. Reeve, however, was impenitent. When Sir Arthur told him that, in the Queen's opinion, 'the book degraded royalty,' he replied: 'Not at all; it elevates it by the contrast it offers between the present and the defunct state of affairs.' But this adroit defence failed to make any impression upon Victoria; and Mr. Reeve, when he retired from the public service, did not receive the knighthood which custom entitled him to expect. Perhaps if the Queen had known how many caustic comments upon herself Mr. Reeve had quietly suppressed in the published Memoirs, she would have been almost grateful to him; but, in that case, what would she have said of Greville? Imagination boggles at the thought. As for more modern essays upon the same topic, Her Majesty, it is to be feared, would have characterised them as 'not discreet.'

But as a rule the leisure hours of that active life were occupied with recreations of a less intangible quality than the study of literature or the appreciation of art. Victoria was a woman not only of vast property but of innumerable possessions. She had inherited an immense quantity of furniture, of ornaments, of china, of plate, of valuable objects of every kind; her purchases, throughout a long life, made a formidable addition to these stores; and there flowed in upon her, besides, from every quarter of the globe, a constant stream of gifts. Over this enormous mass she exercised an unceasing and minute supervision, and the arrangement and the contemplation of it, in all its details, filled her with an intimate satisfaction. The collecting instinct has its roots in the very depths of human nature; and, in the case of Victoria, it seemed to owe its force to two of her dominating impulses—the intense sense, which had always been hers, of her own personality, and the craving which, growing with the years, had become in her old age almost an obsession, for fixity, for solidity, for the setting up of palpable barriers against the outrages of change and time. When she considered the multitudinous objects which belonged to her, or, better still, when, choosing out some section of them as the fancy took her, she actually savoured the vivid richness of their individual qualities, she saw herself deliciously reflected from a million facets, felt herself magnified miraculously over a boundless area, and was well pleased. That was just as it should be; but then came the dismaying thought—everything slips away, crumbles, vanishes; Sèvres dinner-services get broken; even golden basins go unaccoun-

*The Queen's own etching of Islay, a favourite terrier who was also drawn and etched by Landseer. Lord Melbourne had a low opinion of the intelligence of this dog, but allowed him to jump on his lap and lick his spectacles. In old age the Queen derived great consolation from the presence about her of all manner of mementoes of the past, including pictures and sculptures of her favourite animals.*

194

tably astray; even one's self, with all the recollections and experiences that make up one's being, fluctuates, perishes, dissolves . . . But no! It could not, should not be so! There should be no changes and no losses! Nothing should ever move—neither the past nor the present—and she herself least of all! And so the tenacious woman, hoarding her valuables, decreed their immortality with all the resolution of her soul. She would not lose one memory or one pin.

She gave orders that nothing should be thrown away—and nothing was. There, in drawer after drawer, in wardrobe after wardrobe, reposed the dresses of seventy years. But not only the dresses—the furs and the mantles and subsidiary frills and the muffs and the parasols and the bonnets—all were ranged in chronological order, dated and complete. A great cupboard was devoted to the dolls; in the china-room at Windsor a special table held the mugs of her childhood, and her children's mugs as well. Mementoes of the past surrounded her in serried accumulations. In every room the tables were powdered thick with the photographs of relatives; their portraits, revealing them at all ages, covered the walls; their figures, in solid marble, rose up from pedestals, or gleamed from brackets in the form of gold and silver statuettes. The dead, in every shape—in miniatures, in porcelain, in enormous life-size oil-paintings—were perpetually about her. John Brown stood upon her writing-table in solid gold. Her favourite horses and dogs, endowed with a new durability, crowded round her footsteps. Sharp, in silver-gilt, dominated the dinner-table; Boy and Boz lay together among unfading flowers, in bronze. And it was not enough that each particle of the past should be given the stability of metal or of marble: the whole collection, in its arrangement, no less than its entity, should be immutably fixed. There might be additions, but there might never be alterations. No chintz might change, no carpet, no curtain, be replaced by another; or, if long use at last made it necessary, the stuffs and patterns must be so identically reproduced that the keenest eye might not detect the difference. No new picture could be hung upon the walls of Windsor, for those already there had been put in their places by Albert, whose decisions were eternal. So, indeed, were Victoria's. To ensure that they should be the aid of the camera was called in. Every single article in the Queen's possession was photographed from several points of view. These photographs were submitted to Her Majesty, and when, after careful inspection, she approved of them, they were placed in a series of albums, richly bound. Then, opposite each photograph, an entry was made, indicating the number of the article, the number of the room in which it was kept, its exact position in the room and all its principal characteristics. The fate of every object which had undergone this process was henceforth irrevocably sealed. The whole multitude, once and for all, took up its steadfast station. And Victoria, with a gigantic volume or two of the endless catalogue always beside her, to look through, to ponder upon, to expatiate over, could feel, with a double contentment, that the transitoriness of this world had been arrested by the amplitude of her might.

Thus the collection, ever multiplying, ever encroaching upon new fields of consciousness, ever rooting itself more firmly in the depths of instinct, became one of the dominating influences of that strange existence. It was a

*Eos, a favourite greyhound brought over from Coburg by Prince Albert, etched by the Queen. His portrait was also painted by Landseer, and he was tended by the royal children's apothecary when he was accidentally shot in 1842.*

collection not merely of things and of thoughts, but of states of mind and ways of living as well. The celebration of anniversaries grew to be an important branch of it—of birthdays and marriage days and death days, each of which demanded its appropriate feeling, which, in its turn, must be itself expressed in an appropriate outward form. And the form, of course—the ceremony of rejoicing or lamentation—was stereotyped with the rest: it was part of the collection. On a certain day, for instance, flowers must be strewn on John Brown's monument at Balmoral; and the date of the yearly departure for Scotland was fixed by that fact. Inevitably it was around the central circumstances of death—death, the final witness to human mutability—that these commemorative cravings clustered most thickly. Might not even death itself be humbled, if one could recall enough?—if one asserted, with a sufficiently passionate and reiterated emphasis, the eternity of love? Accordingly, every bed in which Victoria slept had attached to it, at the back, on the right-hand side, above the pillow, a photograph of the head and shoulders of Albert as he lay dead, surmounted by a wreath of immortelles. At Balmoral, where memories came crowding so closely, the solid signs of memory appeared in surprising profusion. Obelisks, pyramids, tombs, statues, cairns, and seats of inscribed granite, proclaimed Victoria's dedication to the dead. There, twice a year, on the days that followed her arrival, a solemn pilgrimage of inspection and meditation was performed. There, on August 26—Albert's birthday—at the foot of the bronze statue of him in Highland dress, the Queen, her family, her Court, her servants, and her tenantry, met together and in silence drank to the memory of the dead. In England the tokens of remembrance pullulated hardly less. Not a day passed without some addition to the multifold assemblage—a gold statuette of Ross, the piper—a life-sized marble group of Victoria and Albert, in medieval costume, inscribed upon the base with the words: 'Allured to brighter worlds and led the way'—a granite slab in the shrubbery at Osborne, informing the visitor of 'Waldmann: the very favourite little dachshund of Queen Victoria; who brought him from Baden, April 1872; died, July 11, 1881.'

At Frogmore, the great mausoleum, perpetually enriched, was visited almost daily by the Queen when the Court was at Windsor. But there was another, a more secret and a hardly less holy shrine. The suite of rooms which Albert had occupied in the Castle was kept for ever shut away from the eyes of any save the most privileged. Within those precincts everything remained as it had been at the Prince's death; but the mysterious preoccupation of Victoria had commanded that her husband's clothing should be laid afresh, each evening, upon the bed, and that, each evening, the water should be set ready in the basin, as if he were still alive; and this incredible rite was performed with scrupulous regularity for nearly forty years.

Such was the inner worship; and still the flesh obeyed the spirit; still the daily hours of labour proclaimed Victoria's consecration to duty and to the ideal of the dead. Yet, with the years, the sense of self-sacrifice had faded; the natural energies of that ardent being discharged themselves with satisfaction into the channel of public work; the love of business which, from her girlhood, had been strong within her, reasserted itself in all its vigour, and, in her old age, to have been cut off from her papers and her boxes would have been, not a relief, but an agony to Victoria. Thus, though toiling Ministers might sigh and suffer, the whole process of government continued, till the very end, to pass before her. Nor was that all; ancient precedent had made the validity of an enormous number of official transactions dependent upon the application of the royal sign-manual; and a great proportion of the Queen's working hours was spent in this mechanical task. Nor did she show any desire to diminish it. On the contrary, she voluntarily resumed the duty of signing commissions in the Army, from which she had been set free by Act of Parliament, and from which, during the years of middle life, she had abstained. In no case would she countenance the proposal that she should use a stamp. But, at last, when the increasing pressure of business made the delays of the antiquated system intolerable, she consented that, for certain classes of documents, her oral sanction should be sufficient. Each paper was read aloud to her, and she said at the end 'Approved.' Often, for hours at a time, she would sit, with Albert's bust in front of her, while the word 'Approved' issued at intervals from her lips. The word came forth with a majestic sonority; for her voice now—how changed from the silvery treble of her girlhood!—was a contralto, full and strong.

## IV

The final years were years of apotheosis. In the dazzled imagination of her subjects Victoria soared aloft towards the regions of divinity through a nimbus of purest glory. Criticism fell dumb; deficiencies which, twenty years earlier, would have been universally admitted, were now as universally ignored. That the nation's idol was a very incomplete representative of the nation was a circumstance that was hardly noticed, and yet it was conspicuously true. For the vast changes which, out of the England of 1837, had produced the England of 1897, seemed scarcely to have touched the Queen. The immense industrial development of the period, the significance of which had been so thoroughly understood by Albert, meant little indeed to Victoria. The amazing scientific movement, which Albert had appreciated no less, left Victoria perfectly cold. Her conception of the universe, and of man's place in it, and of the stupendous problems of nature and philosophy remained, throughout her life, entirely unchanged. Her religion was the religion which she had learnt from the Baroness Lehzen and the Duchess of Kent. Here, too, it might be supposed that Albert's views would have influenced her. For Albert, in matters of religion, was advanced. Disbelieving altogether in evil spirits, he had had his doubts about the miracle of the Gadarene Swine. Stockmar, even, had thrown out, in a remarkable memorandum on the education of the Prince of Wales, the suggestion that while the child 'must unquestionably be brought up in the creed of the Church of England,' it might nevertheless be in accordance with the spirit of the times to exclude from his religious training the inculcation of a belief in 'the supernatural doctrines of Christianity.' This, however, would have been going too far; and all the royal children were brought up in complete orthodoxy. Anything else would have grieved Victoria, though her own conceptions of the orthodox were not very precise. But her nature, in which imagination and subtlety held so small a place, made her instinctively recoil from the intricate ecstasies of High Anglicanism; and she seemed to feel most at home in the simple faith of the Presbyterian Church of Scotland. This was what might have been expected; for Lehzen was the daughter of a Lutheran pastor, and the Lutherans and the Presbyterians have much in common. For may years Dr. Norman Macleod, an innocent Scotch minister, was her principal spiritual adviser; and, when he was taken from her, she drew much comfort from quiet chats about life and death with the cottagers at Balmoral. Her piety, absolutely genuine, found what it wanted in the sober exhortations of old John Grant and the devout saws of Mrs. P. Farquharson. They possessed the qualities, which, as a child of fourteen, she had so sincerely admired in the Bishop of Chester's 'Exposition of the Gospel of St. Matthew'; they were 'just plain and comprehensible and full of truth and good feeling.' The Queen, who gave her name to the Age of Mill and of Darwin, never got any further than that.

From the social movements of her time Victoria was equally remote. Towards the smallest no less than towards the greatest changes she remained inflexible. During her youth and middle-age smoking had been forbidden in polite society, and so long as she lived she would not withdraw her anathema against it. Kings might protest; bishops and ambassadors, invited to Windsor, might be reduced, in the privacy of their bedrooms, to lie full-length upon the floor and smoke up the chimney—the interdict continued. It might have been supposed that a female sovereign would have lent her countenance to one of the most vital of all the reforms to which her epoch gave birth—the emancipation of women—but, on the contrary, the mere mention of such a proposal sent the blood rushing to her head. In 1870, her eye having fallen upon the report of a meeting in favour of Women's Suffrage, she wrote to Mr. Martin in royal rage—'The Queen is most anxious to enlist everyone who can speak or write to join in checking this mad, wicked folly of "Woman's Rights," with all its attendant horrors, on which her poor feeble sex is bent, forgetting every sense of womanly feeling and propriety. Lady —— ought to get a *good whipping*. It is a subject which makes the Queen so furious that she cannot contain herself. God created men and women different—then let them remain each in their own position. Tennyson has some beautiful lines on the difference of men and women in "The Princess." Woman would become the most hateful, heartless, and disgusting of human beings were she allowed to unsex herself; and where would be the protection which man was intended to give the weaker sex? The Queen is sure that Mrs. Martin agrees with her.' The argument was irrefutable; Mrs. Martin agreed; and yet the canker spread.

In another direction Victoria's comprehension of the spirit of her age has been constantly asserted. It was for long the custom for courtly historians and polite politicians to compliment the Queen upon the correctness of her attitude towards the Constitution. But such praises seem hardly to be justified by the facts. In her later years Victoria more than once alluded with regret to her conduct during the Bedchamber crisis, and let it be understood that she had grown wiser since. Yet in truth it is difficult to trace any fundamental change either in her theory or her practice in constitutional matters throughout her life. The same despotic and personal spirit which led her to break off the negotiations with Peel is equally visible in her animosity towards Palmerston, in her threats of abdication to Disraeli, and in her desire to prosecute the Duke of Westminster for attending a meeting upon Bulgarian atrocities. The complex and delicate principles of the Constitution cannot be said to have come within the compass of her mental faculties; and in the actual developments which it underwent during her reign she played a passive part. From 1840 to 1861 the power of the Crown steadily increased in England; from 1861 to 1901 it steadily declined. The first process was due to the influence of the Prince Consort, the second to that of a series of great Ministers. During the first Victoria was in effect a mere accessory; during the second the threads of power, which Albert had so laboriously collected, inevitably fell from her hands into the vigorous grasp of Mr. Gladstone, Lord Beaconsfield, and Lord Salisbury. Perhaps, absorbed as she was in routine, and difficult as she found it to distinguish at all clearly between the trivial and the essential, she was only dimly aware of what was happening. Yet, at the end of her reign, the Crown was weaker than at any other time in English history. Paradoxically enough, Victoria received the highest eulogiums for assenting to a political evolution which, had she completely realised its import, would have filled her with supreme displeasure.

Nevertheless it must not be supposed that she was a second George III. Her desire to impose her will, vehement as it was, and unlimited by any principle, was yet checked by a certain shrewdness. She might oppose her Ministers with extraordinary violence; she might remain utterly impervious to arguments and supplications; the pertinacity of her resolution might seem to be unconquerable; but, at the very last moment of all, her obstinacy would give way. Her innate respect and capacity for business, and perhaps, too, the memory of Albert's scrupulous avoidance of extreme courses, prevented her from ever entering an *impasse*. By instinct she understood when the facts were too much for her, and to them she invariably yielded. After all, what else could she do?

But if, in all these ways, the Queen and her epoch were profoundly separated, the points of contact between them also were not few. Victoria understood very well the meaning and the attractions of power and property, and in such learning the English nation, too, had grown to be more and more proficient. During the last fifteen years of the reign—for the short Liberal Administration of 1892 was a mere interlude—imperialism was the dominant creed of the country. It was Victoria's as well. In this direction, if in no other, she had allowed her mind to develop. Under Disraeli's tutelage the British Dominions over the seas had come to mean much more to her than ever before, and, in particular, she had grown enamoured of the East. The thought of India fascinated her; she set to, and learnt a little Hindustani; she engaged some Indian servants, who became her inseparable attendants, and one of whom, Munshi Abdul Karim, eventually almost succeeded to the position which had once been John Brown's. At the same time, the imperialist temper of the nation invested her office with a new significance exactly harmonising with her own inmost proclivities. The English polity was in the main a common-sense structure; but there was always a corner in it

*Mrs. Amelia Bloomer's new fashions, and habits, for 'strong-minded women' were satirized in Punch in 1851. Acute disapproval prevented the startling American import from catching on in mid-Victorian England, but with the bicycling mania of the later decades of the reign women at last began to discard their long skirts and restrictive corsets.*

Cape Town's Diamond Jubilee celebrations on 22 June 1897 were a demonstration of loyalty in a troubled area. Early the previous year, tensions between the Boers and the British had been increased by the Jameson Raid, Cecil Rhodes's ill-judged invasion of the Transvaal in an attempt to overthrow the Boer government. With the German Kaiser declaring support for the Boer President Kruger, the British government hastily repudiated Rhodes's action, in the hope of avoiding major conflict. Jubilee year saw Lord Milner's arrival as Governor of Cape Colony; the situation deteriorated further under his rule and the second Boer War broke out in 1899.

The Queen receives a Diamond Jubilee address from the Mayor of Newport in the Isle of Wight. Thanks partly to royal patronage, the island was a popular Victorian holiday resort, and straw-hatted holiday-makers can be seen among the loyal crowd in the gaily decorated street. As 'Chatelaine of Osborne' the Queen was the most famous resident, but for some years the Poet Laureate, Lord Tennyson, and the pioneer photographer Julia Margaret Cameron also had homes on the island.

where common-sense could not enter—where, somehow or other, the ordinary measurements were not applicable and the ordinary rules did not apply. So our ancestors had laid it down, giving scope, in their wisdom, to that mystical element which, as it seems, can never quite be eradicated from the affairs of men. Naturally it was in the Crown that the mysticism of the English polity was concentrated—the Crown, with its venerable antiquity, its sacred associations, its imposing spectacular array. But, for nearly two centuries, common-sense had been predominant in the great building, and the little, unexplored, inexplicable corner had attracted small attention. Then, with the rise of imperialism, there was a change. For imperialism is a faith as well as a business; as it grew, the mysticism in English public life grew with it; and simultaneously a new importance began to attach to the Crown. The need for a symbol—a symbol of England's might, of England's worth, of England's extraordinary and mysterious destiny—became felt more urgently than ever before. The Crown was that symbol: and the Crown rested upon the head of Victoria. Thus it happened that while by the end of the reign the power of the sovereign had appreciably diminished, the prestige of the sovereign had enormously grown.

Yet this prestige was not merely the outcome of public changes; it was an intensely personal matter, too. Victoria was the Queen of England, the Empress of India, the quintessential pivot round which the whole magnificent machine was revolving—but how much more besides! For one thing, she was of a great age—an almost indispensable qualification for popularity in England. She had given proof of one of the most admired characteristics of the race—persistent vitality. She had reigned for sixty years, and she was not out. And then, she was a character. The outlines of her nature were firmly drawn, and, even through the mists which envelop royalty, clearly visible. In the popular imagination her familiar figure filled, with satisfying ease, a distinct and memorable place. It was, besides, the kind of figure which naturally called forth the admiring sympathy of the great majority of the nation. Goodness they prized above every other human quality; and Victoria, who, at the age of twelve, had said that she would be good, had kept her word. Duty, conscience, morality—yes! in the light of those high beacons the Queen had always lived. She had passed her days in work and not in pleasure—in public responsibilities and family cares. The standard of solid virtue which had been set up so long ago amid the domestic happiness of Osborne had never been lowered for an instant. For more than half a century no divorced lady had approached the precincts of the court. Victoria, indeed, in her enthusiasm for wifely fidelity, had laid down a still stricter ordinance: she frowned severely upon any widow who married again. Considering that she herself was the offspring of a widow's second marriage, this prohibition might be regarded as an eccentricity; but, no doubt, it was an eccentricity on the right side. The middle-classes, firm in the triple brass of their respectability, rejoiced with a special joy over the most respectable of Queens. They almost claimed her, indeed, as one of themselves; but this would have been an exaggeration. For, though many of her characteristics were most often found among the middle-classes, in other respects—in her manners, for instance—Victoria was decidedly aristocratic. And, in one important particular, she was neither aristocratic nor middle-class: her attitude toward herself was simply regal.

Such qualities were obvious and important; but, in the impact of a personality, it is something deeper, something fundamental and common to all its qualities, that really tells. In Victoria, it is easy to discern the nature of this underlying element: it was a peculiar sincerity. Her truthfulness, her single-mindedness, the vividness of her emotions and her unrestrained expression of them, were the varied forms which this central characteristic assumed. It was her sincerity which gave her at once her impressiveness, her charm, and her absurdity. She moved through life with the imposing certitude of one to whom concealment was impossible—either towards her surroundings or towards herself. There she was, all of her—the Queen of England, complete and obvious; the world might take her or leave her; she had nothing more to show, or to explain, or to modify; and, with her peerless carriage, she swept along her path. And not only was concealment out of the question; reticence, reserve, even dignity itself, as it sometimes seemed, might be very well dispensed with. As Lady Lyttelton said: 'There is a transparency in her truth that is very striking—not a shade of exaggeration in describing feelings or facts; like very few other people I ever knew. Many may be as true, but I think it goes often along with some reserve. She talks all out; just as it is, no more and no less.' She talked all out; and she wrote all out, too. Her letters, in the surprising jet of their expression, remind one of a turned-on tap. What is within pours forth in an immediate, spontaneous rush. Her utterly unliterary style has at least the merit of being a vehicle exactly suited to her thoughts and feelings; and even the platitude of her phraseology carries with it a curiously personal flavour. Undoubtedly it was through her writings that she touched the heart of the public. Not only in her 'Highland Journals,' where the mild chronicle of her private proceedings was laid bare without a trace either of affectation or of embarrassment, but also in those remarkable messages to the nation which, from time to time, she published in the newspapers, her people found her very close to them indeed. They felt instinctively Victoria's irresistible sincerity, and they responded. And in truth it was an endearing trait.

The personality and the position, too—the wonderful combination of them—that, perhaps, was what was finally fascinating in the case. The little old lady, with her white hair and her plain mourning clothes, in her wheeled chair or her donkey-carriage—one saw her so; and then—close behind—with their immediate suggestion of singularity, of mystery, and of power—the Indian servants. That was the familiar vision, and it was admirable; but, at chosen moments, it was right that the widow of Windsor should step forth

*Britannia on a bicycle was Punch's suggested design for a commemorative Diamond Jubilee coin in 1897.*

apparent Queen. The last and the most glorious of such occasions was the Jubilee of 1897. Then, as the splendid procession passed along, escorting Victoria through the thronged re-echoing streets of London on her progress of thanksgiving to St. Paul's Cathedral, the greatness of her realm and the adoration of her subjects blazed out together. The tears welled to her eyes, and, while the multitude roared round her, 'How kind they are to me! How kind they are!' she repeated over and over again. That night her message flew over the Empire: 'From my heart I thank my beloved people. May God bless them!' The long journey was nearly done. But the traveller, who had come so far, and through such strange experiences, moved on with the old unfaltering step. The girl, the wife, the aged woman, were the same: vitality, conscientiousness, pride, and simplicity were hers to the latest hour.

*The Queen attends to her papers, by this time with the aid of a typewriter, guarded by an Indian attendant. 'I am learning a few words of Hindustani to speak to my servants,' she recorded. 'It is a great interest to me for both the language and the people, I have naturally never come into real contact with before.' Two Indian servants entered the royal household in the Golden Jubilee year of 1887. The younger man, Abdul Karim, eventually came to replace John Brown in the Queen's regard, earning the titles of 'Munshi' (clerk) and 'Hafiz' (secretary). He was extremely unpopular in court circles, being considered a pernicious influence of low origin, as well as a possible security risk, but the Queen warmly defended 'the poor Munshi's sensitive feelings'.*

203

# 10: THE END

THE evening had been golden; but, after all, the day was to close in cloud and tempest. Imperial needs, imperial ambitions, involved the country in the South African War. There were checks, reverses, bloody disasters; for a moment the nation was shaken, and the public distresses were felt with intimate solicitude by the Queen. But her spirit was high, and neither her courage nor her confidence wavered for a moment. Throwing herself heart and soul into the struggle, she laboured with redoubled vigour, interested herself in every detail of the hostilities, and sought by every means in her power to render service to the national cause. In April 1900, when she was in her eighty-first year, she made the extraordinary decision to abandon her annual visit to the South of France, and to go instead to Ireland, which had provided a particularly large number of recruits to the armies in the field. She stayed for three weeks in Dublin, driving through the streets, in spite of the warnings of her advisers, without an armed escort; and the visit was a complete success. But, in the course of it, she began, for the first time, to show signs of the fatigue of age.

For the long strain and the unceasing anxiety, brought by the war, made themselves felt at last. Endowed by nature with a robust constitution, Victoria, though in periods of depression she had sometimes supposed herself an invalid, had in reality throughout her life enjoyed remarkably good health. In her old age, she had suffered from a rheumatic stiffness of the joints, which had necessitated the use of a stick, and, eventually, a wheeled chair; but no other ailments attacked her, until, in 1898, her eyesight began to be affected by incipient cataract. After that, she found reading more and more difficult, though she could still sign her name, and even, with some difficulty, write letters. In the summer of 1900, however, more serious symptoms appeared. Her memory, in whose strength and precision she had so

*The Queen in her donkey cart, one of several solutions to her increasing lack of mobility (a less practical suggestion came from an anonymous correspondent who advised providing Her Majesty with a thick leather jacket to which balloons could be attached). Getting the Queen into her conveyance could be a lengthy business: she 'generally keeps her own carriage waiting for an hour', wrote a lady-in-waiting on an Italian trip in 1893. 'At last she came out, after an infinity of rugs, shawls, parasols and drawing materials had preceded her. Carpeted steps were pushed near the carriage and a grey-headed Highlander on one side and a lemon-turbaned Indian on the other lifted the old lady in.' Until the very end of her life the Queen took regular carriage drives accompanied by her ladies; on one occasion her companion spoke of the consolation of meeting one's deceased relatives in Abraham's bosom. 'I shall NOT meet Abraham,' replied the Queen.*

long prided herself, now sometimes deserted her; there was a tendency towards aphasia; and, while no specific disease declared itself, by the autumn there were unmistakable signs of a general physical decay. Yet, even in these last months, the vein of iron held firm. The daily work continued; nay, it actually increased; for the Queen, with an astonishing pertinacity, insisted upon communicating personally with an ever-growing multitude of men and women who had suffered through the war.

By the end of the year the last remains of her ebbing strength had almost deserted her; and through the early days of the opening century it was clear that her dwindling forces were kept together only by an effort of will. On January 14, she had at Osborne an hour's interview with Lord Roberts, who had returned victorious from South Africa a few days before. She inquired with acute anxiety into all the details of the war; she appeared to sustain the exertion successfully; but, when the audience was over, there was a collapse. On the following day her medical attendants recognised that her state was hopeless; and yet, for two days more, the indomitable spirit fought on; for two days more she discharged the duties of a Queen of England. But after that there was an end of working; and then, and not till then, did the last optimism of those about her break down. The brain was failing, and life was gently slipping away. Her family gathered round her; for a little more she lingered, speechless and apparently insensible; and, on January 22, 1901, she died.

'God knows there is nothing to admire in my ugly old person,' wrote the Queen to her eldest daughter who tried to make her censor unflattering photographs of herself. After about 1890 her eyesight worsened and, in spite of the spectacles she wears in this portrait, she was forced to give up painting and to use Princess Beatrice as an amanuensis, an arrangement which frequently led to errors and misunderstandings.

When, two days previously, the news of the approaching end had been made public, astonished grief had swept over the country. It appeared as if some monstrous reversal of the course of nature was about to take place. The vast majority of her subjects had never known a time when Queen Victoria had not been reigning over them. She had become an indissoluble part of their whole scheme of things, and that they were about to lose her appeared a scarcely possible thought. She herself, as she lay blind and silent, seemed to those who watched her to be divested of all thinking—to have glided already, unawares, into oblivion. Yet, perhaps, in the secret chambers of consciousness, she had her thoughts, too. Perhaps her fading mind called up once more the shadows of the past to float before it, and retraced, for the last time, the vanished visions of that long history—passing back and back, through the cloud of years, to older and ever older memories—to the spring woods at Osborne, so full of primroses for Lord Beaconsfield—to Lord Palmerston's queer clothes and high demeanour, and Albert's face under the green lamp, and Albert's first stag at Balmoral, and Albert in his blue and silver uniform, and the Baron coming in through a doorway, and Lord M. dreaming at Windsor with the rooks cawing in the elm-trees, and the Archbishop of Canterbury on his knees in the dawn, and the old King's turkey-cock ejaculations, and Uncle Leopold's soft voice at Claremont, and Lehzen with the globes, and her mother's feathers sweeping down towards her, and a great old repeater-watch of her father's in its tortoise-shell case, and a yellow rug, and some friendly flounces of sprigged muslin, and the trees and the grass at Kensington.

# NOTES

Lytton Strachey drew on a wide range of sources, published and private, for his biography of Queen Victoria, and was meticulous in giving page references and in indicating, where appropriate, the receipt of private information. Such references have been omitted in this edition; but those notes in which he provided additional material of interest are given below. The reading list on the following page cites the most important of his sources, as well as works that have appeared since his time.

**page 35** 'The cause of the Queen's alienation from the Duchess and hatred of Conroy, the Duke [of Wellington] said, was unquestionably owing to her having witnessed some familiarities between them. What she had seen she repeated to Baroness Späth, and Späth not only did not hold her tongue, but (he thinks) remonstrated with the Duchess herself on the subject. The consequence was that they got rid of Späth, and they would have got rid of Lehzen, too, if they had been able, but Lehzen, who knew very well what was going on, was prudent enough not to commit herself, and she was, besides, powerfully protected by George IV, so that they did not dare to attempt to expel her.' (Greville)

**page 44** 'March 1, 1835. Called on Lord Melbourne, and found him reading the Acts, with a quarto Greek Testament that belonged to Samuel Johnson.' (Benjamin Robert Haydon, *Autobiography*, 3 vols., 1853)

**page 57** The Duke of Bedford told Greville he was 'sure there was a battle between her and Melbourne. . . . He is sure there was one about the men's sitting after dinner, for he heard her say to him rather angrily, "it is a horrid custom"—but when the ladies left the room (he dined there) directions were given that the men should remain *five minutes* longer.' (Greville)

**page 68** The exclamation 'They wished to treat me like a girl, but I will show them that I am Queen of England!' often quoted as the Queen's, is apocryphal. It is merely part of Greville's summary of the two letters to Melbourne, printed in *Letters*, 162.

**page 71** Greville's statement (November 27, 1839) that 'the Queen settled everything about her marriage herself, and without consulting Melbourne at all on the subject, not even communicating to him her intention,' has no foundation in fact. The Queen's journal proves that she consulted Melbourne at every point.

**page 78** 'I had much talk with Lady Cowper about the Court. She lamented the obstinate character of the Queen, from which she thought that hereafter great evils might be apprehended. She said that her prejudices and antipathies were deep and strong, and her disposition very inflexible. Her hatred of Peel and her resentment against the Duke for having sided with him rather than with her in the old quarrel are unabated.' (Greville)

**page 118**
> 'You jolly Turks, now go to work,
> And show the Bear your power.
> It is rumoured over Britain's isle
> That A—— is in the Tower;
> The Postmen some suspicion had,
> And opened the two letters,
> 'Twas a pity sad the German lad
> Should not have known much better.'

(From *Lovely Albert!*, a broadside preserved at the British Museum)

**page 123** 'Read this carefully, and tell me if there are any mistakes in it.' 'Here is a draft I have made for you. Read it. I should think this would do.'

**page 138** 'One cannot speak with certainty; but it is horrible to think that such a life *may* have been sacrificed to Sir J. Clark's selfish jealousy of every member of his profession.' (The Earl of Clarendon to the Duchess of Manchester, December 17, 1861)

**page 168** In 1889 it was officially stated that the Queen's total savings from the Civil List amounted to £824,025, but that out of this sum much had been spent on special entertainments to foreign visitors. Taking into consideration the proceeds from the Duchy of Lancaster, which were more than £60,000 a year, the savings of the Prince Consort, and Mr. Neild's legacy, it seems probable that, at the time of her death, Victoria's private fortune approached two million pounds.

# FURTHER READING

**By Queen Victoria**

*The Girlhood of Queen Victoria, a Selection from her Majesty's Diaries between the years 1832 and 1840*, ed. Viscount Esher, 2 vols., 1912.

*Leaves from the Journal of our Life in the Highlands, from 1848 to 1861*, 1868.

*More Leaves from the Journal of a Life in the Highlands, from 1862 to 1882*, 1883.

*Letters*, ed. Viscount Esher and A.C. Benson, 1st series, 1908; 2nd series, 1926; 3rd series, ed. G.E. Buckle, 1930.

**Selection of works cited by Lytton Strachey**

Bloomfield, Georgiana, Lady, *Reminiscences of Court and Diplomatic Life*, 2 vols., 1883.

Buckle, G.E., and Monypenny, W.F., *The Life of Benjamin Disraeli, Earl of Beaconsfield*, 6 vols., 1910–20.

Crawford, Emily, *Victoria, Queen and Ruler*, 1903.

*The Creevey Papers*, ed. Sir Herbert Maxwell, 2 vols., 1904.

*The Greville Memoirs*, ed. Henry Reeve, 8 vols., 1896.

Grey, General Charles, *Early Years of the Prince Consort*, 1867.

Jerrold, Clare, *The Early Court of Queen Victoria*, 1912; *The Married Life of Queen Victoria*, 1913; *The Widowhood of Queen Victoria*, 1916.

Lee, Sidney, *Queen Victoria: a biography*, 1902.

Martin, Theodore, *The Life of His Royal Highness the Prince Consort*, 5 vols., 1875–80; *Queen Victoria as I knew her*, 1908.

Maxwell, Sir Herbert, *The Life and Letters of the Fourth Earl of Clarendon*, 2 vols., 1913.

Morley, John, *The Life of William Ewart Gladstone*, 3 vols., 1903.

*The Private Life of the Queen*, by One of Her Majesty's Servants, 1897.

*Correspondence of Sarah Spencer, Lady Lyttelton, 1787–1870*, ed. Mrs. Hugh Wyndham, 1912.

Torrens, W.M., *Memoirs of William Lamb, second Viscount Melbourne*, 1890.

**Other works**

Blake, Robert, *Disraeli*, 1966.

*Dearest Child: Letters between Queen Victoria and the Princess Royal*, ed. Roger Fulford, 1964.

*The Greville Memoirs, 1814–1860*, ed. Lytton Strachey and Roger Fulford, 8 vols., 1938.

Longford, Elizabeth, *Victoria R.I.*, 1964.

Magnus, Philip, *Gladstone, a Biography*, 1954.

Marie Louise, Princess, *My Memories of Six Reigns*, 1956.

Rhodes James, Robert, *Albert, Prince Consort*, 1983.

Warner, Marina, *Queen Victoria's Sketchbooks*, 1979.

Weintraub, Stanley, *Victoria, Biography of a Queen*, 1987.

Woodham Smith, Cecil, *Queen Victoria, her Life and Times*, vol. 1, 1972.

Zeigler, Philip, *Melbourne*, 1976.